MW00981597

THE BENT BULKHEAD

CARTOONS FOR THE SAILOR
By Chris Stoyan

DINKADOLLY
PUBLISHING
TORONTO

THE BENT BULKHEAD

CARTOONS FOR THE SAILOR

Canadian Cataloguing in Publication Data

Stoyan, Chris, 1956-
    The bent bulkhead : cartoons for the sailor

ISBN 0-9698138-0-5

1. Sailing - Caricatures and cartoons.
2. Canadian wit and humor, Pictorial. 1. Title

NC1449.S86A4 1994   741.5'971   C94-930971-0

Printed in Canada
MSI Graphics Pickering, Ontario

For information write: **Dinkadolly Publishing
P.O. Box 275 Station "D"
Scarborough, Ontario,
Canada M1R 5B7**

Attention: Yacht Clubs, Businesses and other organizations, quantity discounts available with bulk purchase for sales and promotional use. Please write or FAX (416) 431-5343

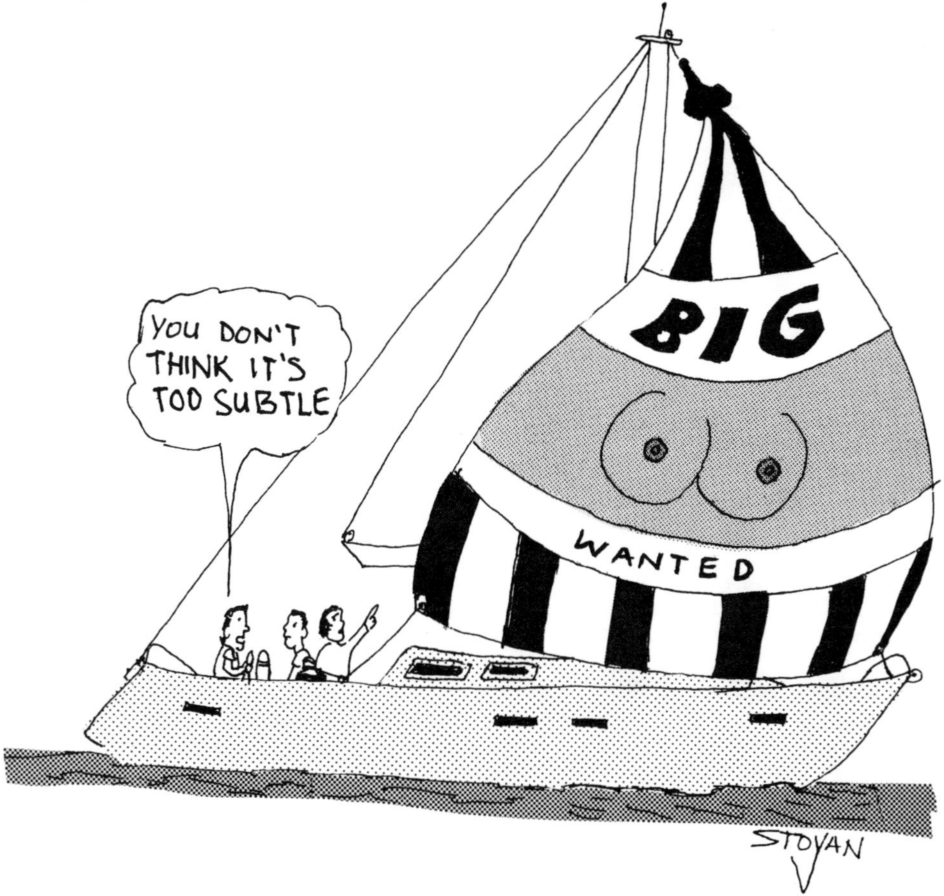
YOU DON'T THINK IT'S TOO SUBTLE
BIG
WANTED
STOYAN

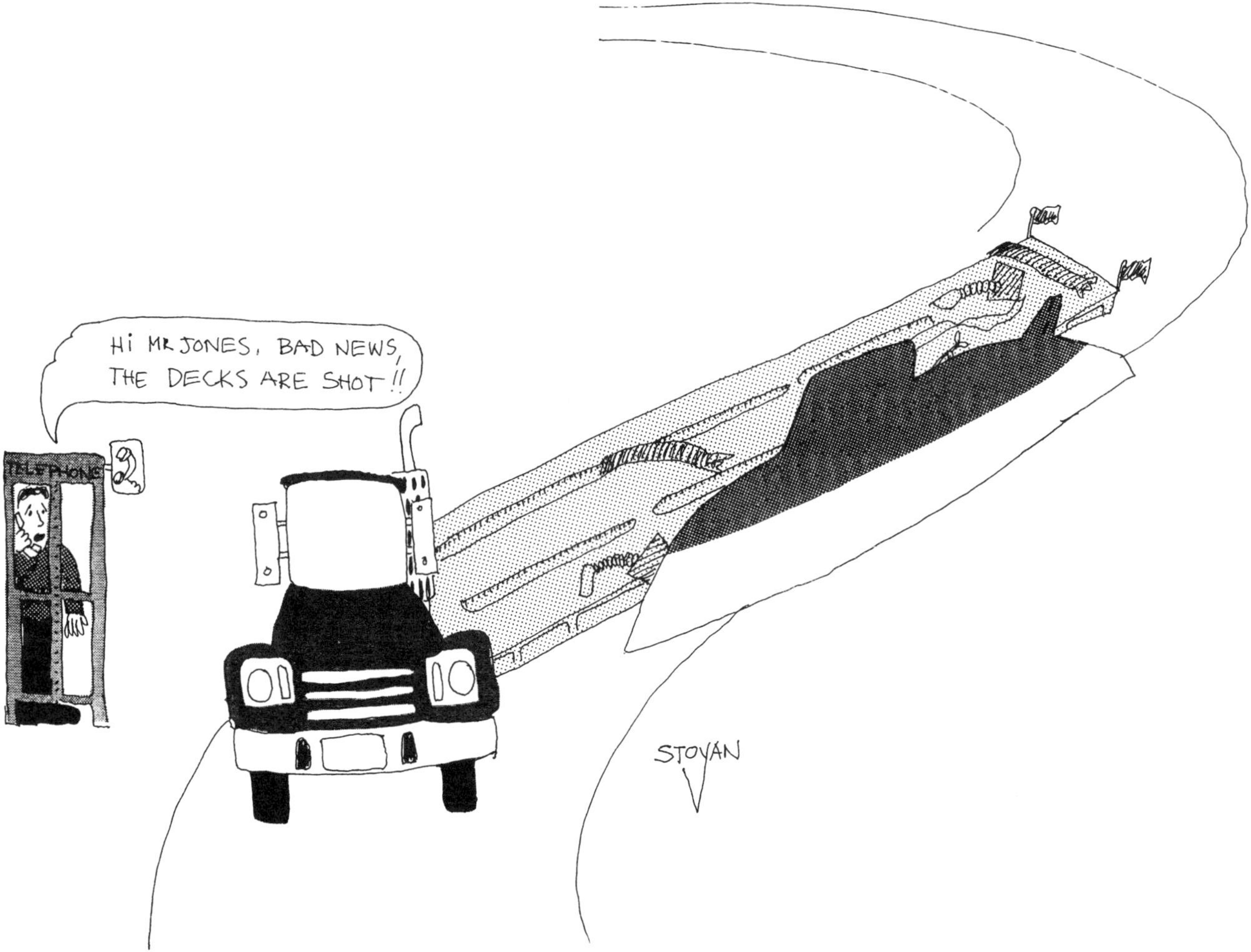
HI MR JONES, BAD NEWS, THE DECKS ARE SHOT!!
TELEPHONE
STOYAN

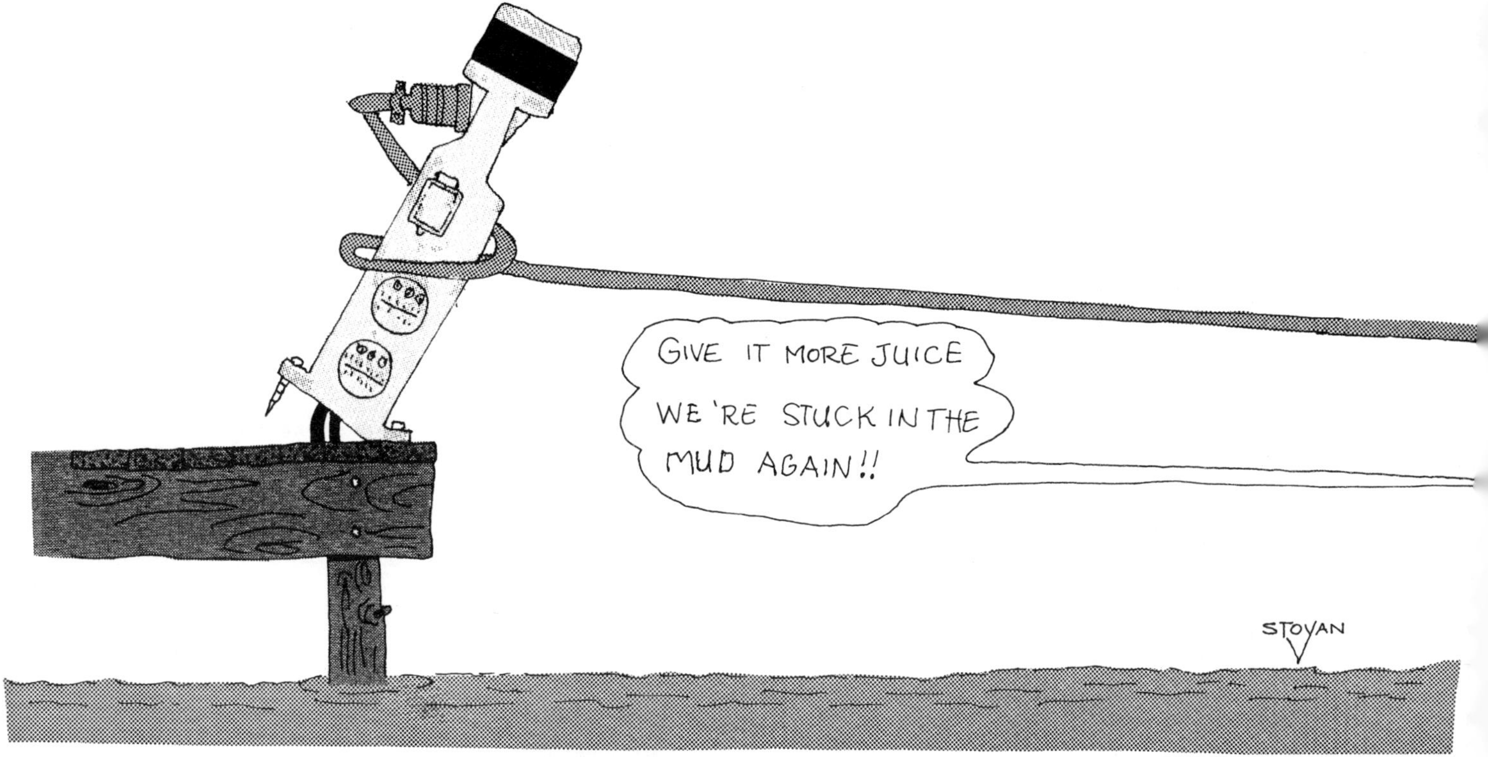
GIVE IT MORE JUICE WE'RE STUCK IN THE MUD AGAIN!!
STOYAN

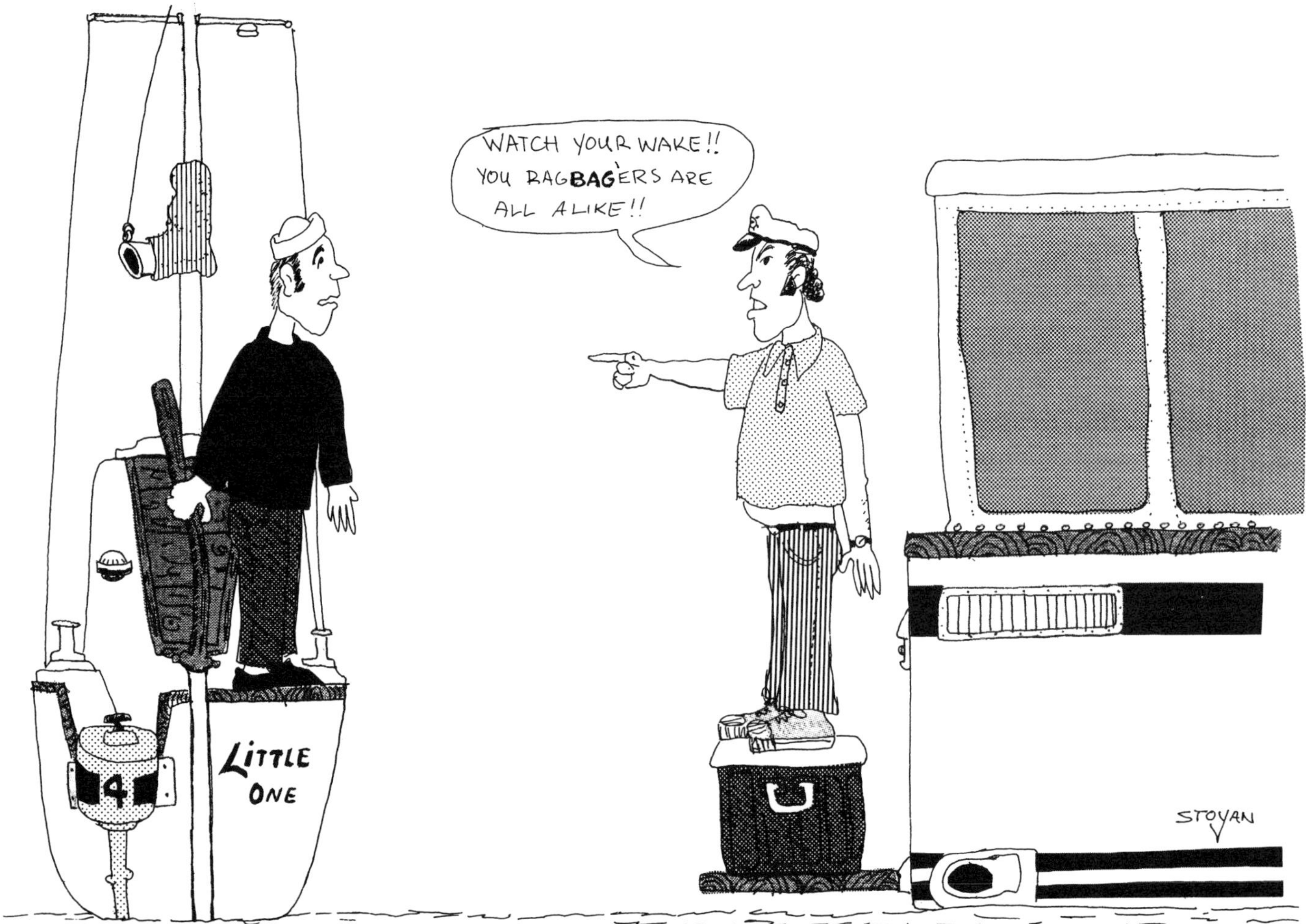
WATCH YOUR WAKE!! YOU RAGBAG'ERS ARE ALL ALIKE!!
LITTLE ONE
4
STOYAN

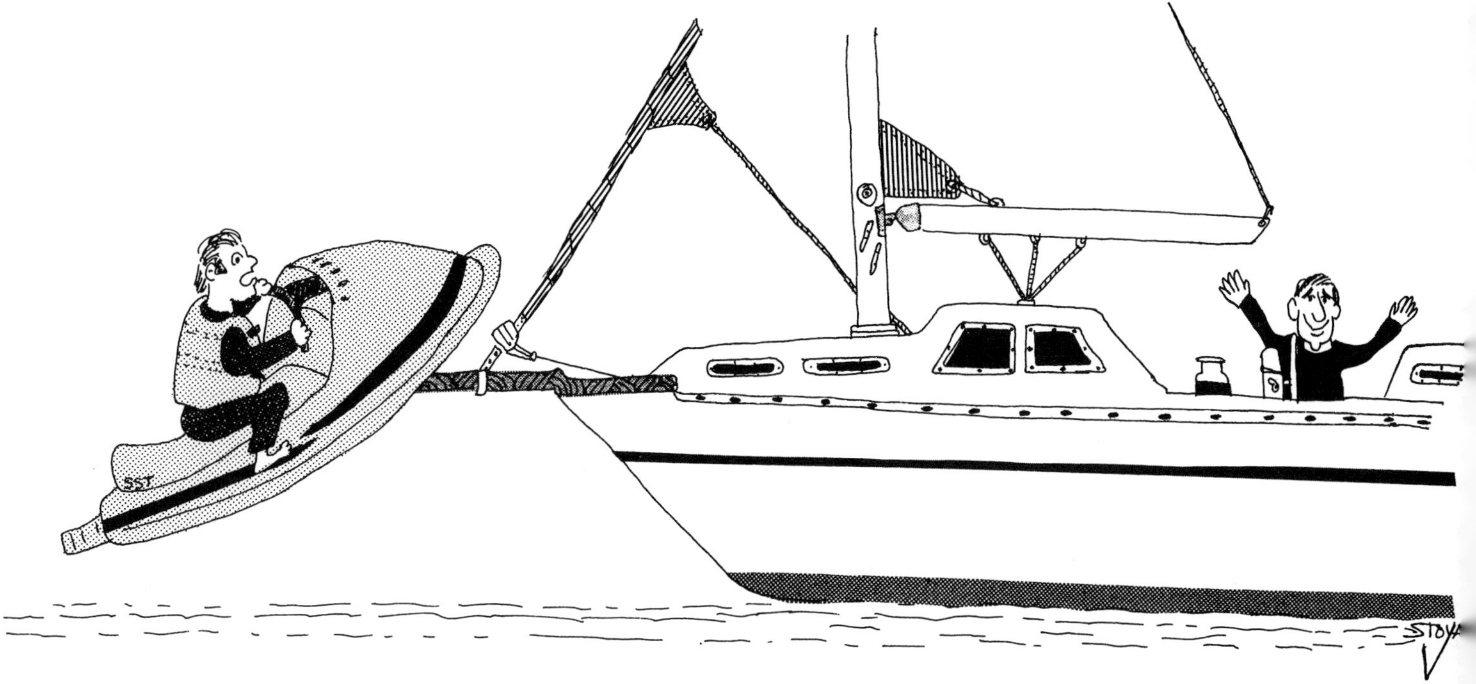
SST

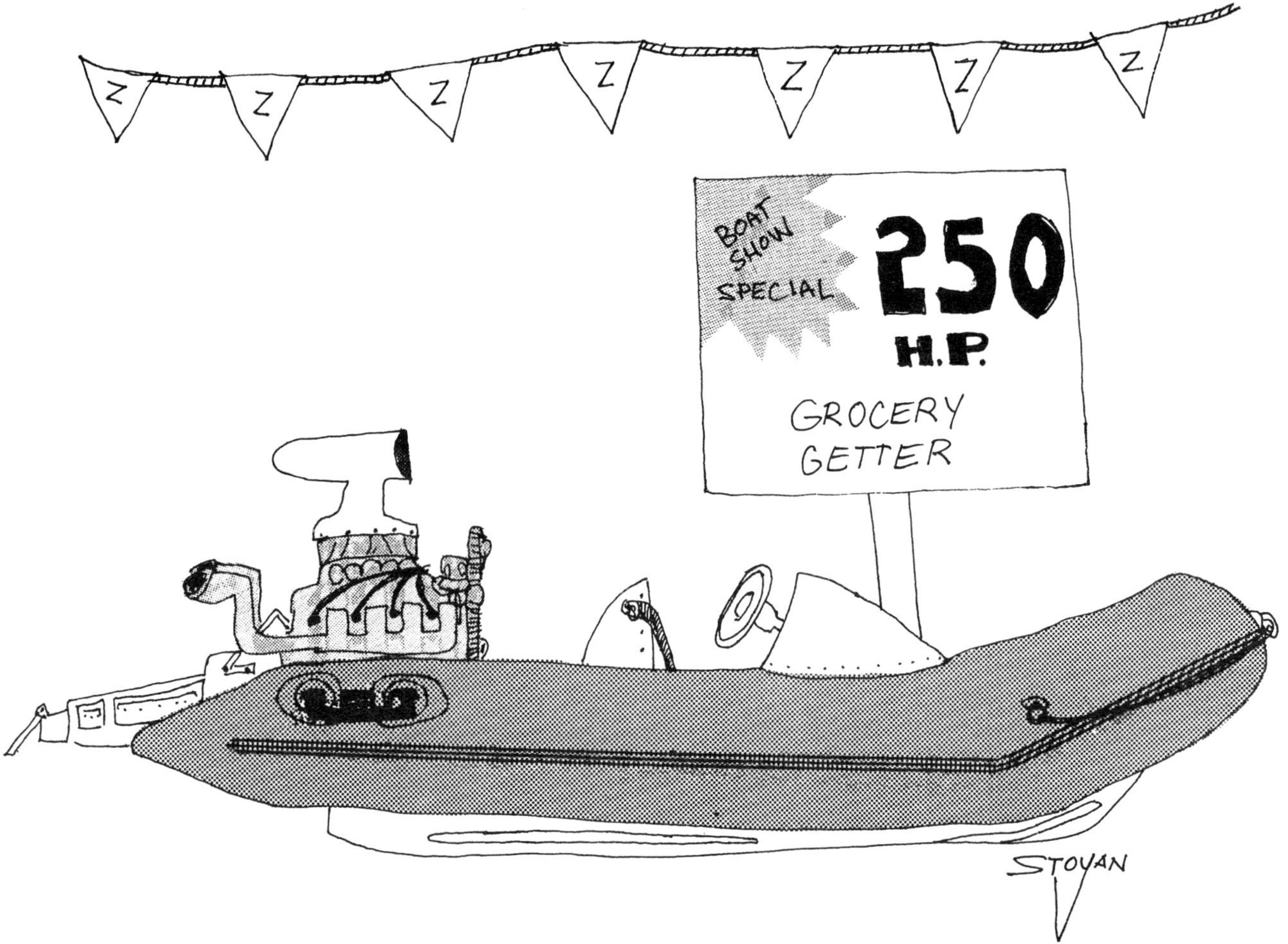
Z Z Z Z Z Z Z
BOAT SHOW SPECIAL
250
H.P.
GROCERY GETTER
STOYAN

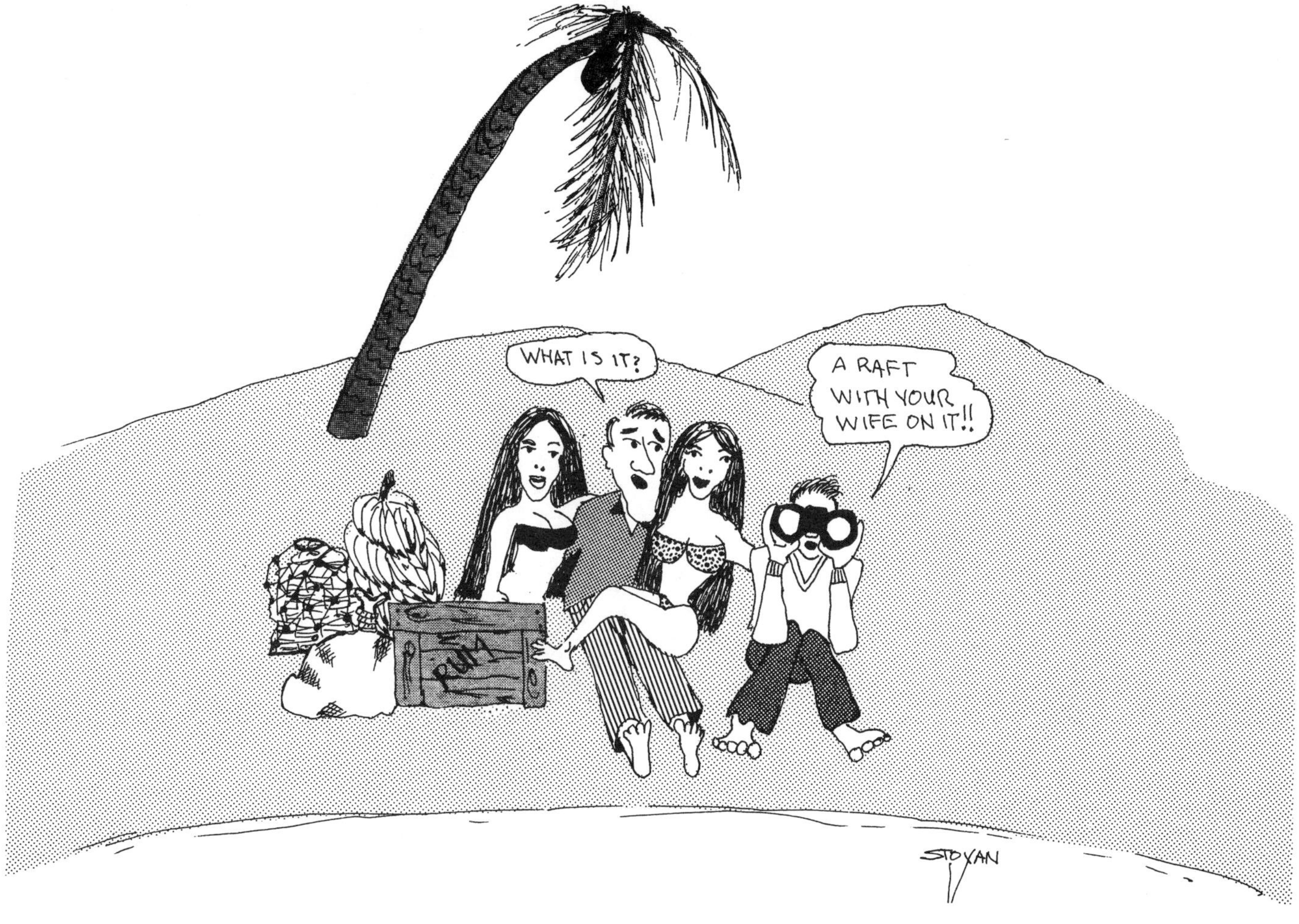
WHAT IS IT?
A RAFT WITH YOUR WIFE ON IT!!
RUM
STOYAN

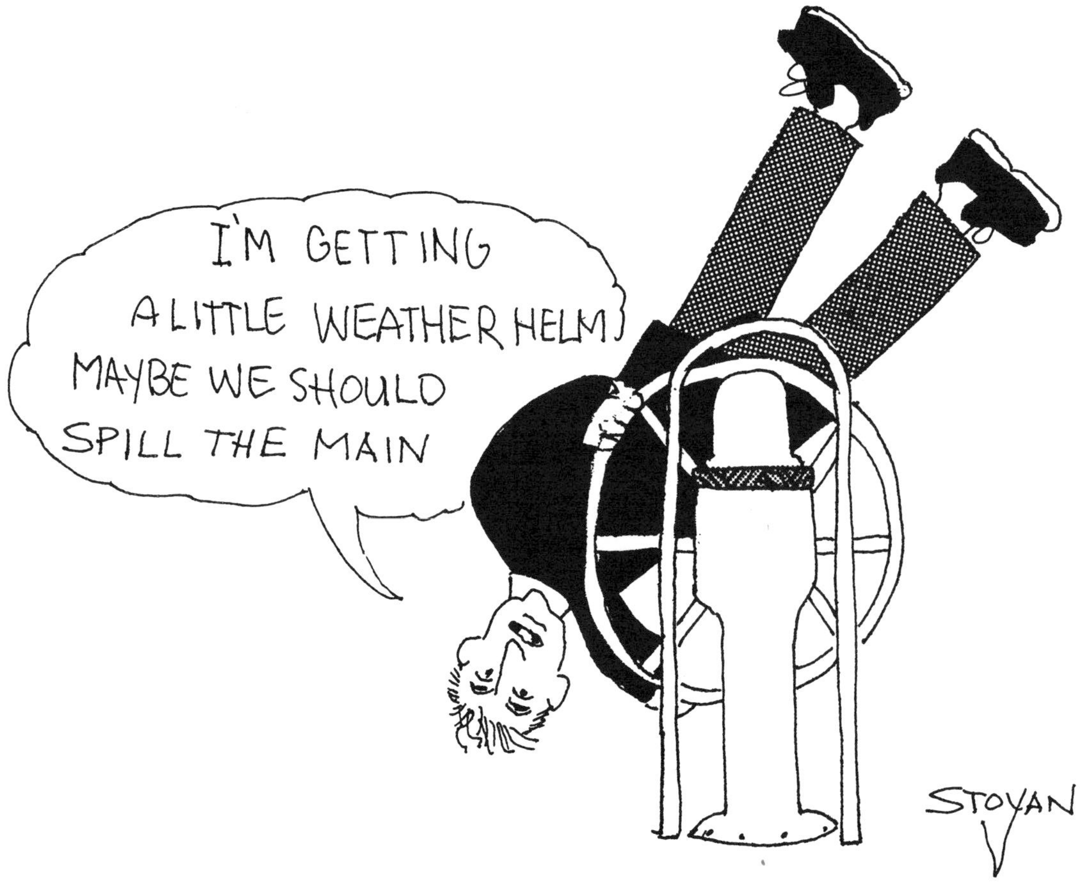
I'M GETTING A LITTLE WEATHER HELM, MAYBE WE SHOULD SPILL THE MAIN
STOYAN

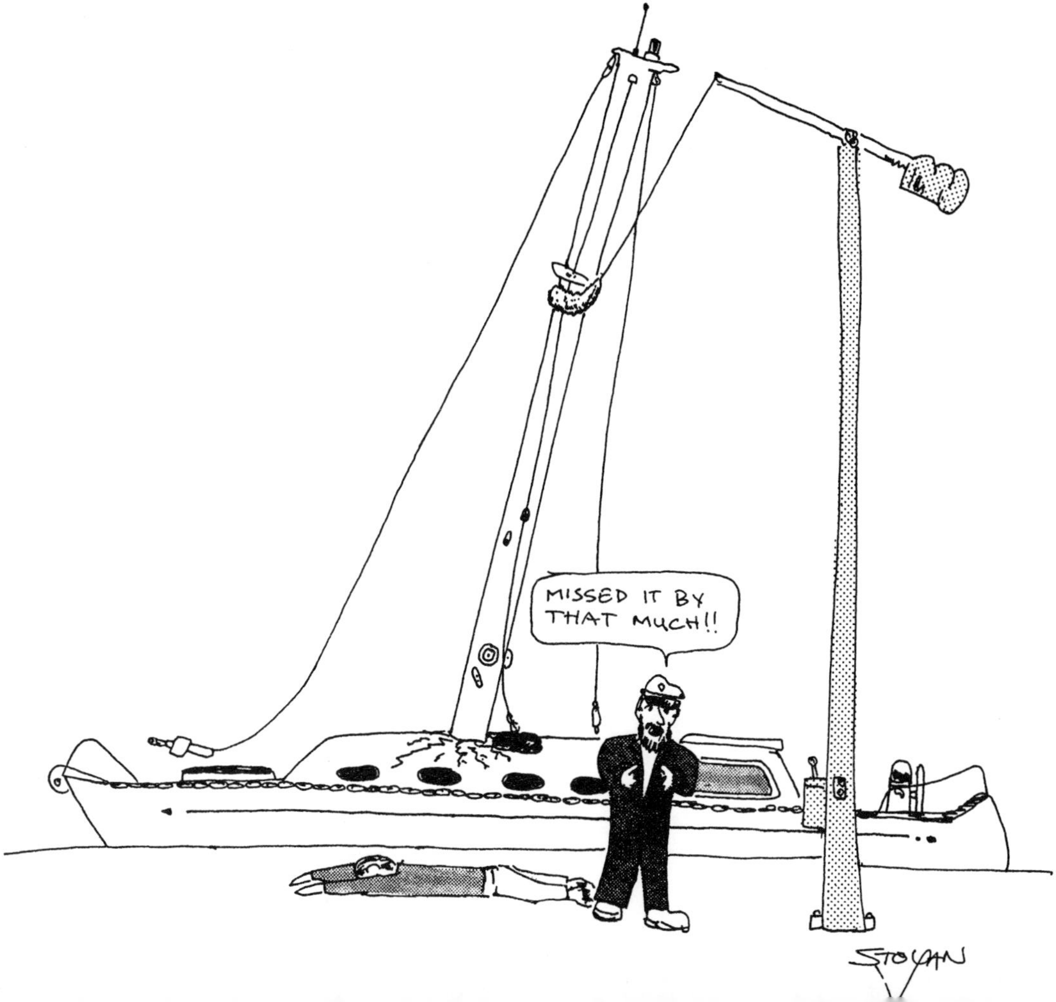
MISSED IT BY THAT MUCH!!
STOYAN

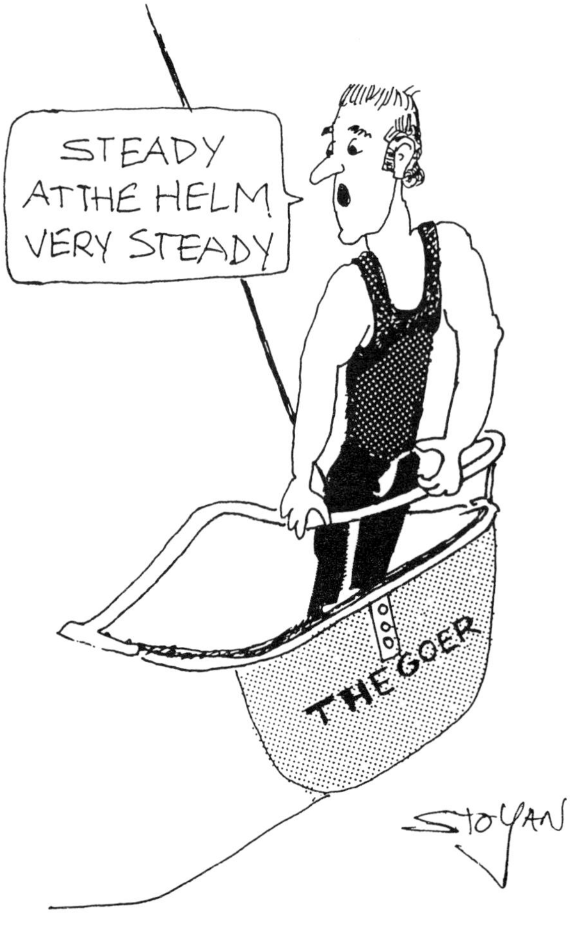
STEADY AT THE HELM VERY STEADY
THE GOER
STOYAN

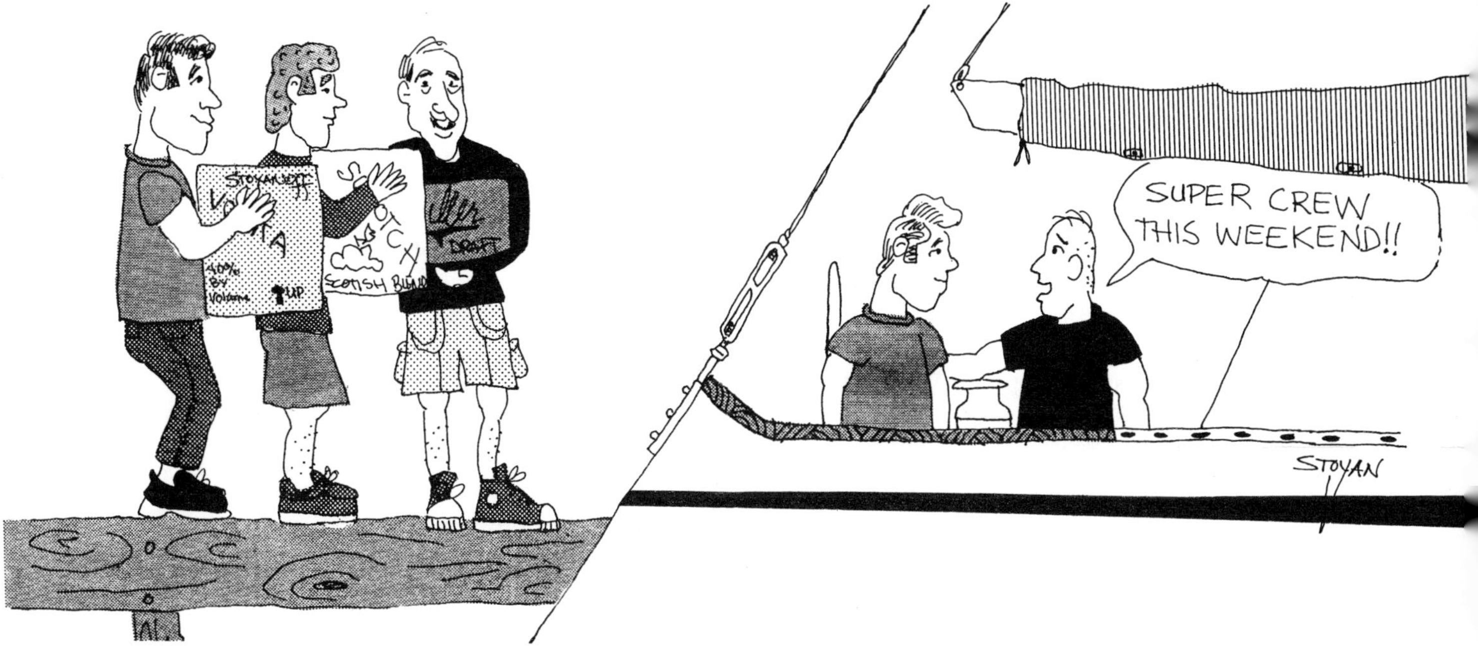
SUPER CREW
THIS WEEKEND!!
SCOTISH BLEND
DRAFT
STOYAN

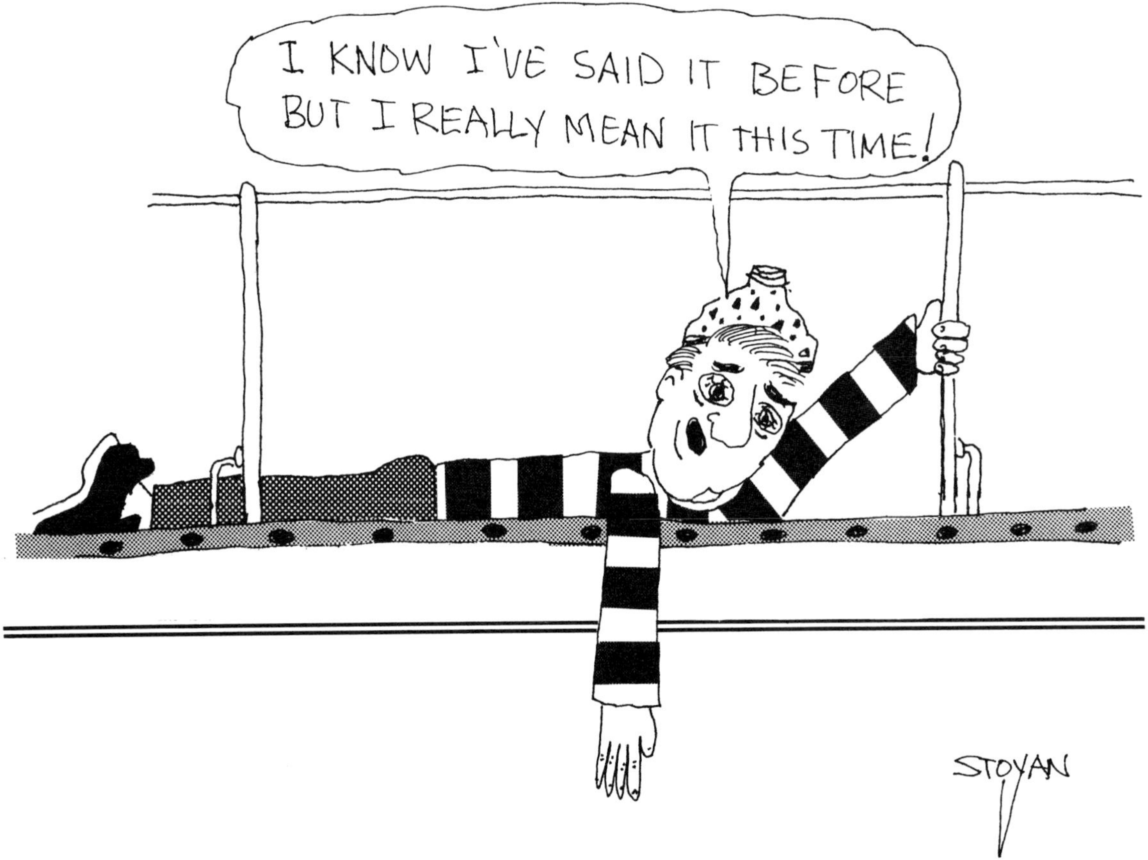
I KNOW I'VE SAID IT BEFORE BUT I REALLY MEAN IT THIS TIME!
STOYAN

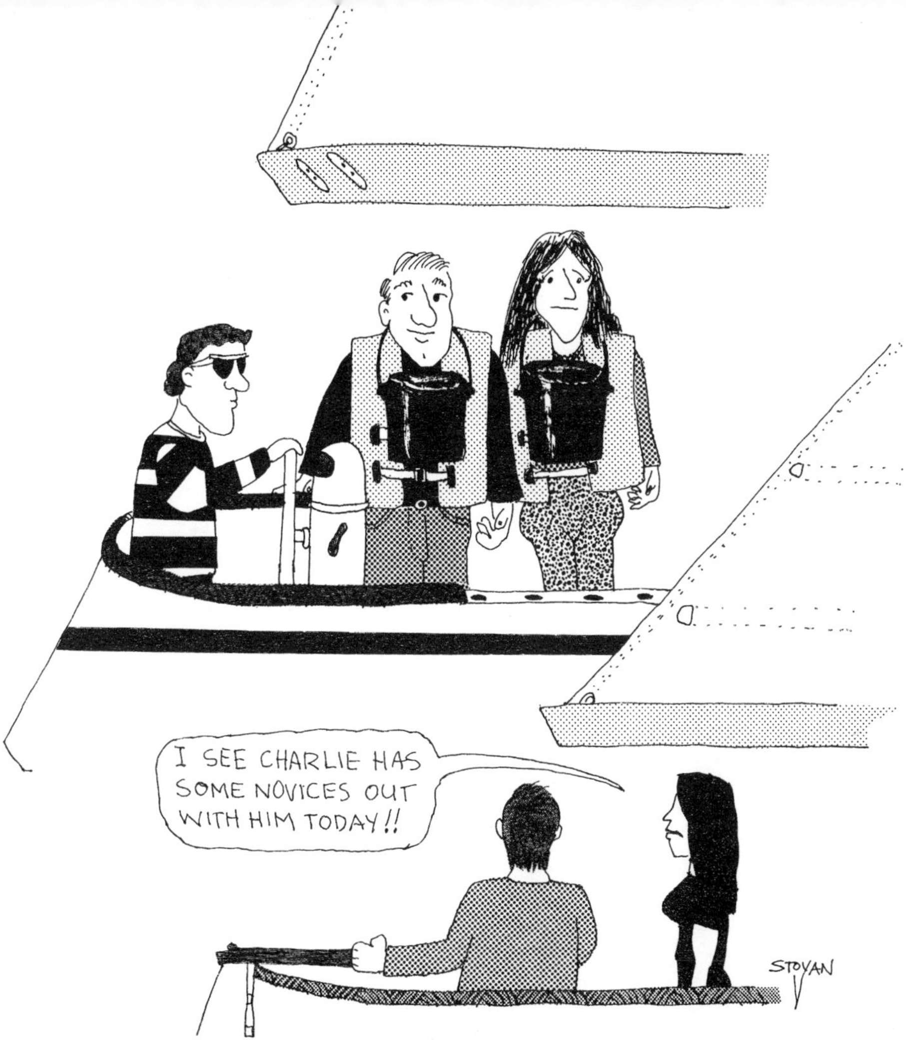
I SEE CHARLIE HAS SOME NOVICES OUT WITH HIM TODAY!!
STOYAN

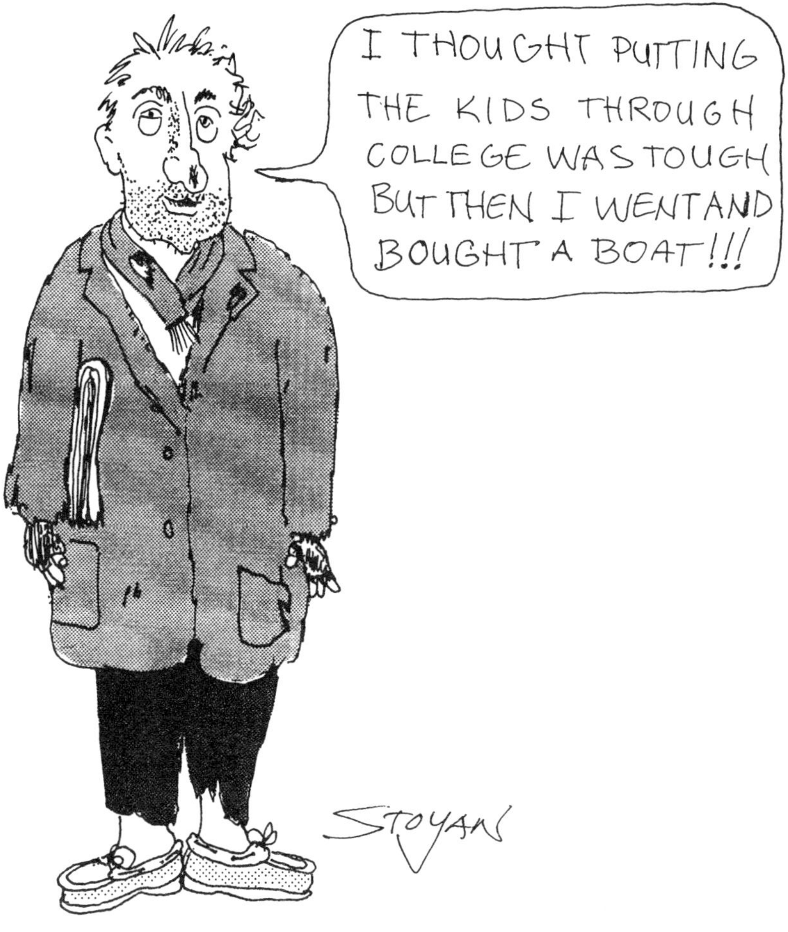
I THOUGHT PUTTING THE KIDS THROUGH COLLEGE WAS TOUGH BUT THEN I WENT AND BOUGHT A BOAT!!!
STOYAN

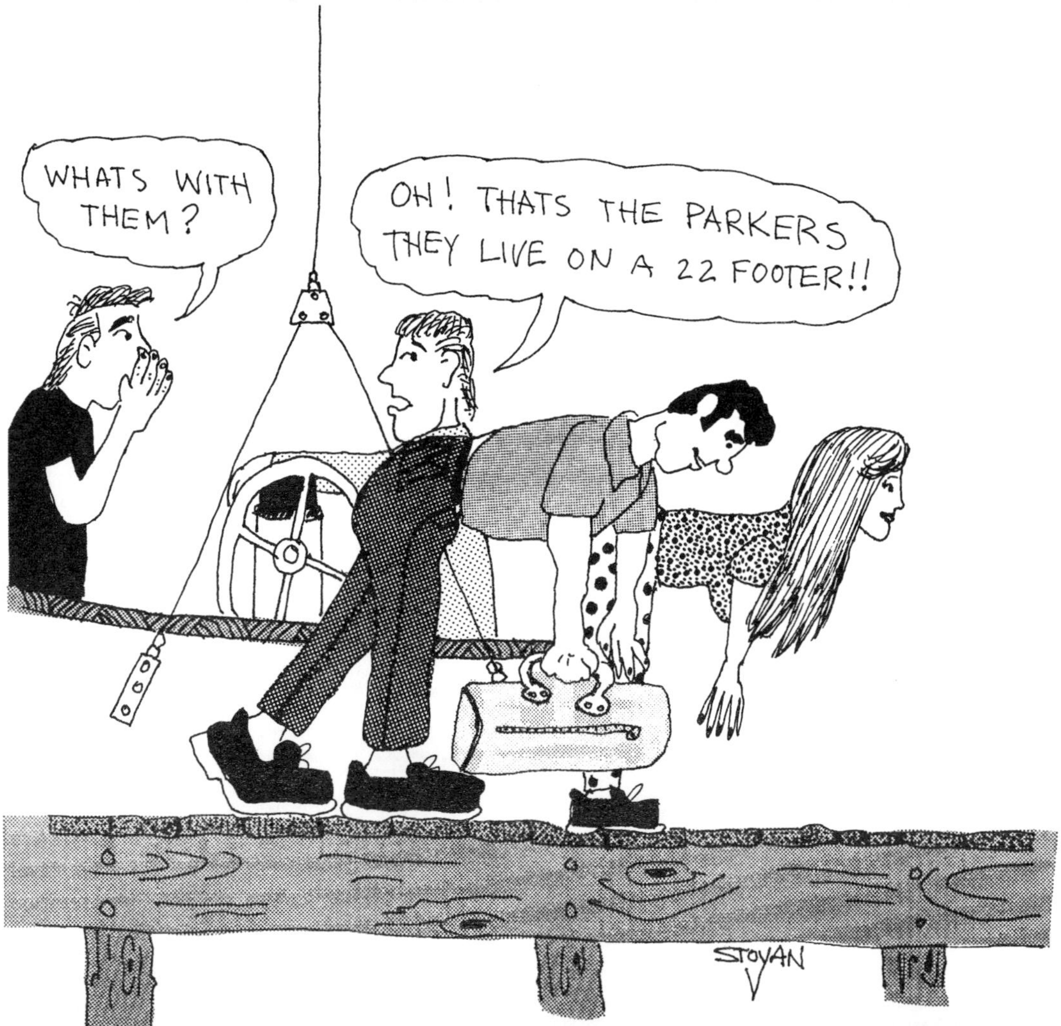
WHATS WITH THEM?
OH! THATS THE PARKERS THEY LIVE ON A 22 FOOTER!!
STOYAN

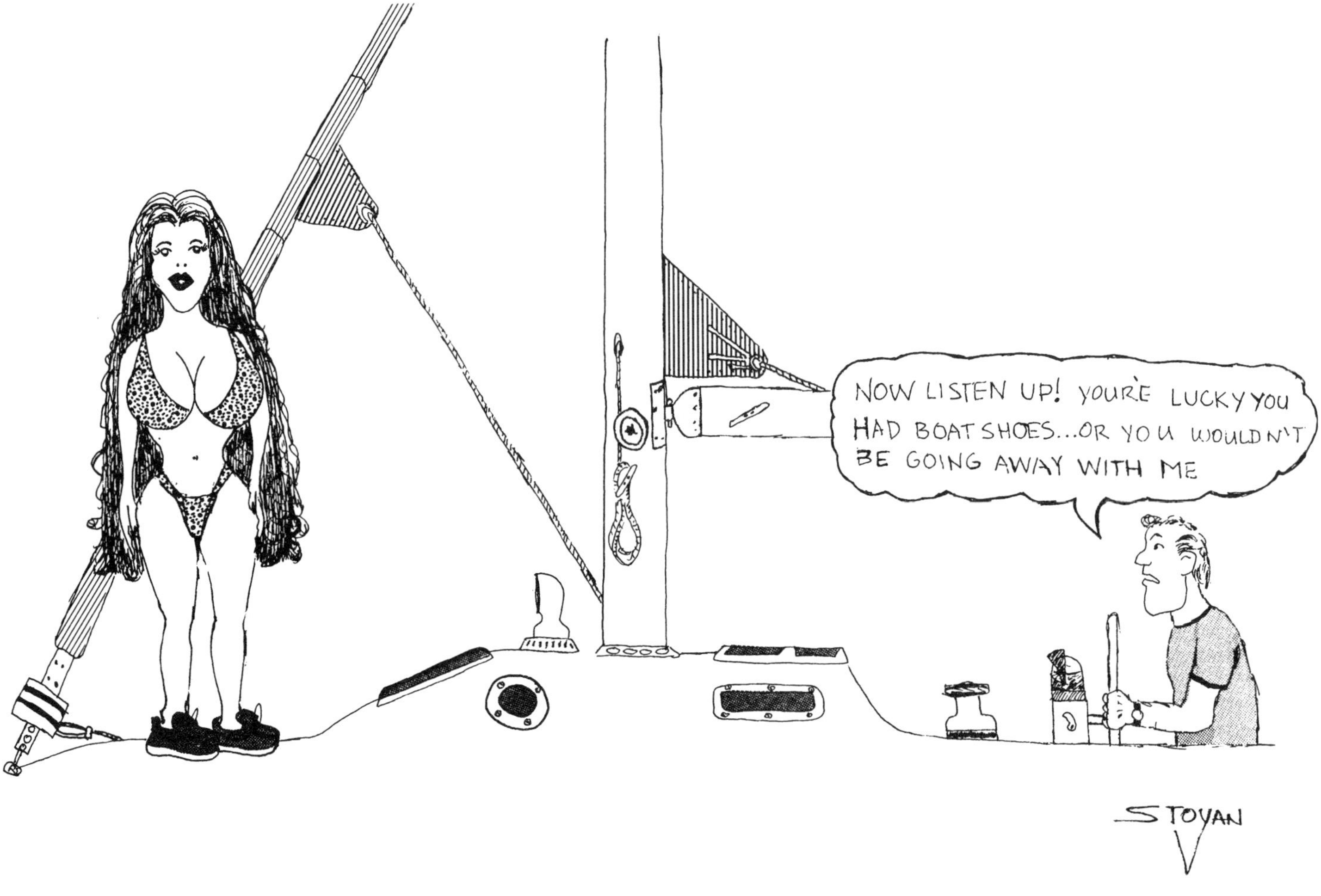
NOW LISTEN UP! YOU'RE LUCKY YOU HAD BOAT SHOES...OR YOU WOULDN'T BE GOING AWAY WITH ME
STOYAN

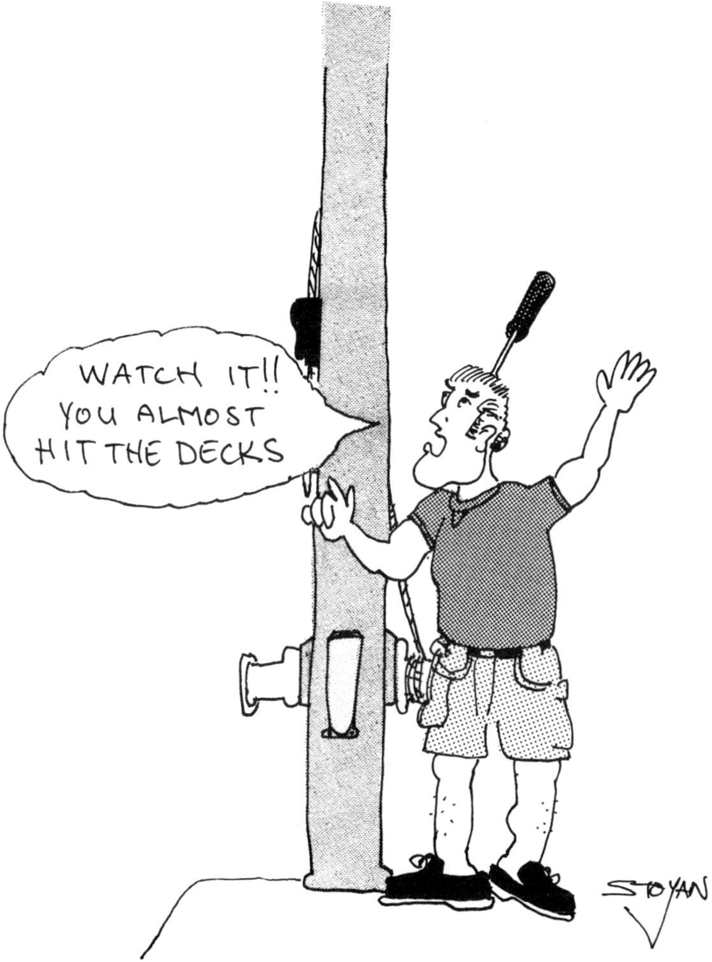
WATCH IT!! YOU ALMOST HIT THE DECKS
STOYAN

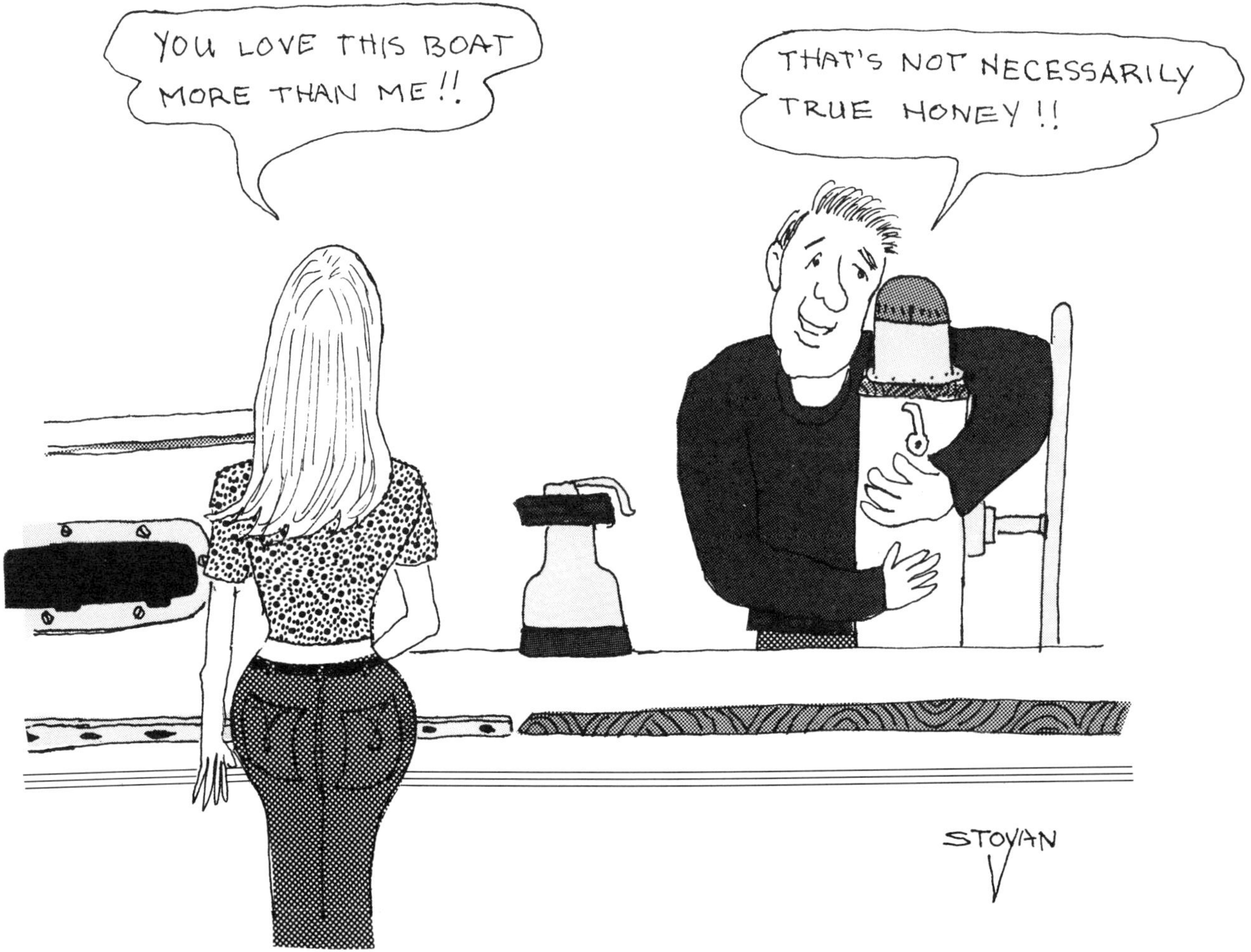
YOU LOVE THIS BOAT MORE THAN ME!!
THAT'S NOT NECESSARILY TRUE HONEY!!
STOYAN

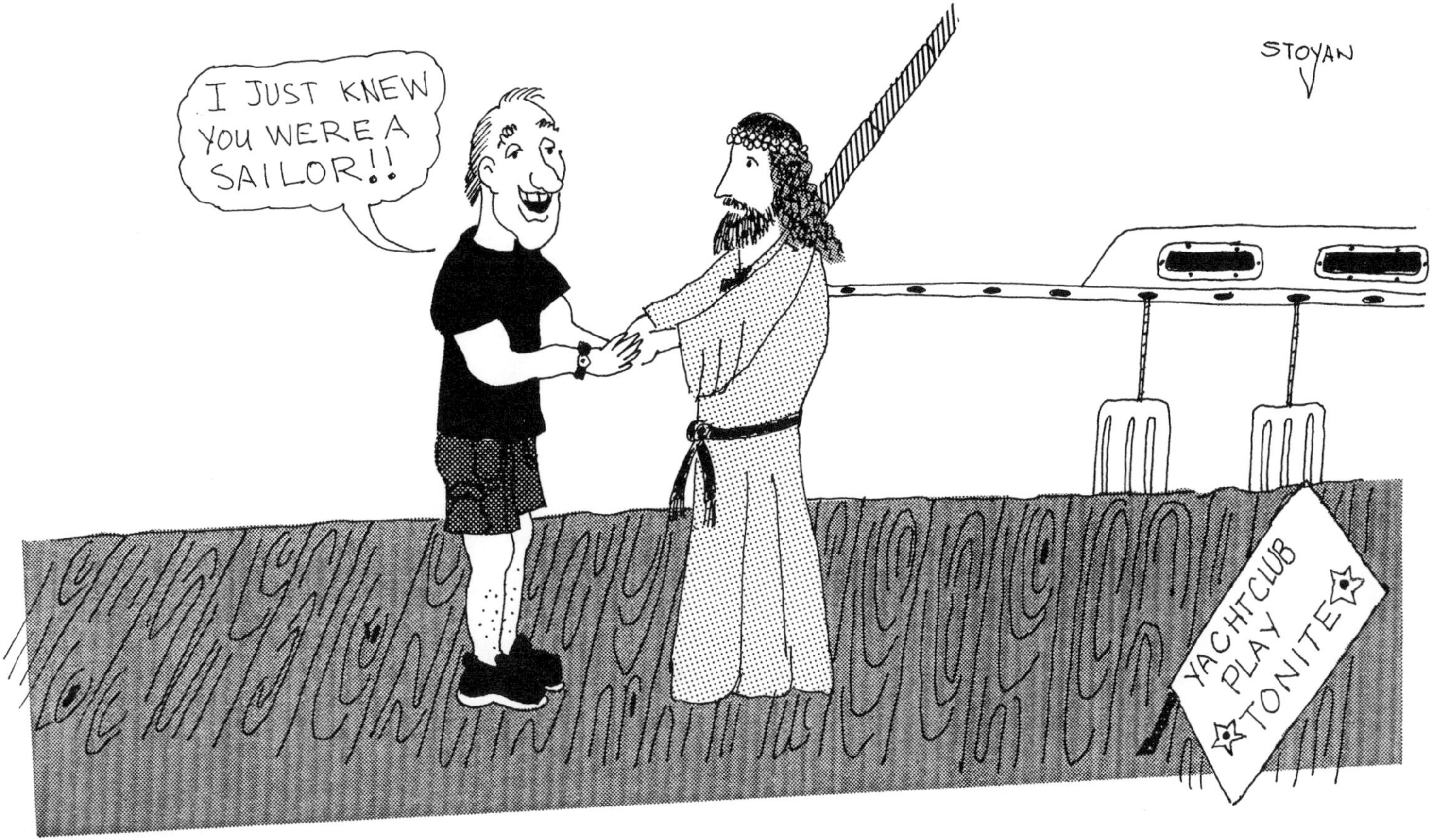
STOYAN
I JUST KNEW YOU WERE A SAILOR!!
YACHTCLUB PLAY TONITE

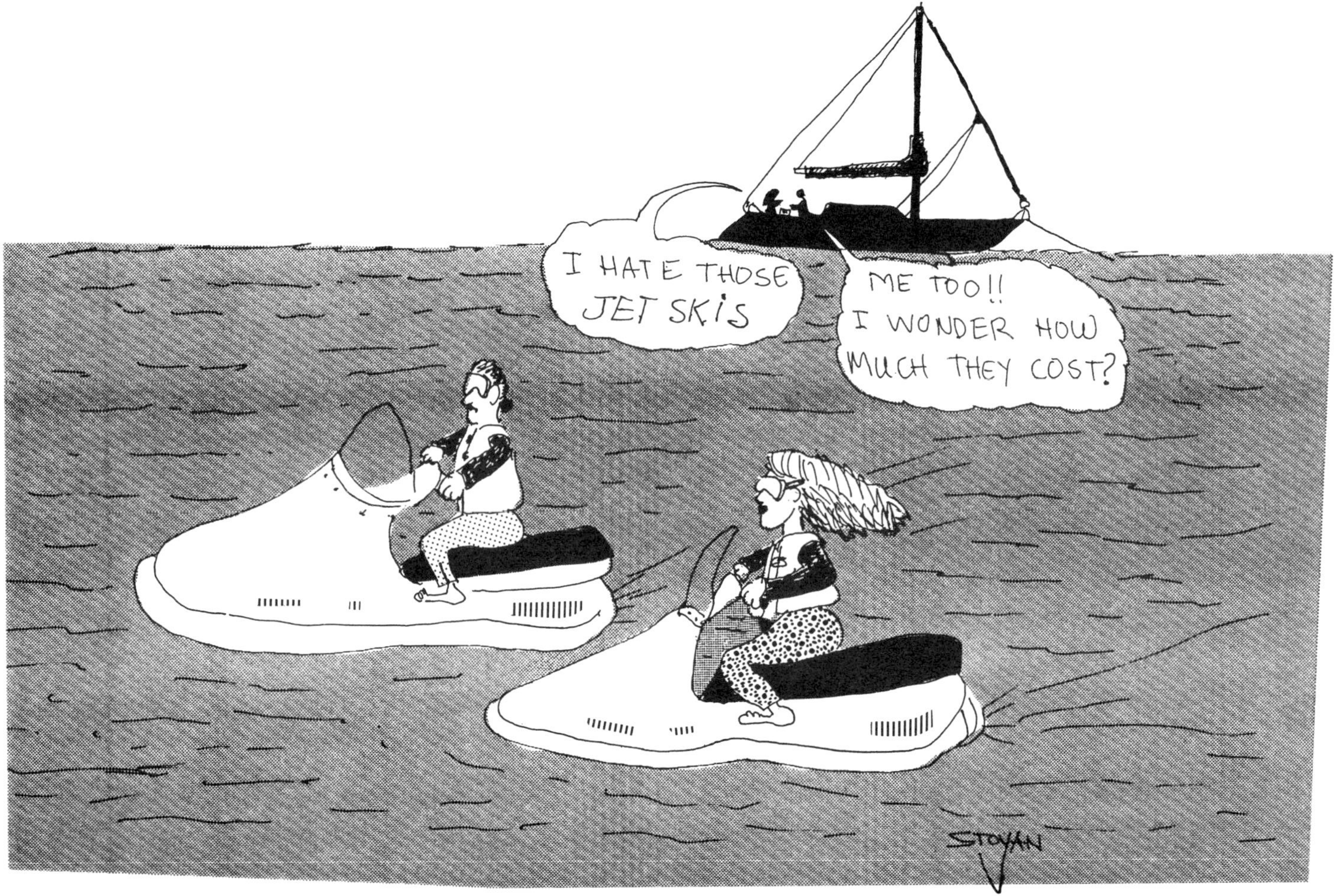
I HATE THOSE JET SKIS
ME TOO!! I WONDER HOW MUCH THEY COST?
STOYAN

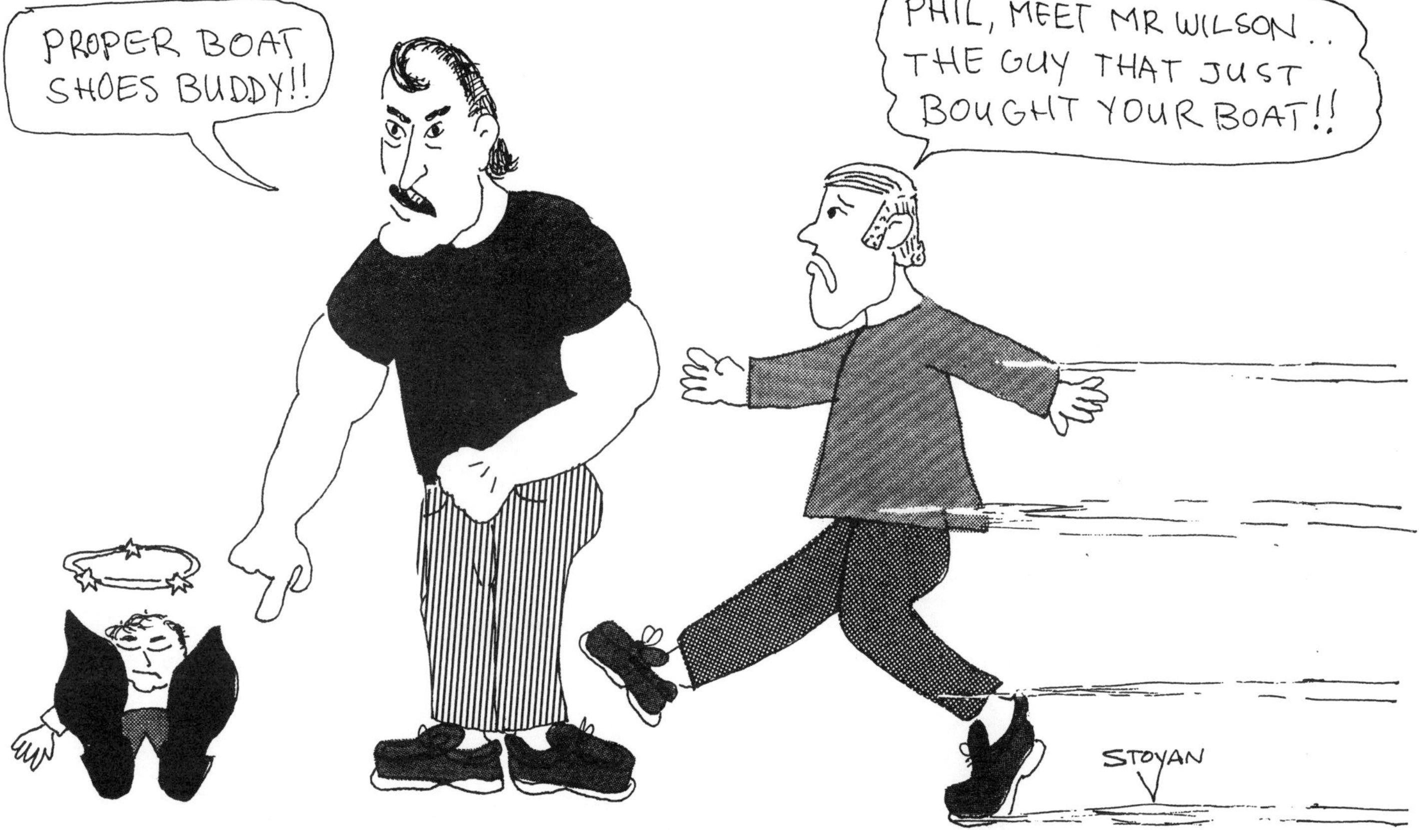
PROPER BOAT SHOES BUDDY!!
PHIL, MEET MR WILSON.. THE GUY THAT JUST BOUGHT YOUR BOAT!!
STOYAN

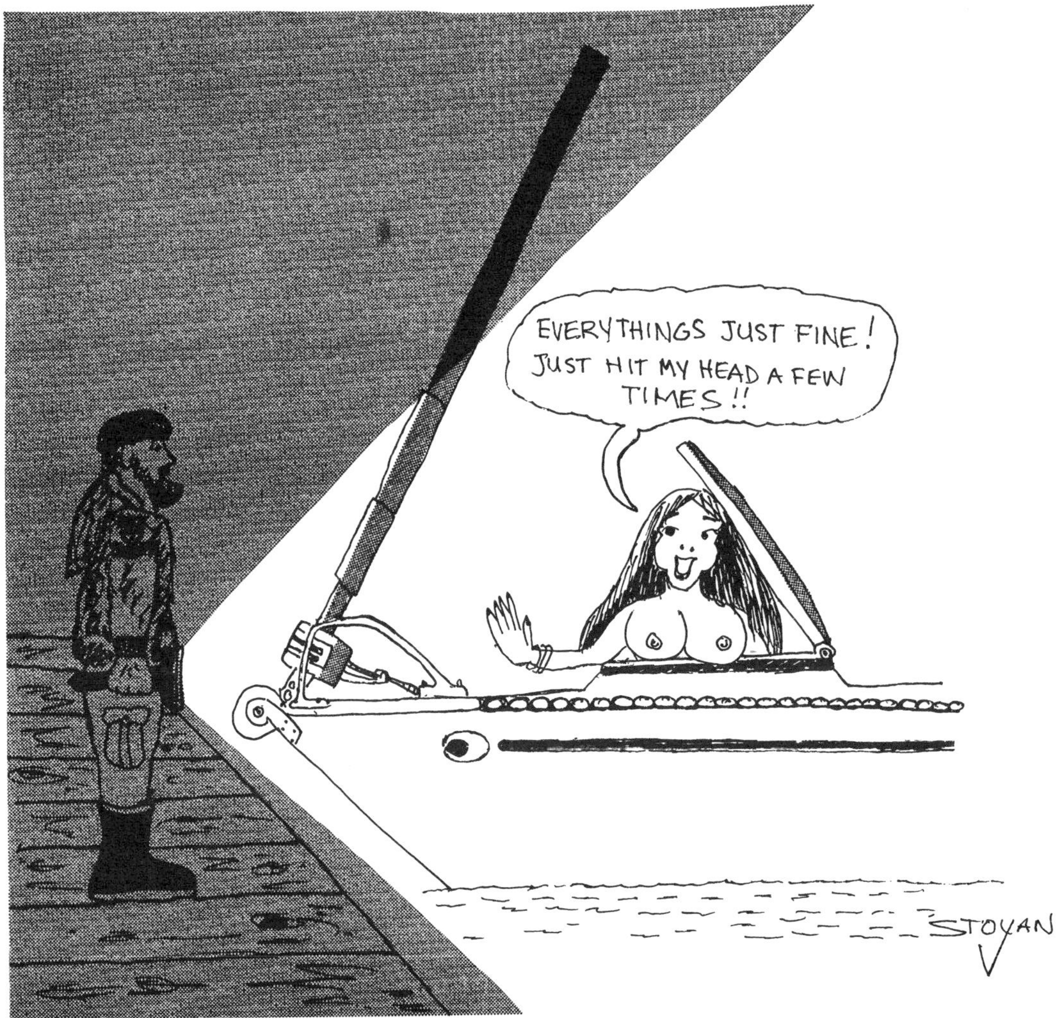
EVERYTHINGS JUST FINE!
JUST HIT MY HEAD A FEW TIMES!!
STOYAN

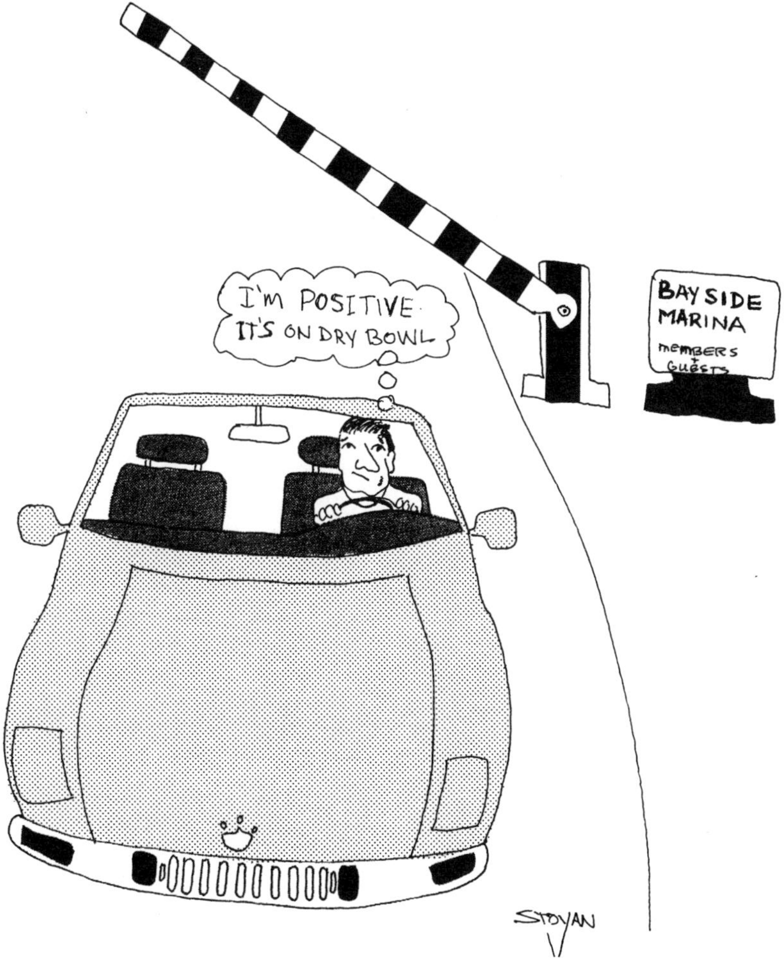
I'M POSITIVE IT'S ON DRY BOWL
BAYSIDE MARINA
members + GUESTS
STOYAN

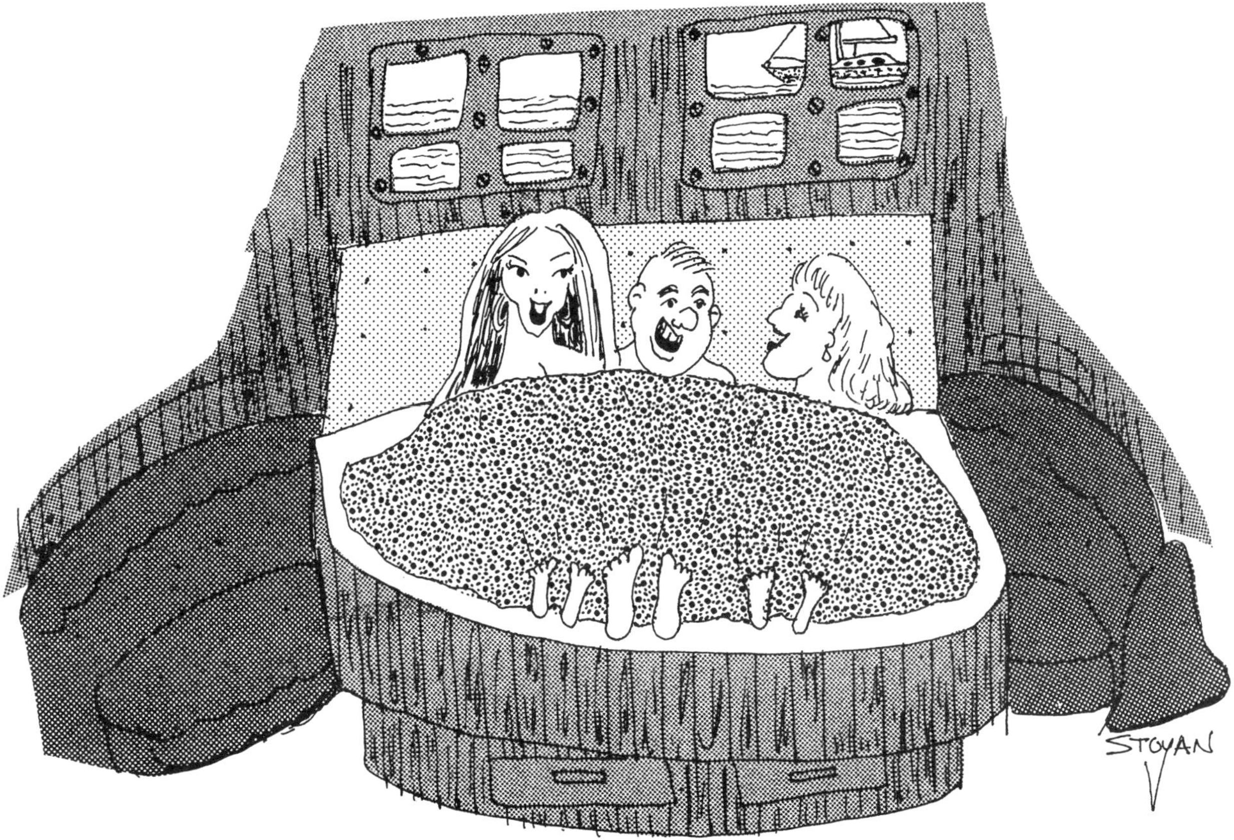
STOYAN

AND WE STILL HAVE TIME TO SQUEEZE IN
A LITTLE SAILING!!

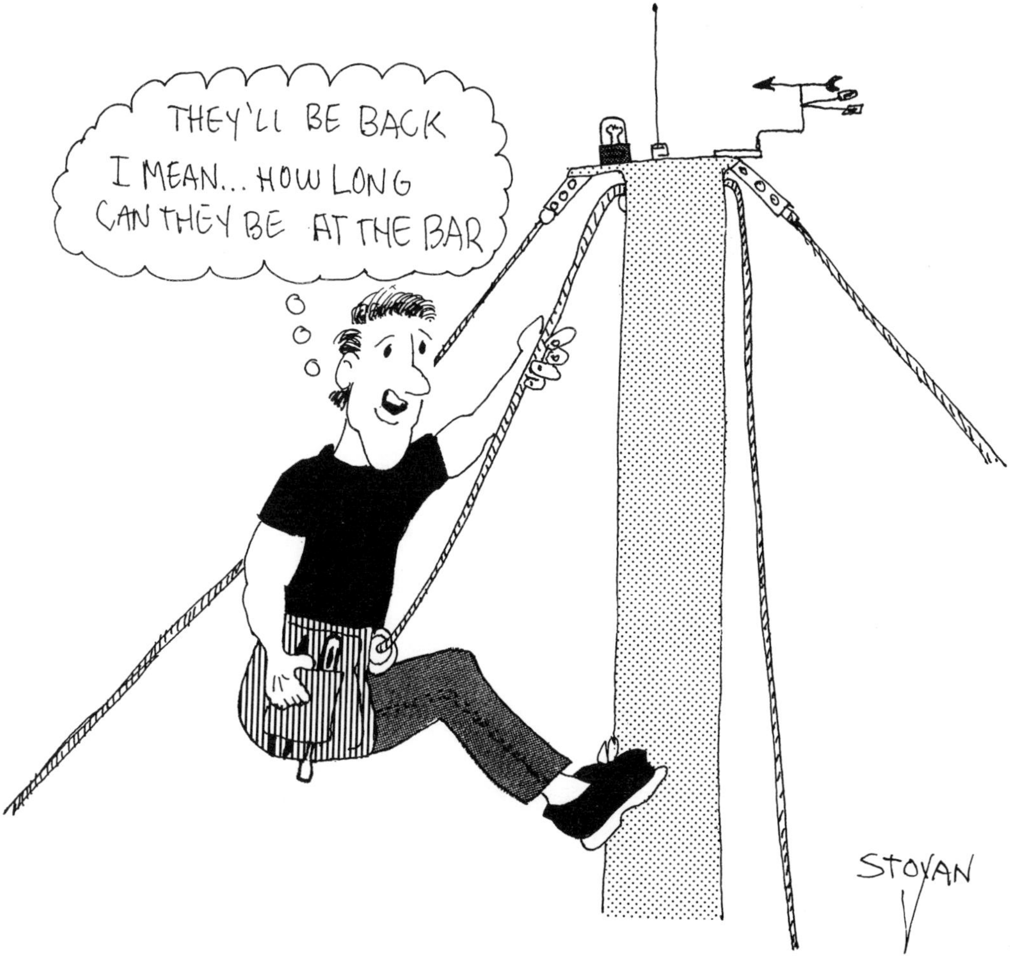
THEY'LL BE BACK
I MEAN... HOW LONG
CAN THEY BE AT THE BAR
STOYAN

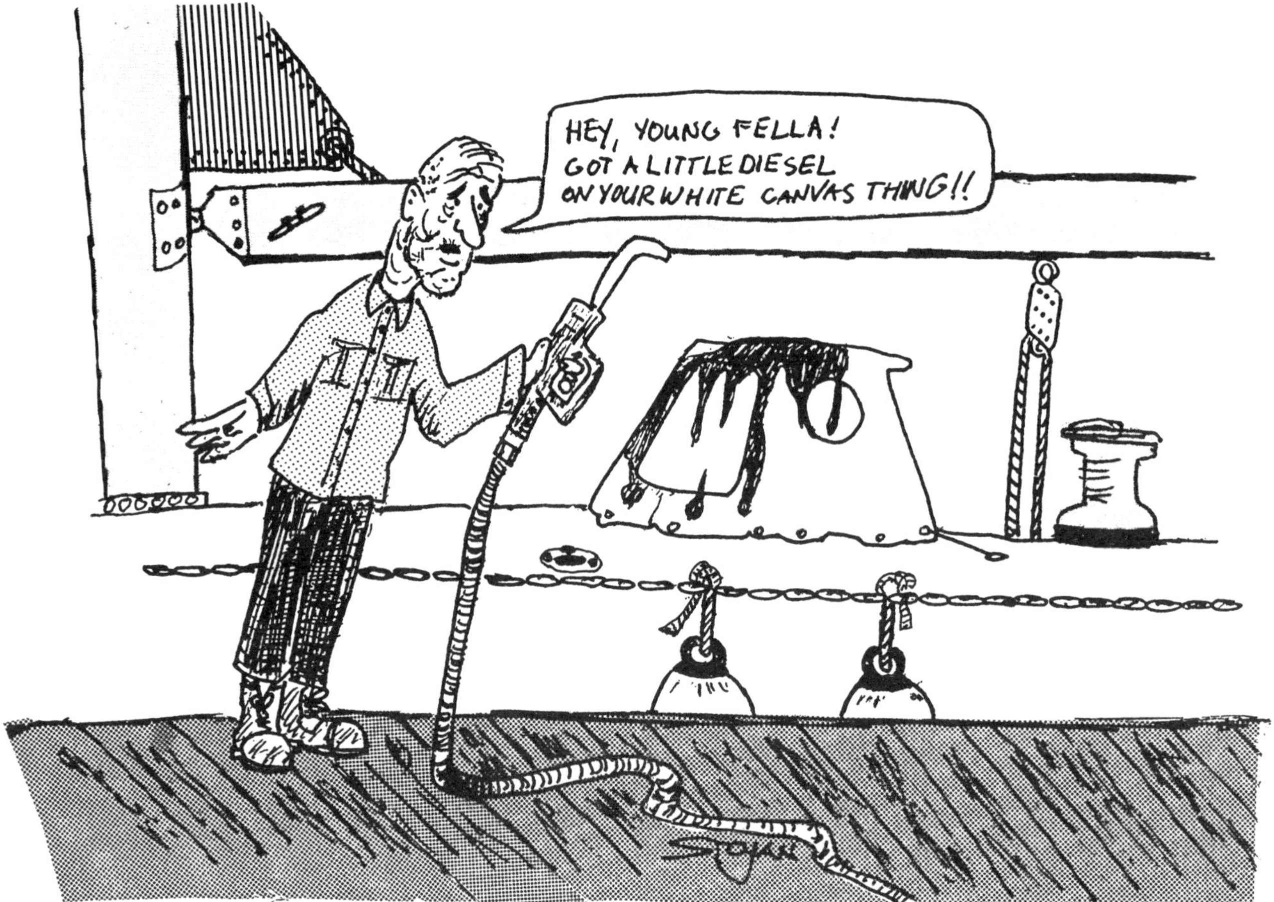
HEY, YOUNG FELLA!
GOT A LITTLE DIESEL
ON YOUR WHITE CANVAS THING!!

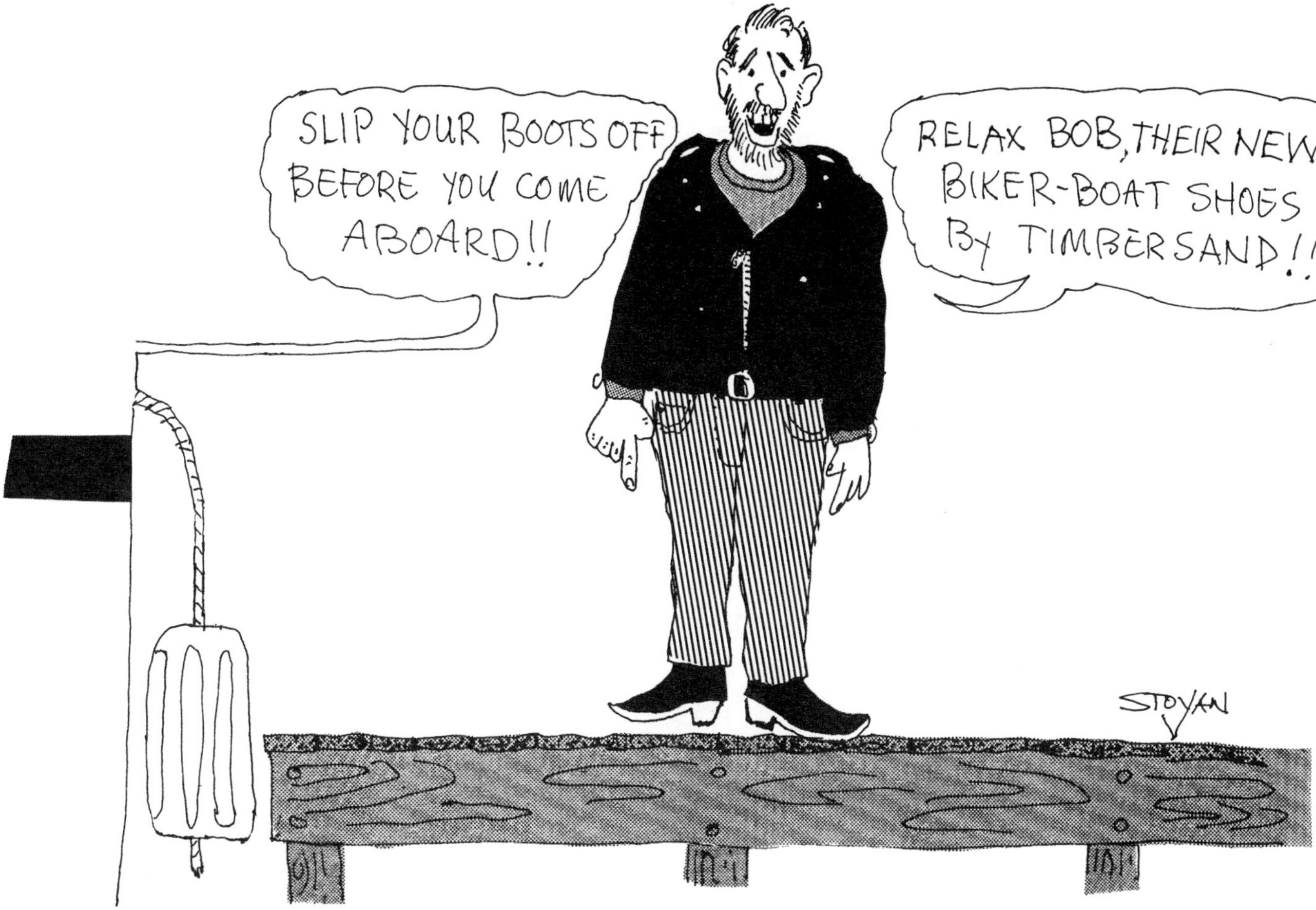
SLIP YOUR BOOTS OFF BEFORE YOU COME ABOARD!!
RELAX BOB, THEIR NEW BIKER-BOAT SHOES BY TIMBERSAND!!
STOYAN

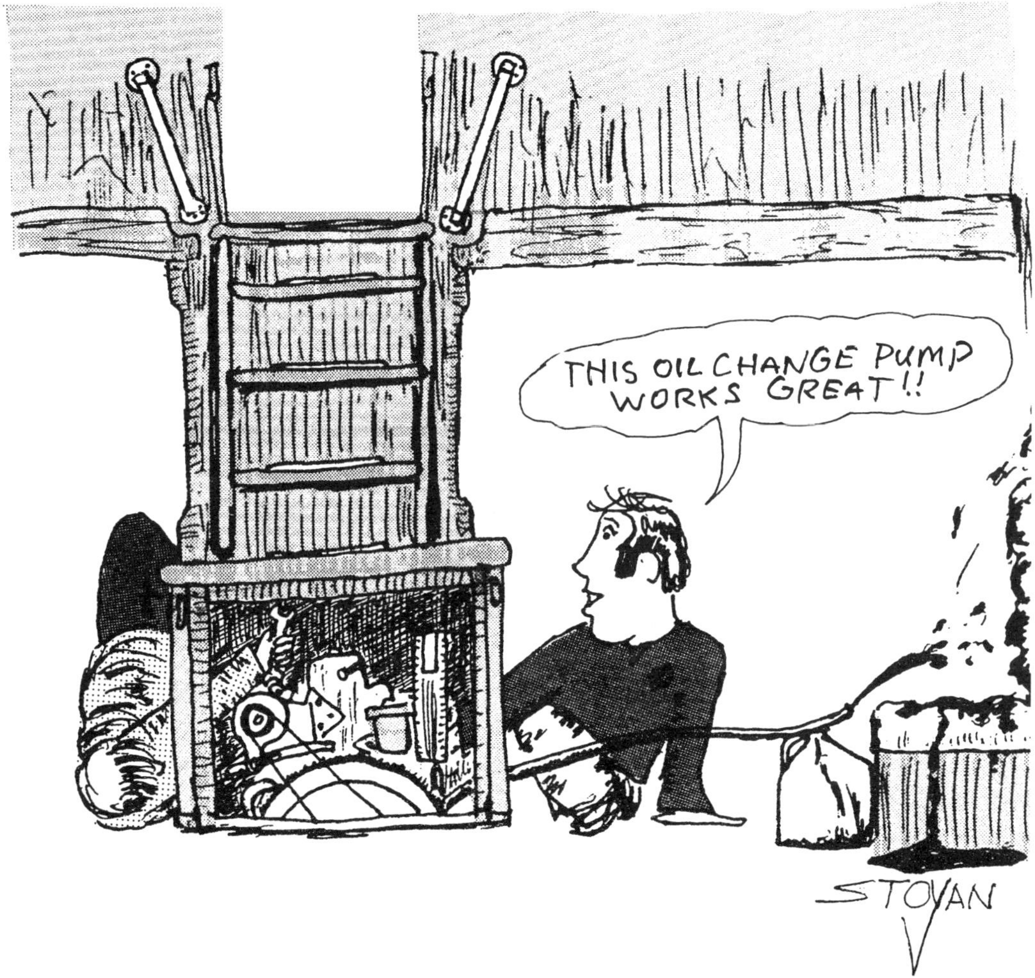
THIS OIL CHANGE PUMP WORKS GREAT!!
STOVAN

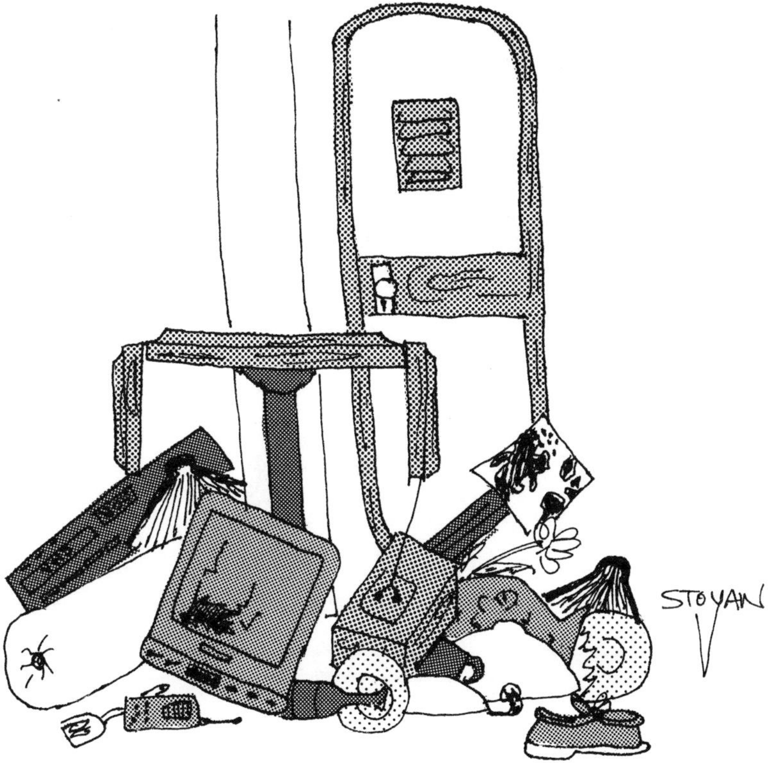
STOYAN

AFTER A DAY OF GOOD WIND WE CALL IT
SALON SCRABBLE!

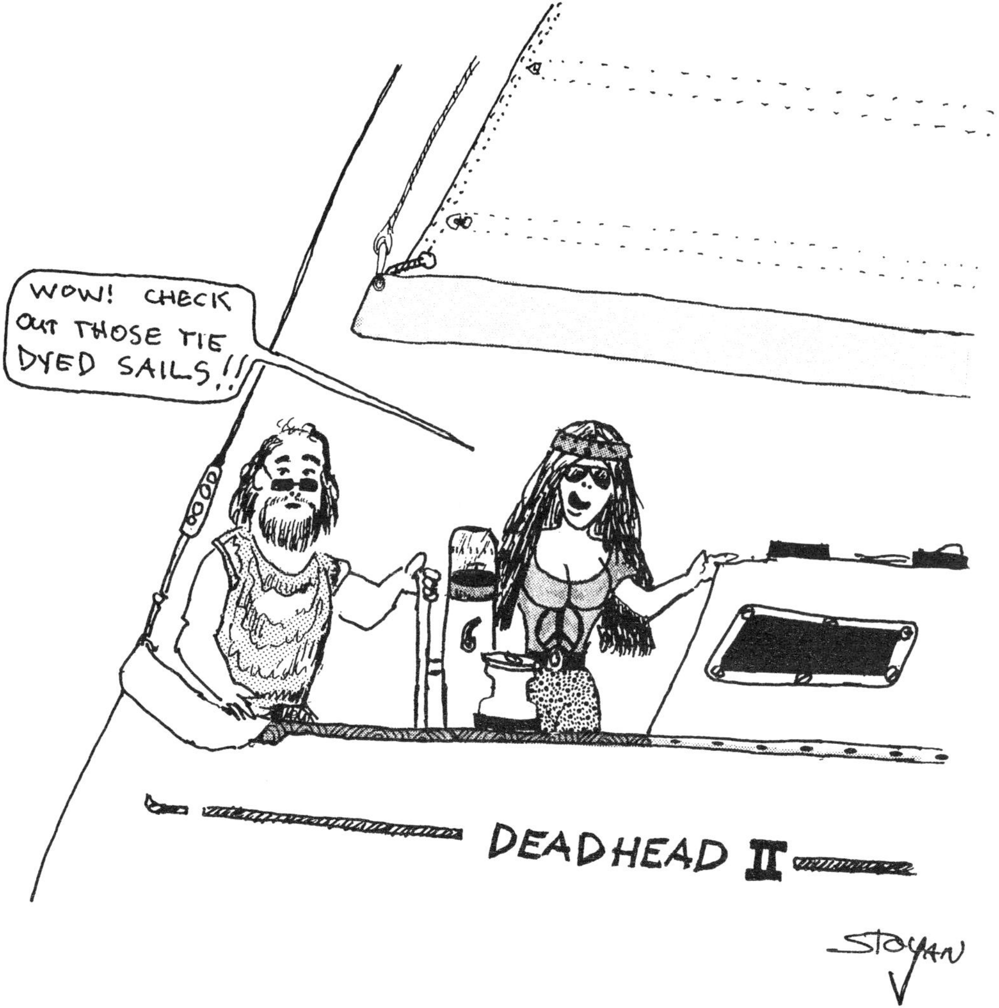
WOW! CHECK OUT THOSE TIE DYED SAILS!!!
DEADHEAD II
STOYAN

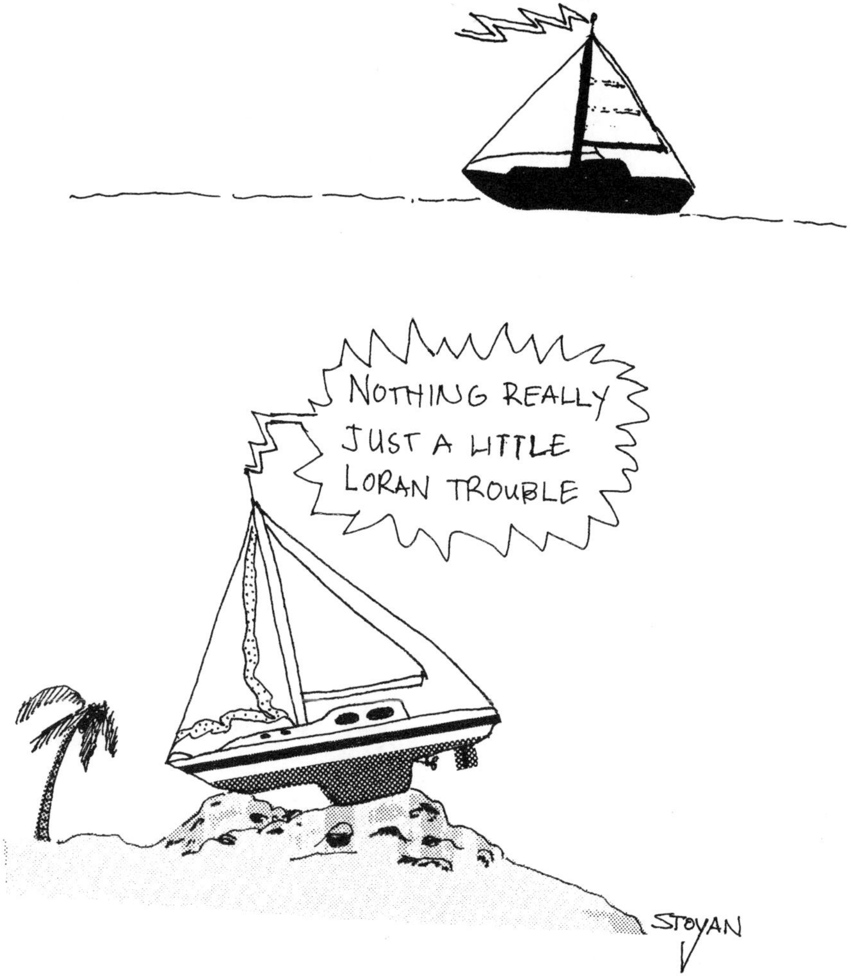
NOTHING REALLY JUST A LITTLE LORAN TROUBLE
STOYAN

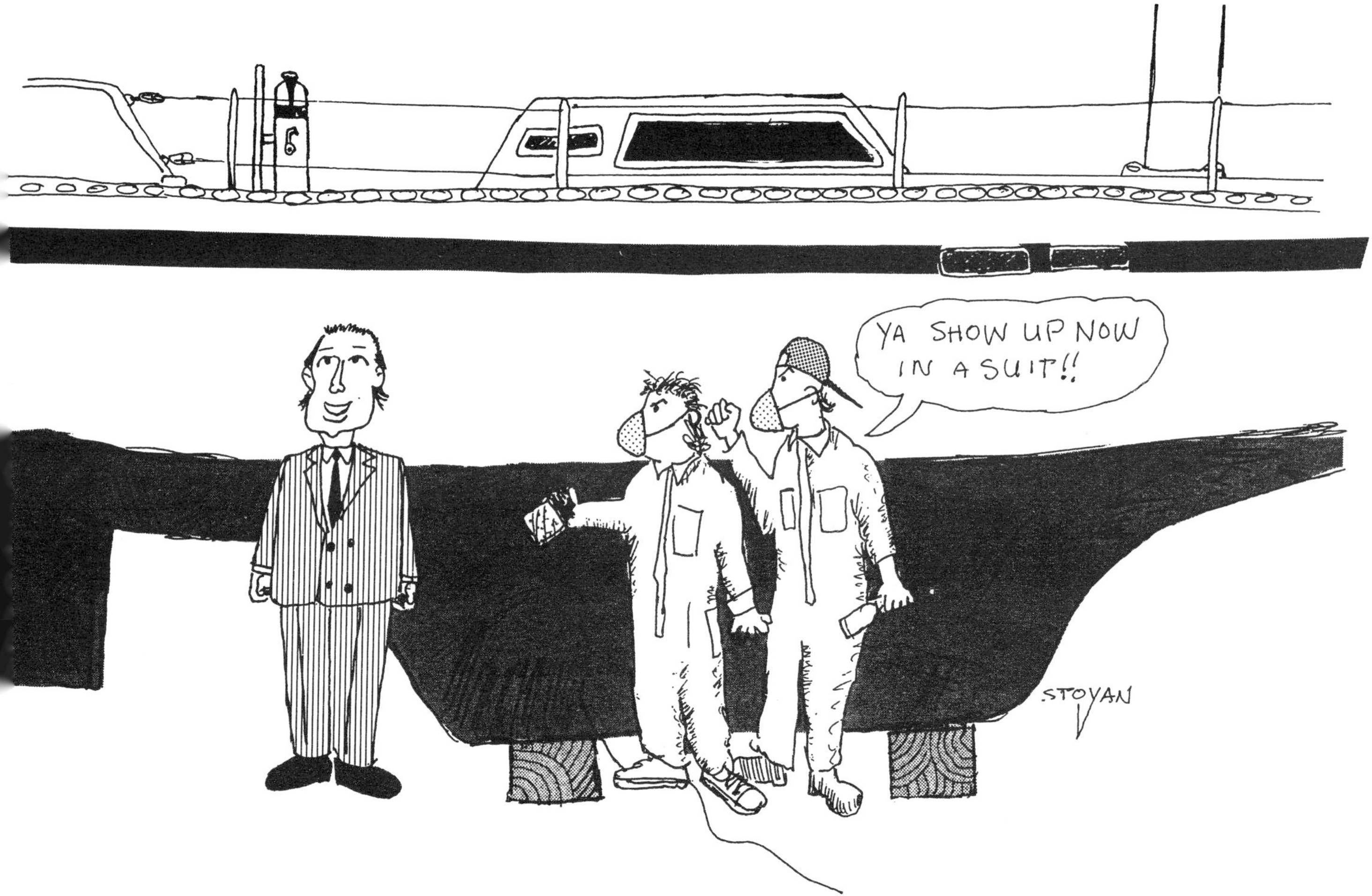
YA SHOW UP NOW IN A SUIT!!
STOYAN

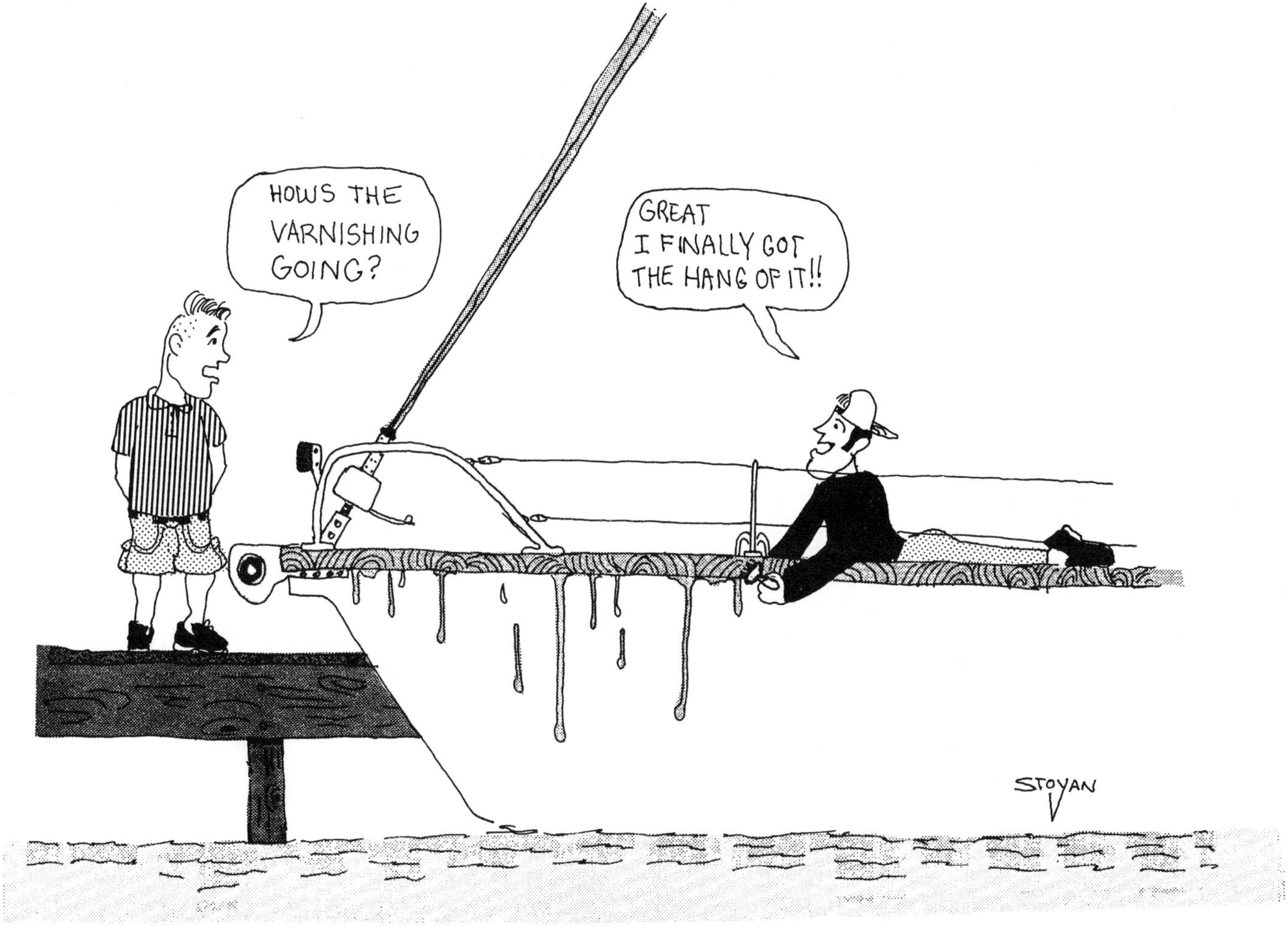
HOWS THE VARNISHING GOING?
GREAT I FINALLY GOT THE HANG OF IT!!
STOYAN

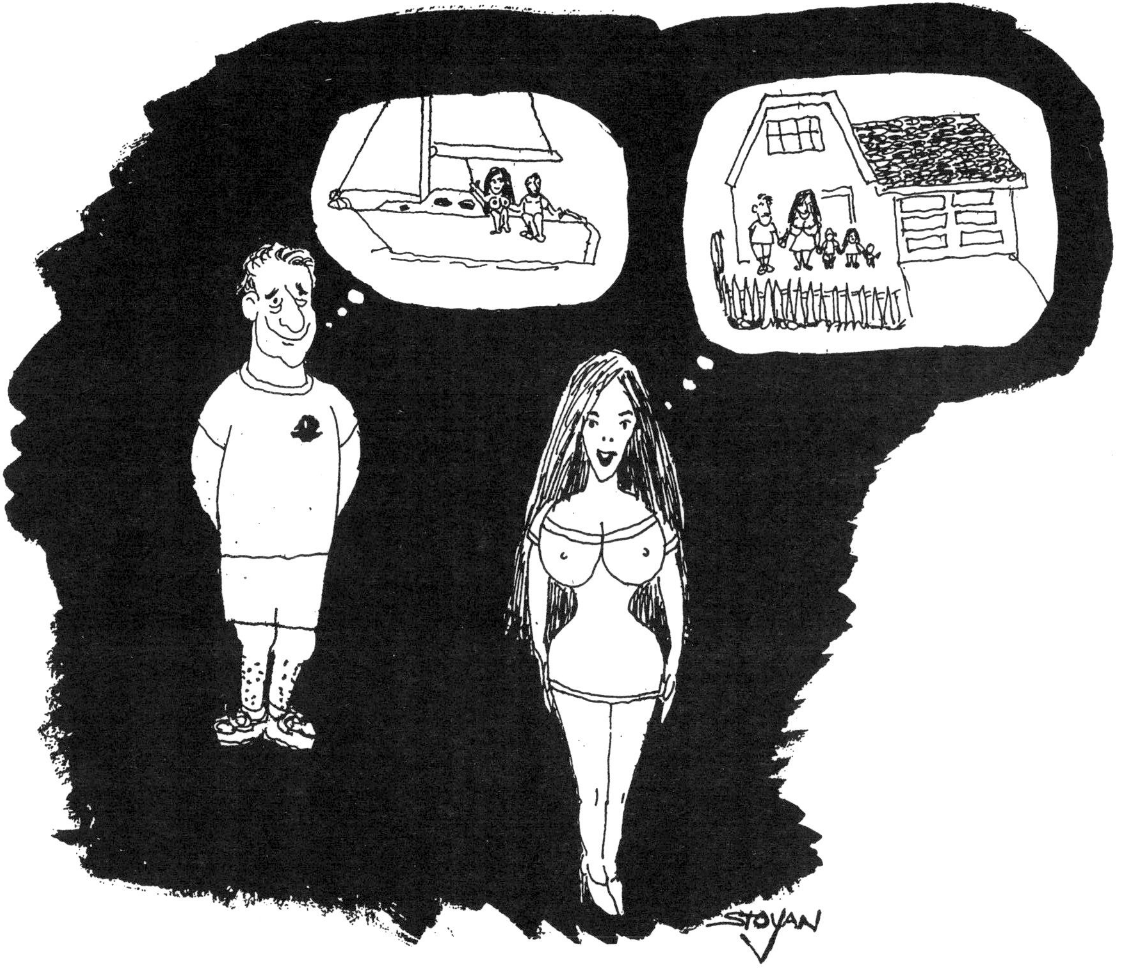
STOYAN

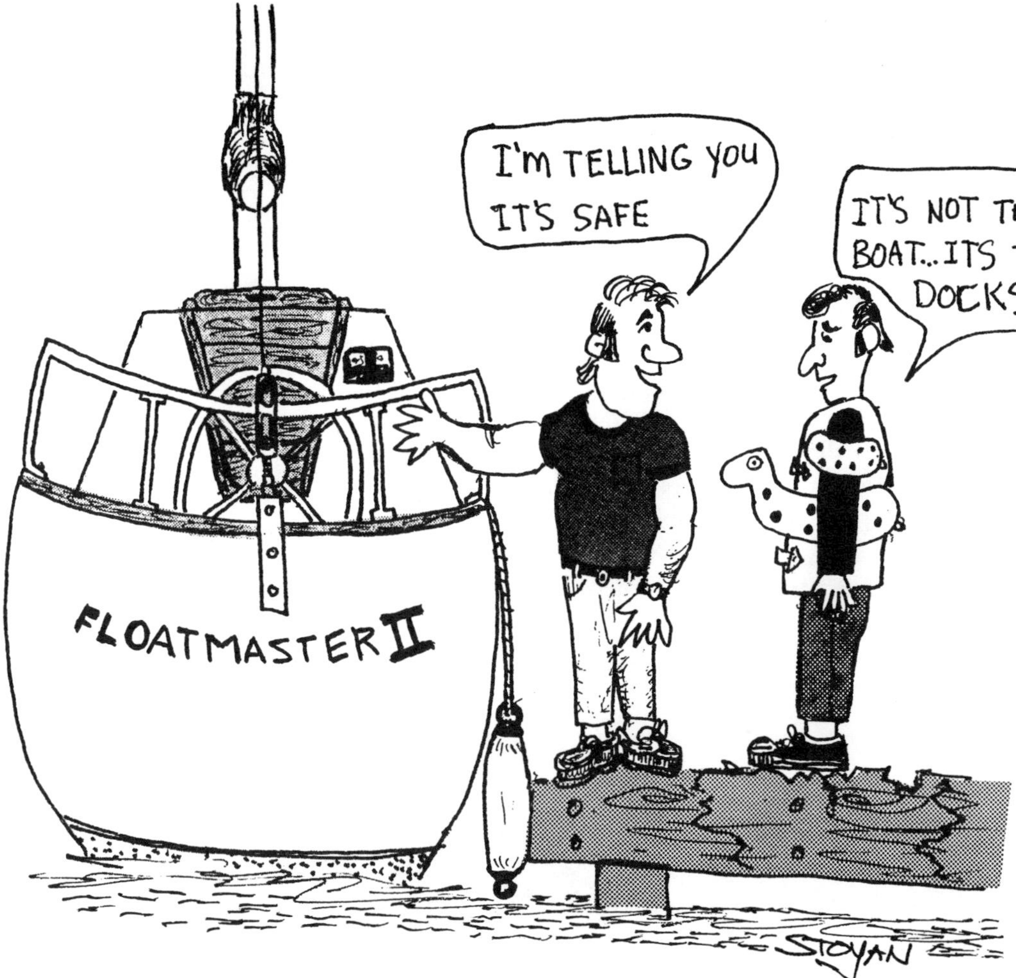

I'M TELLING YOU IT'S SAFE
IT'S NOT THE BOAT...ITS THE DOCKS!!
FLOATMASTER II
STOYAN

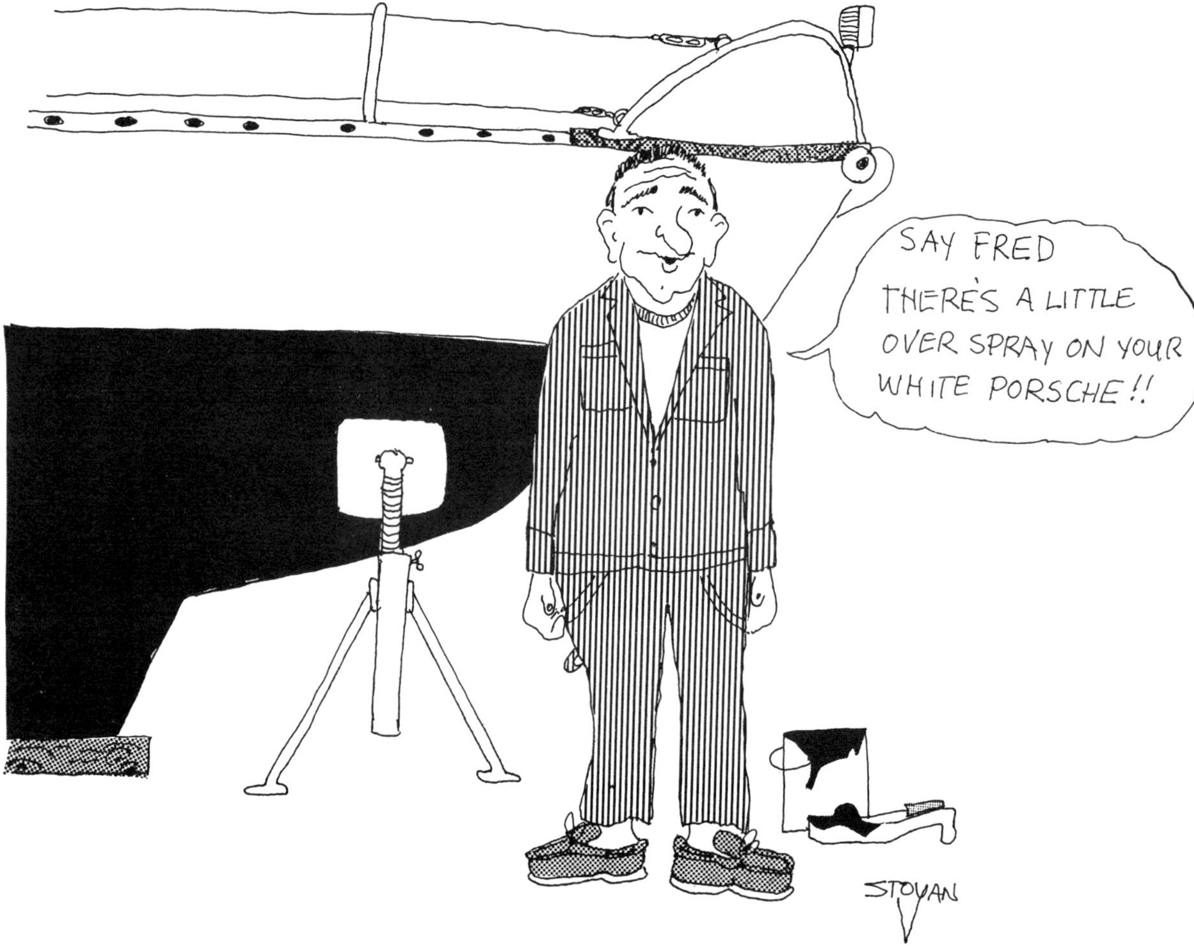
SAY FRED THERE'S A LITTLE OVER SPRAY ON YOUR WHITE PORSCHE!!
STOYAN

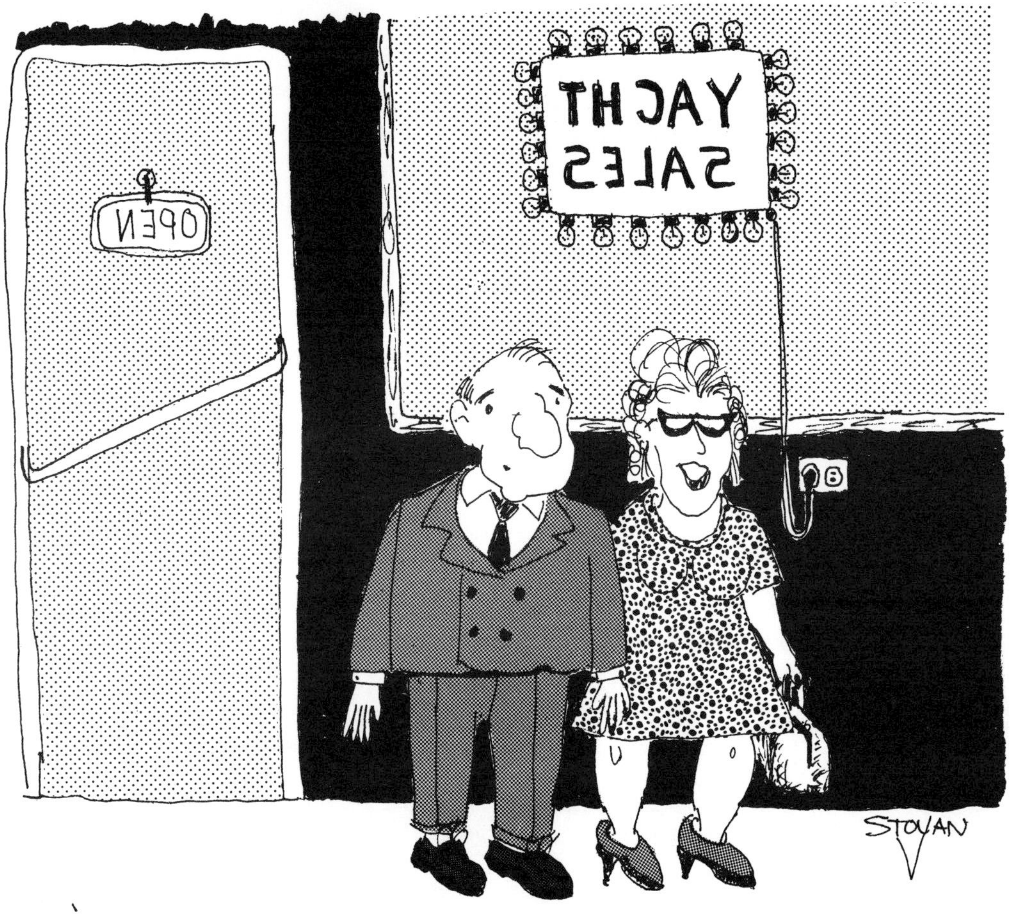
OPEN
YACHT
SALES
STOYAN

WE'RE LOOKING FOR A SAILBOAT... HEADROOM NOT A FACTOR!!

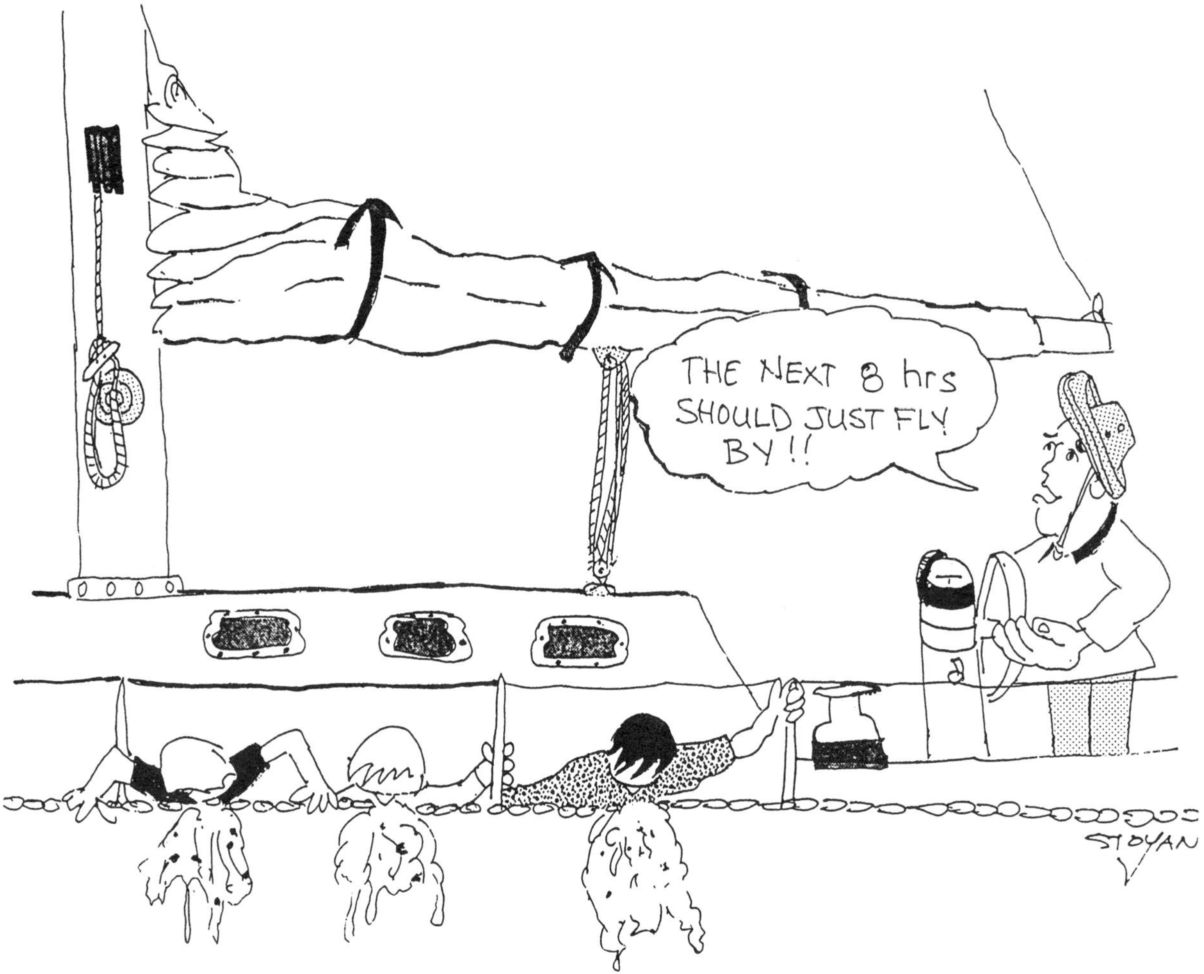
THE NEXT 8 hrs SHOULD JUST FLY BY!!
STOYAN

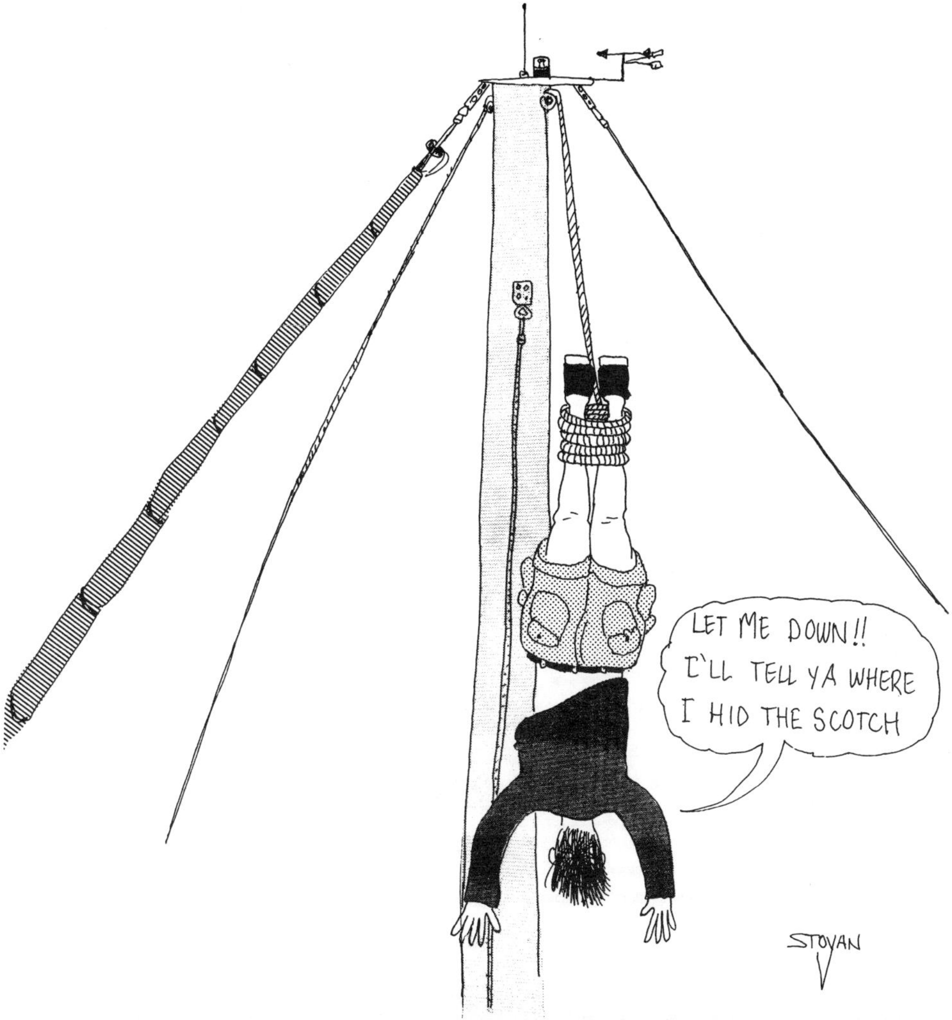
LET ME DOWN!!
I'LL TELL YA WHERE
I HID THE SCOTCH
STOYAN

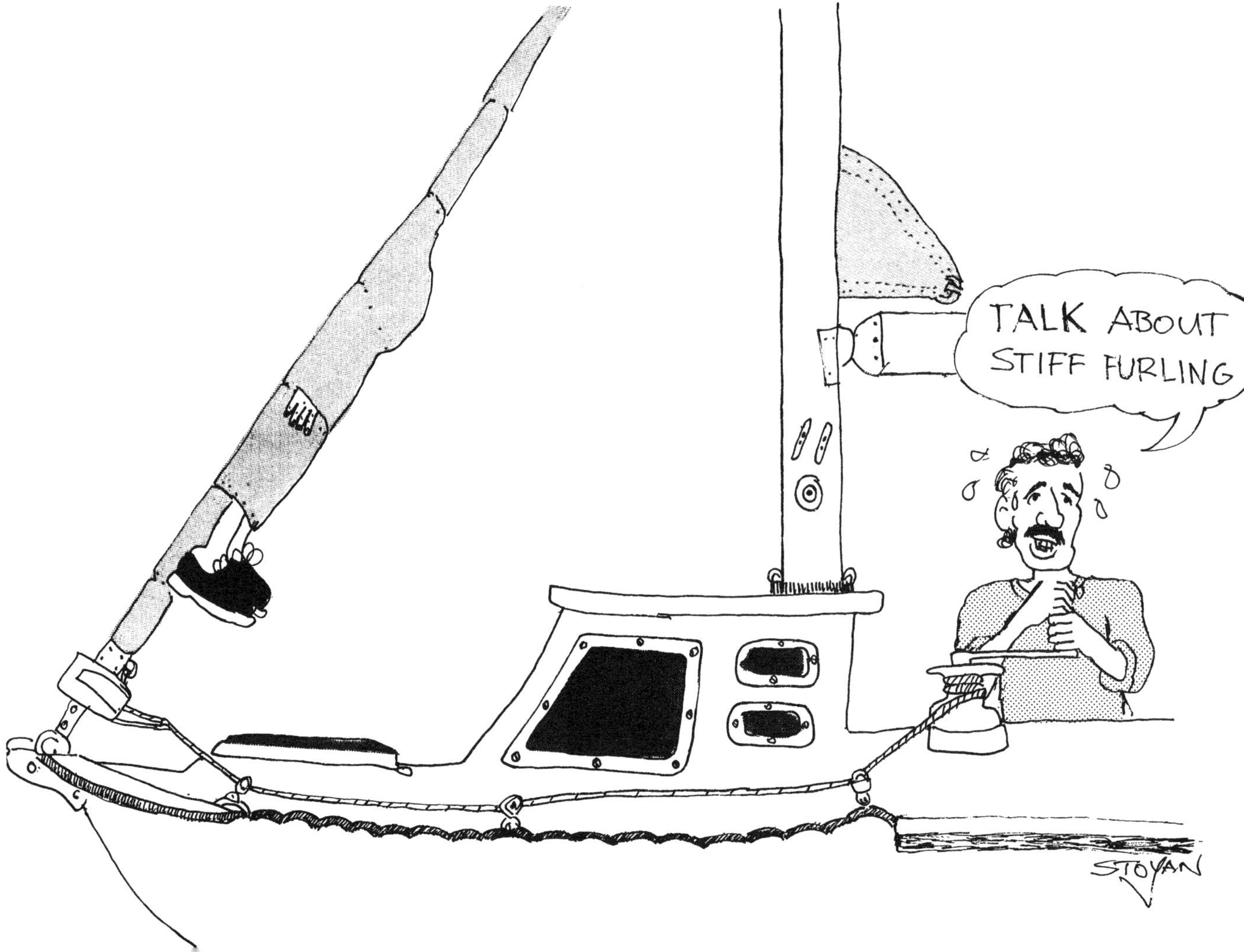
TALK ABOUT STIFF FURLING
STOYAN

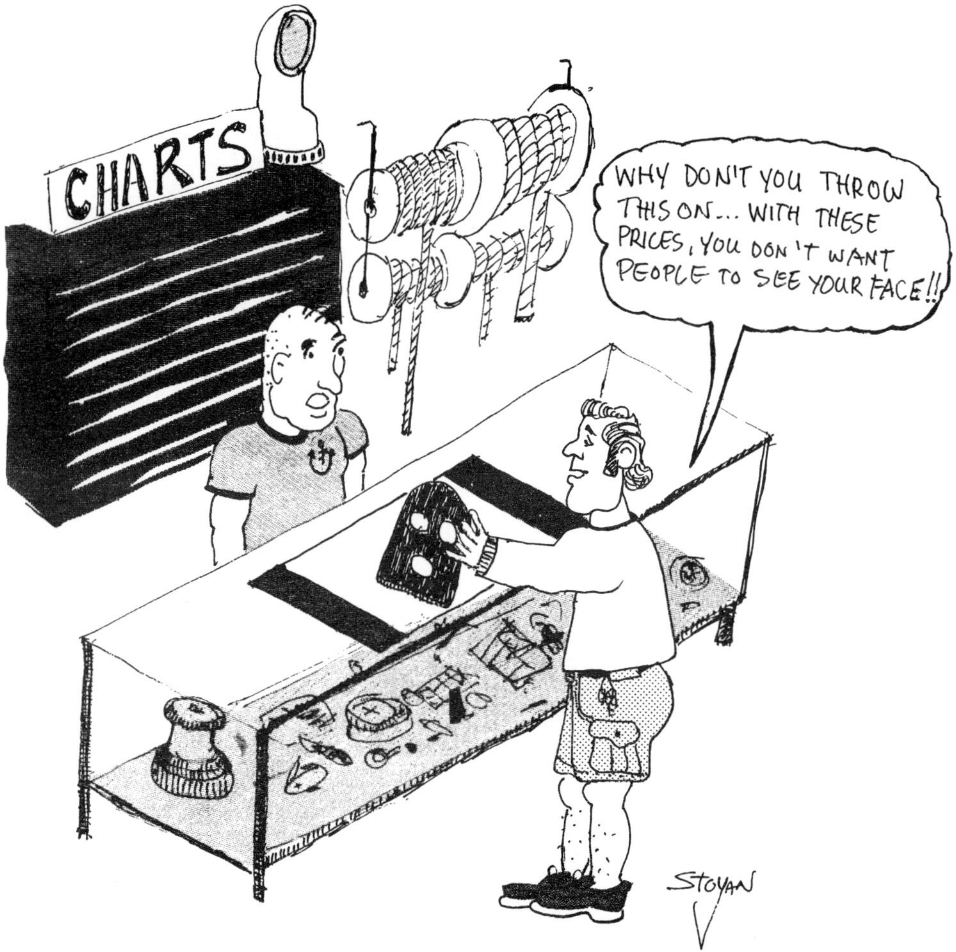
CHARTS
WHY DON'T YOU THROW THIS ON... WITH THESE PRICES, YOU DON'T WANT PEOPLE TO SEE YOUR FACE!!
STOYAN

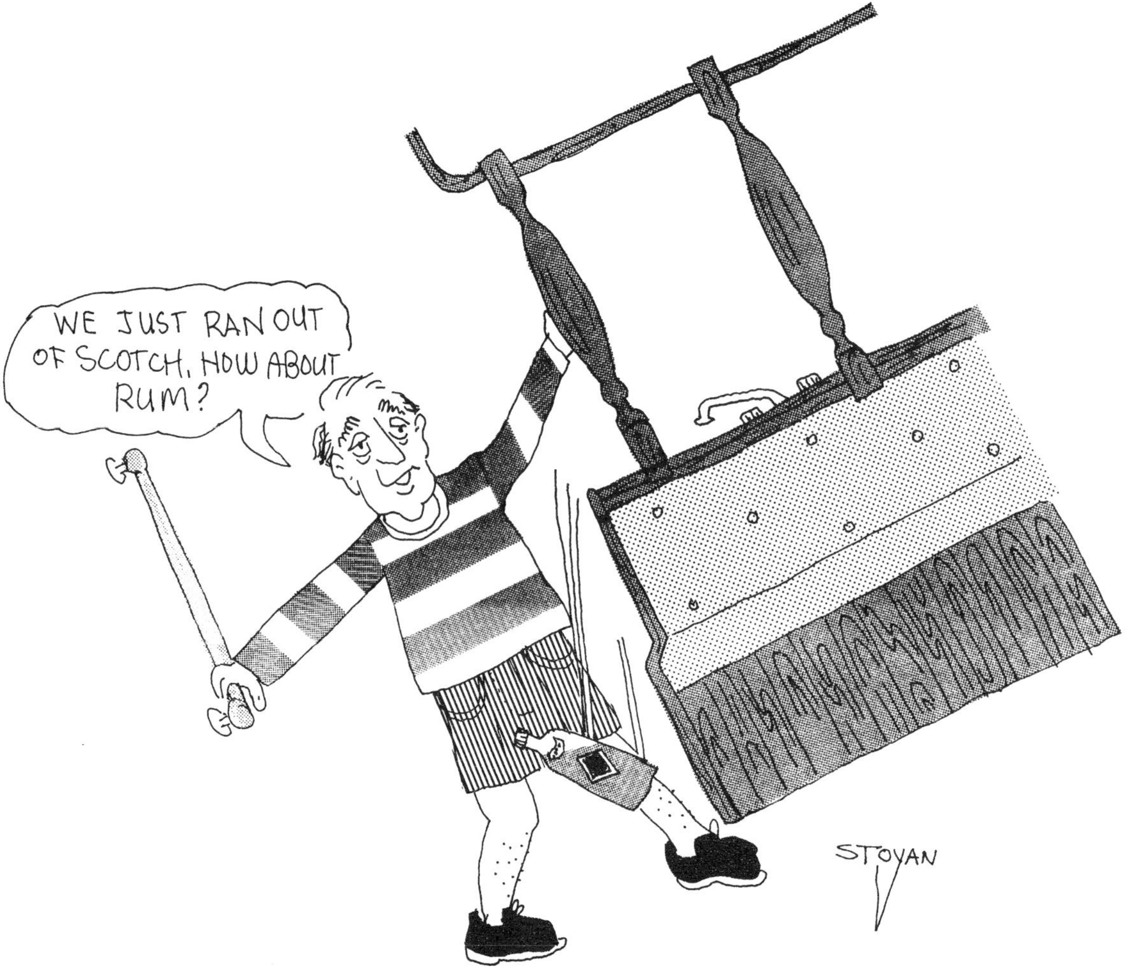
WE JUST RAN OUT OF SCOTCH, HOW ABOUT RUM?
STOYAN

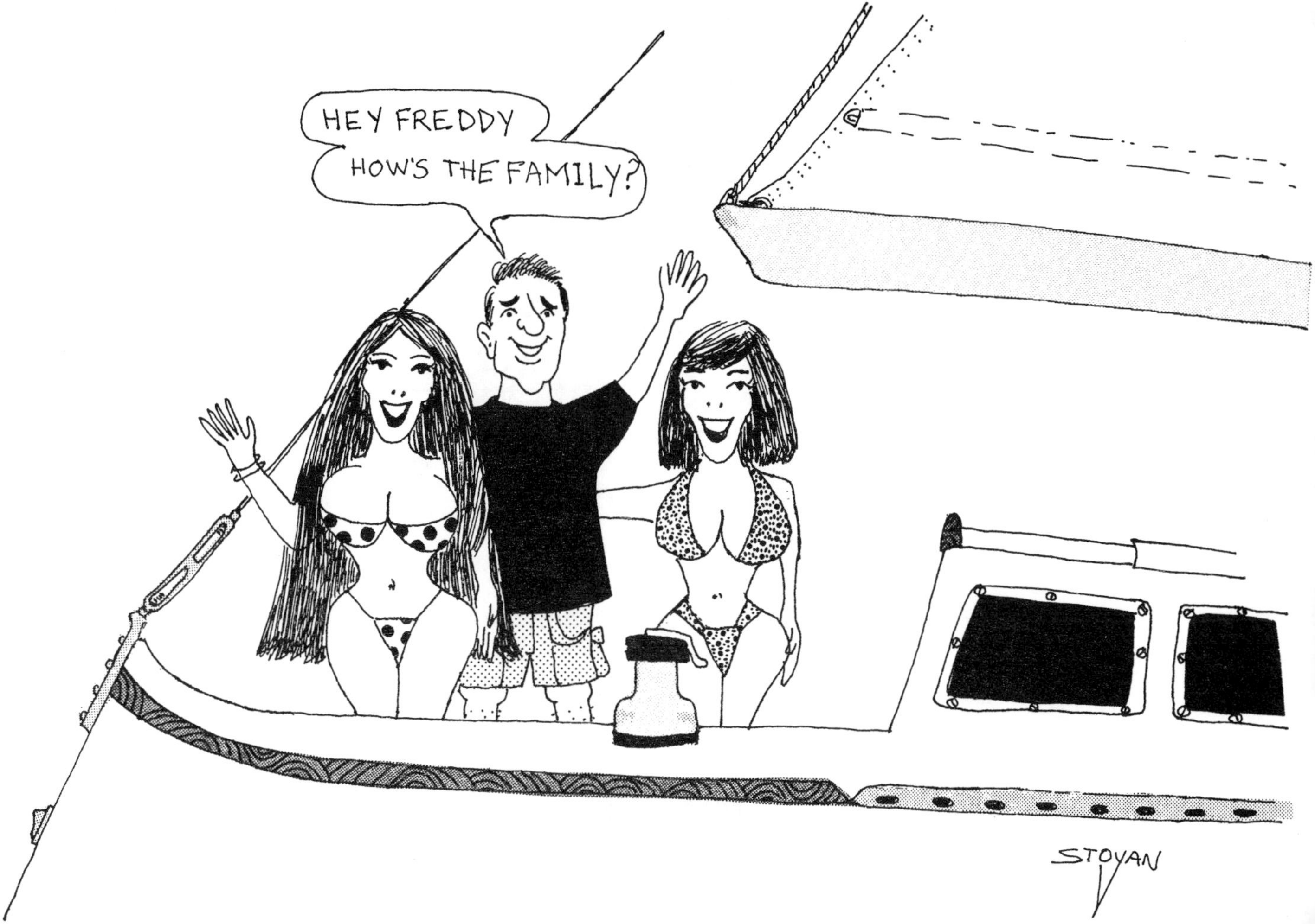
HEY FREDDY
HOW'S THE FAMILY?
STOYAN

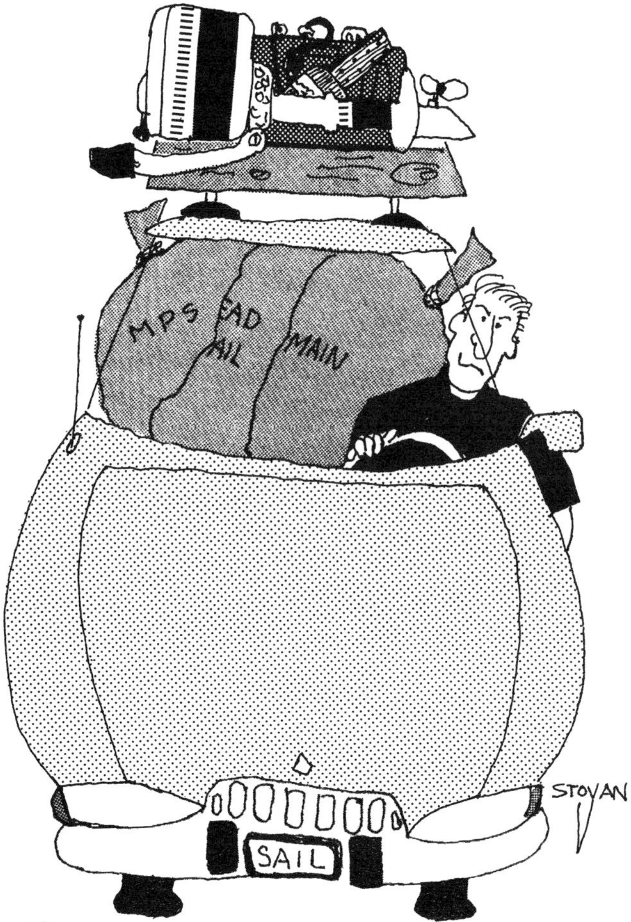
MPS
MAIN
SAIL
STOYAN

"THE SIGNS OF SPRING"

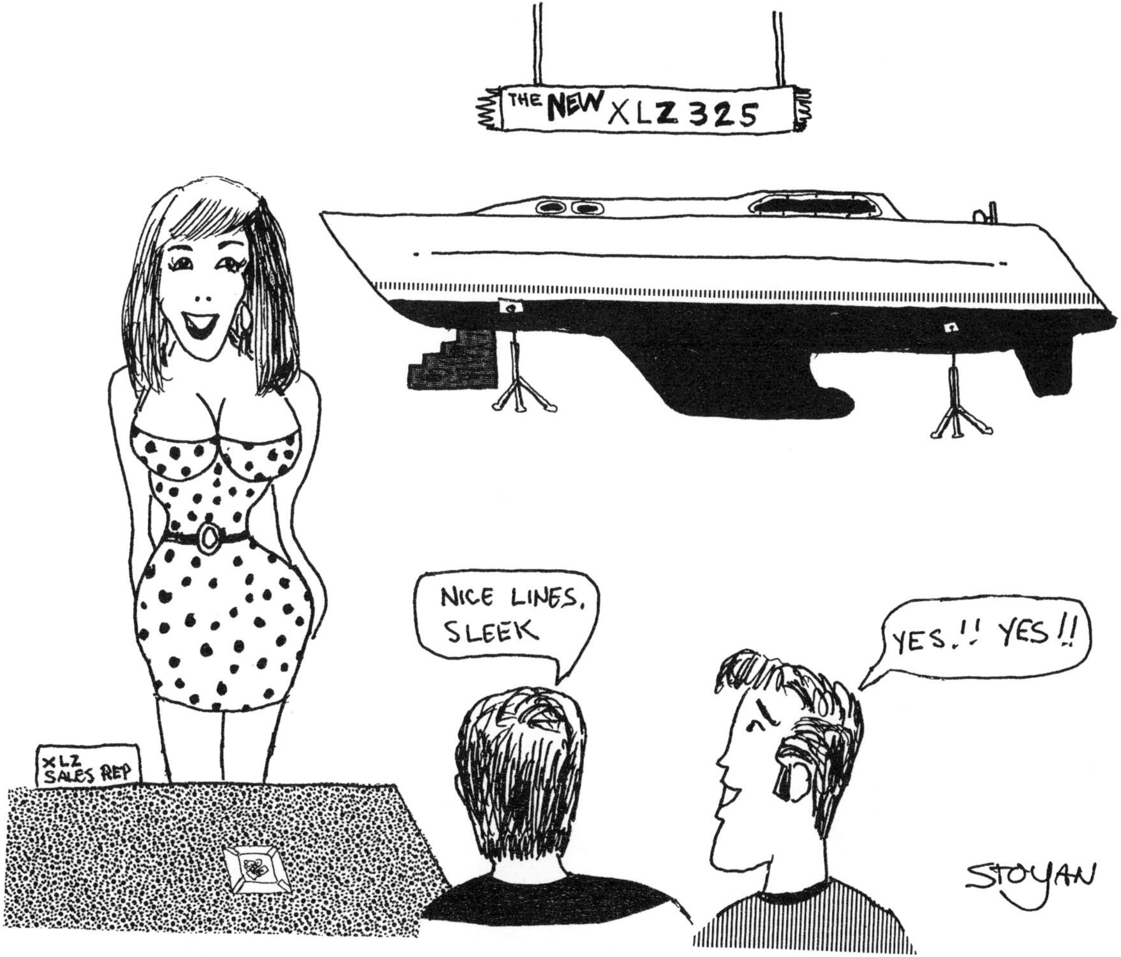
THE NEW XLZ 325
XLZ SALES REP
NICE LINES. SLEEK
YES.!! YES!!
STOYAN

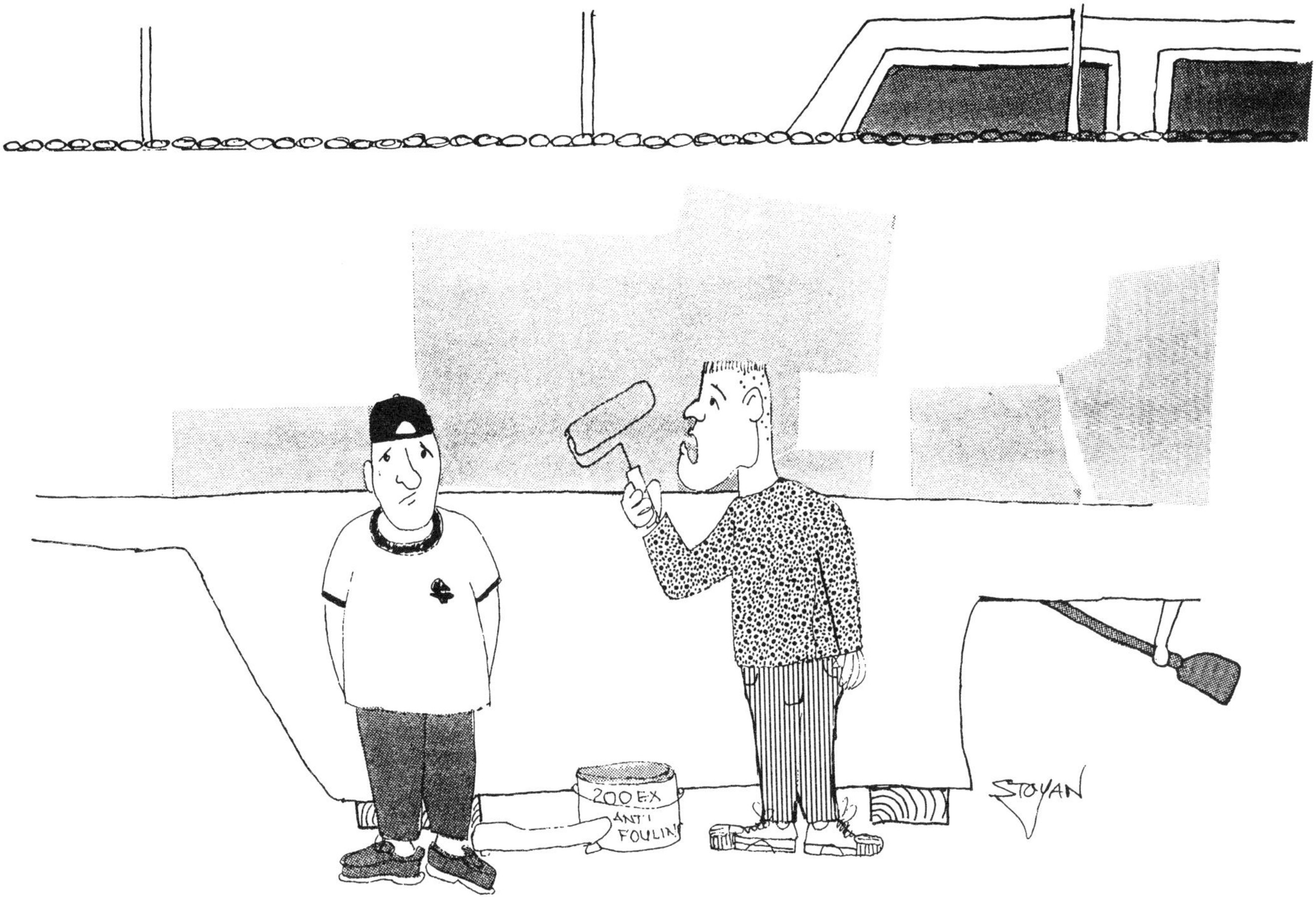
200EX
ANTI FOULIN'
STOYAN

DID I DO SOMETHING WRONG?

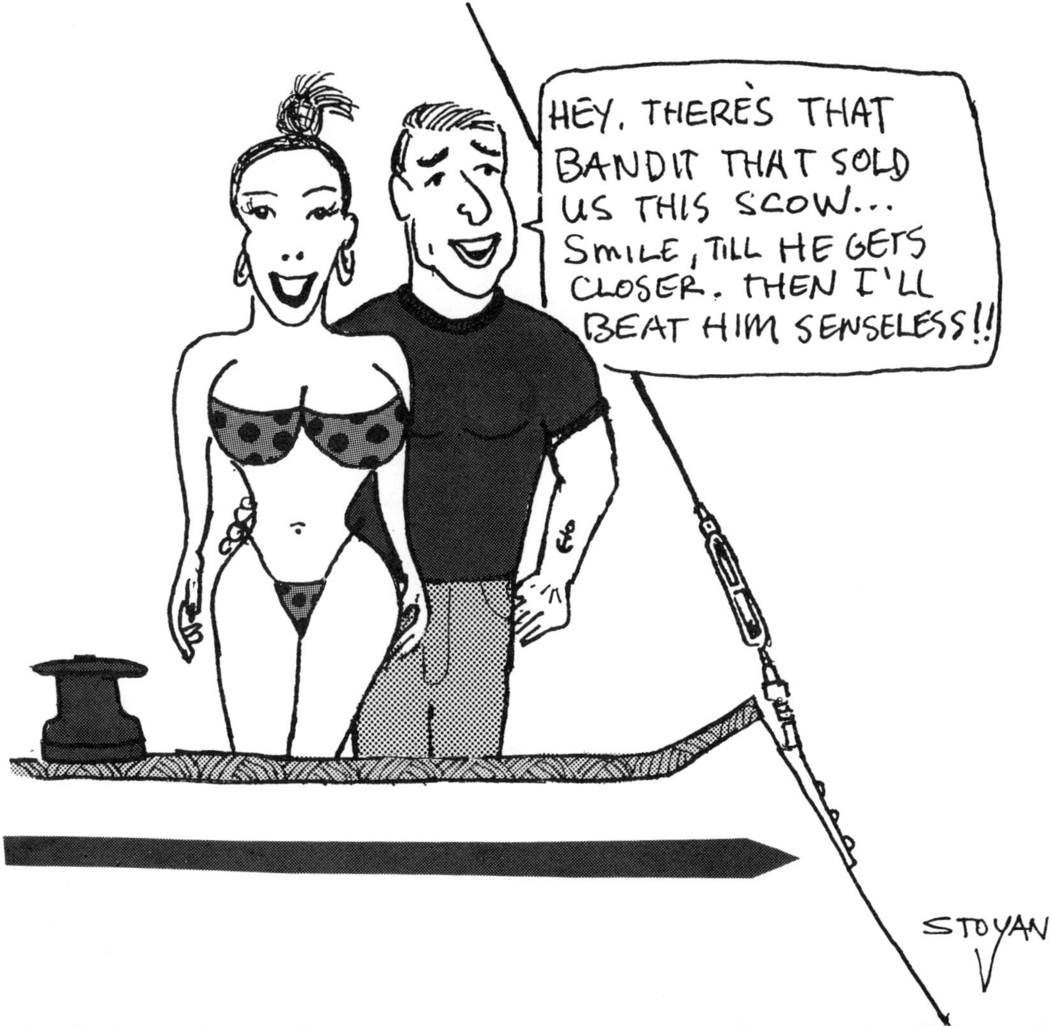
HEY. THERE'S THAT BANDIT THAT SOLD US THIS SCOW... SMILE, TILL HE GETS CLOSER. THEN I'LL BEAT HIM SENSELESS!!
STOYAN

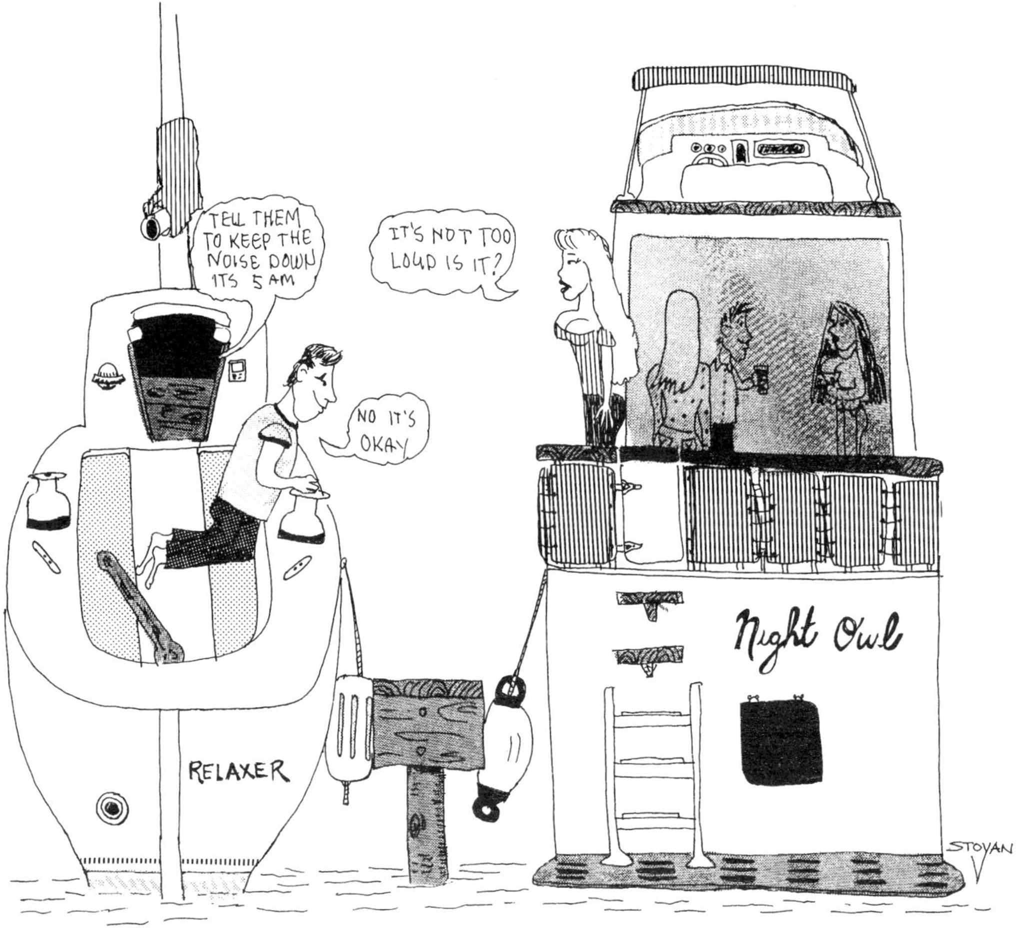
TELL THEM TO KEEP THE NOISE DOWN ITS 5 AM
IT'S NOT TOO LOUD IS IT?
NO IT'S OKAY
RELAXER
Night Owl
STOYAN

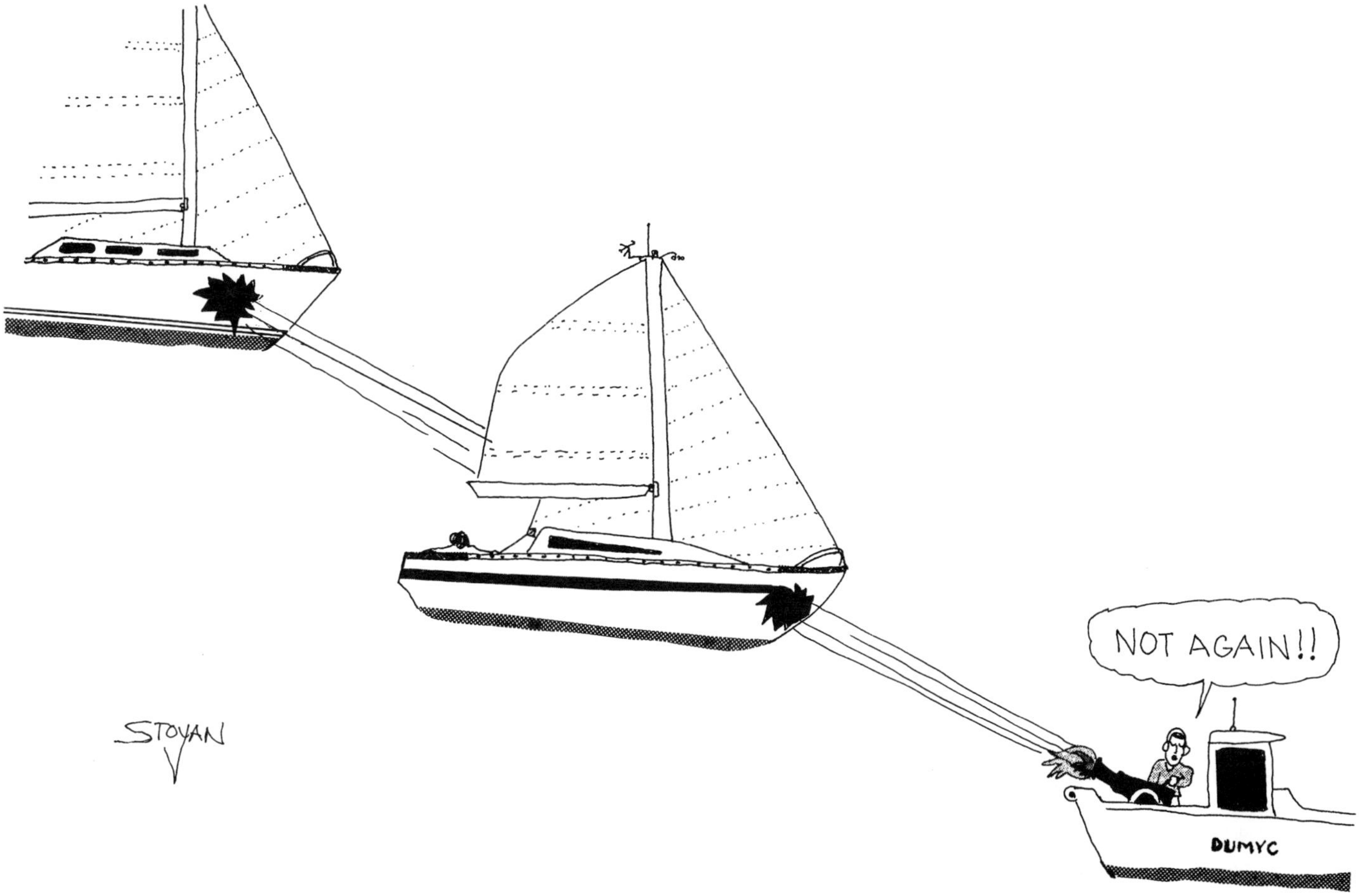
NOT AGAIN!!
DUMYC
STOYAN

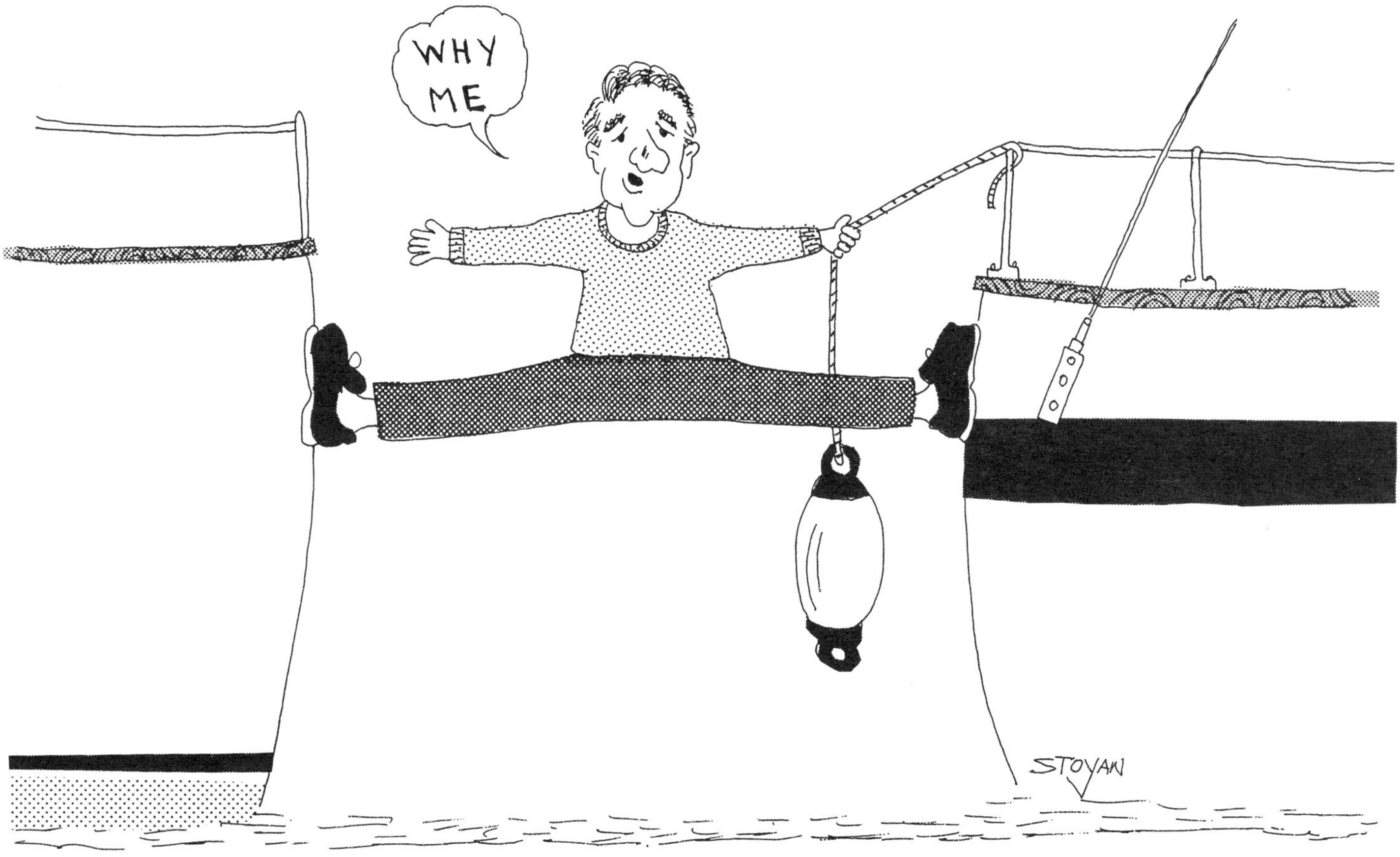
WHY ME
STOYAN

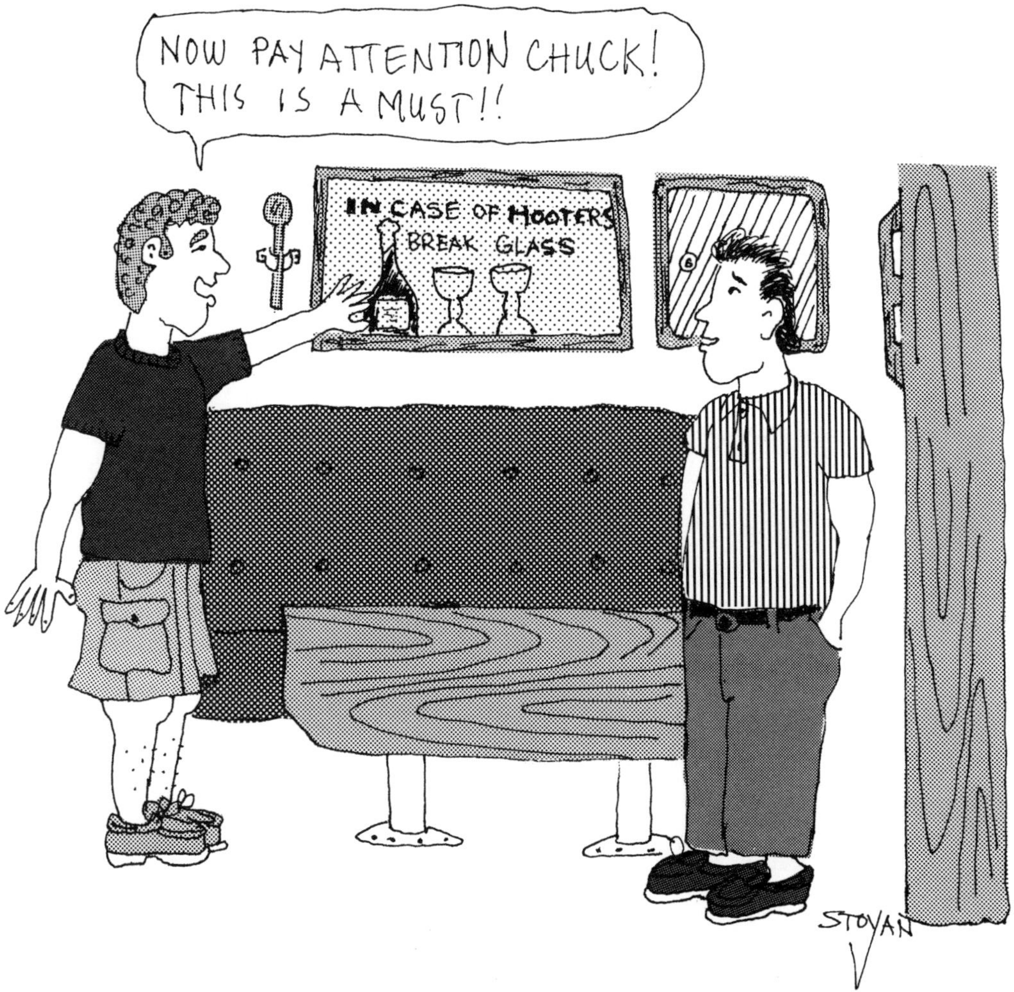
NOW PAY ATTENTION CHUCK! THIS IS A MUST!!
IN CASE OF HOOTERS BREAK GLASS
STOYAN

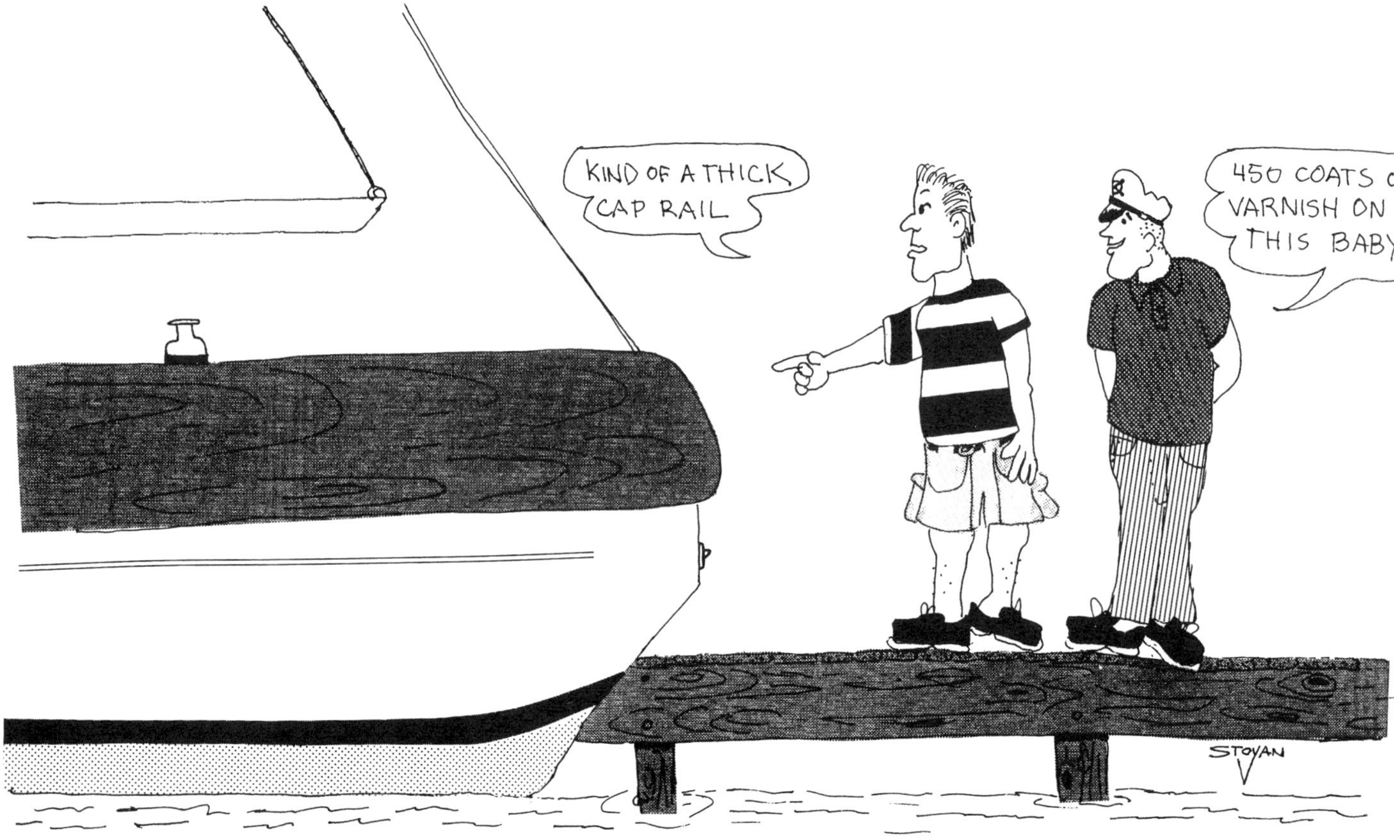
KIND OF A THICK CAP RAIL
450 COATS OF VARNISH ON THIS BABY
STOYAN

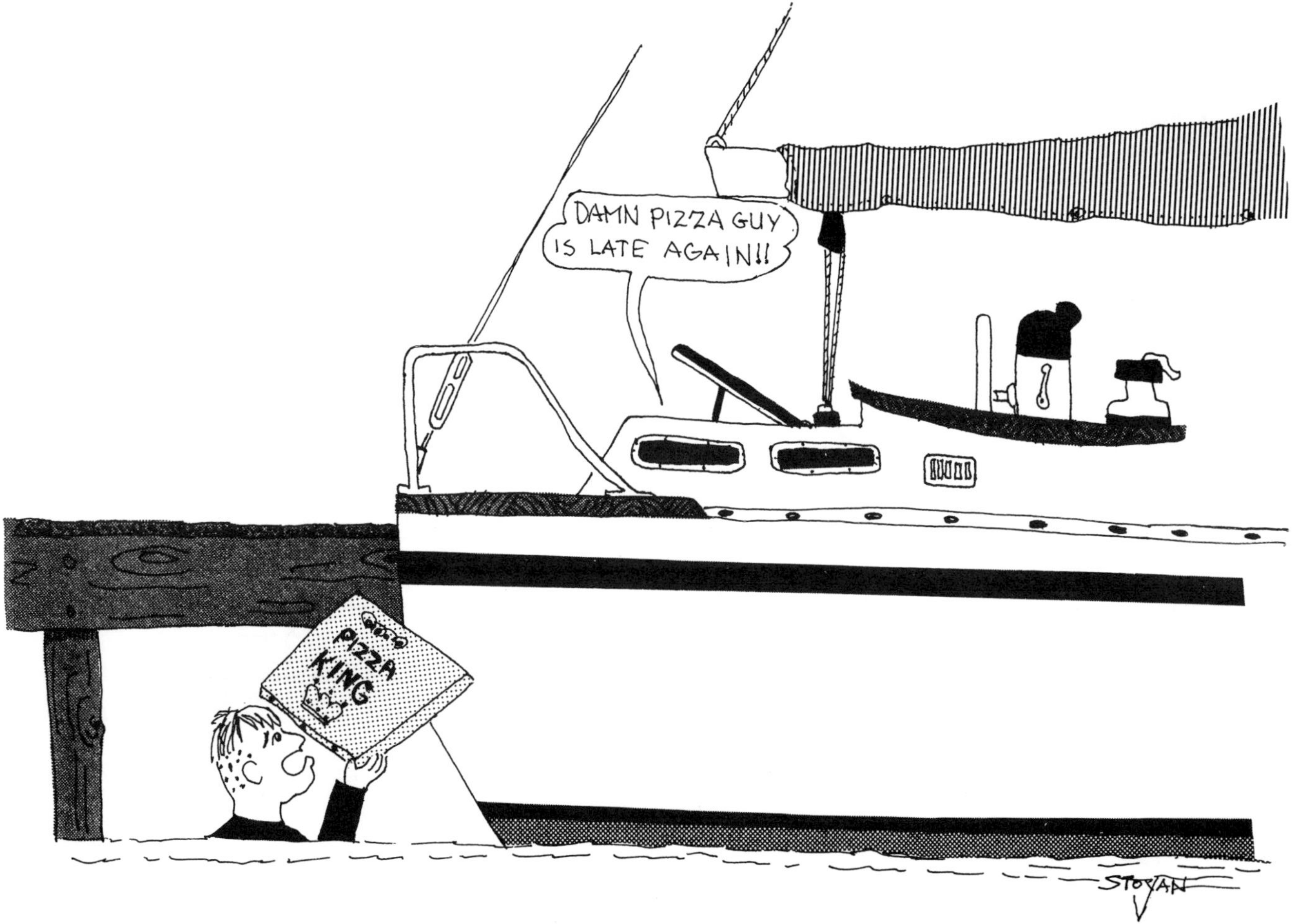
DAMN PIZZA GUY IS LATE AGAIN!!
PIZZA KING
STOYAN

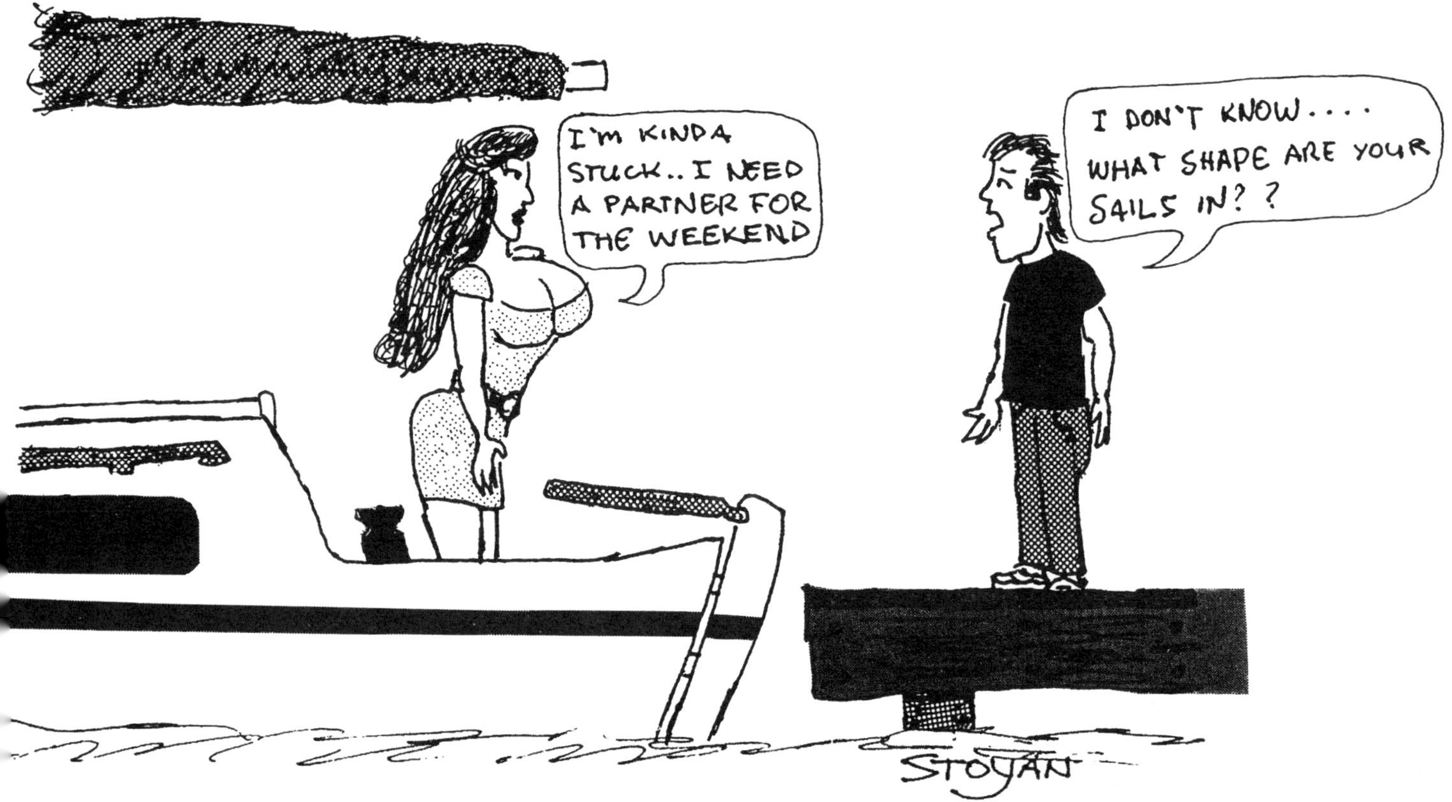
I'M KINDA STUCK.. I NEED A PARTNER FOR THE WEEKEND
I DON'T KNOW.... WHAT SHAPE ARE YOUR SAILS IN??
STOYAN

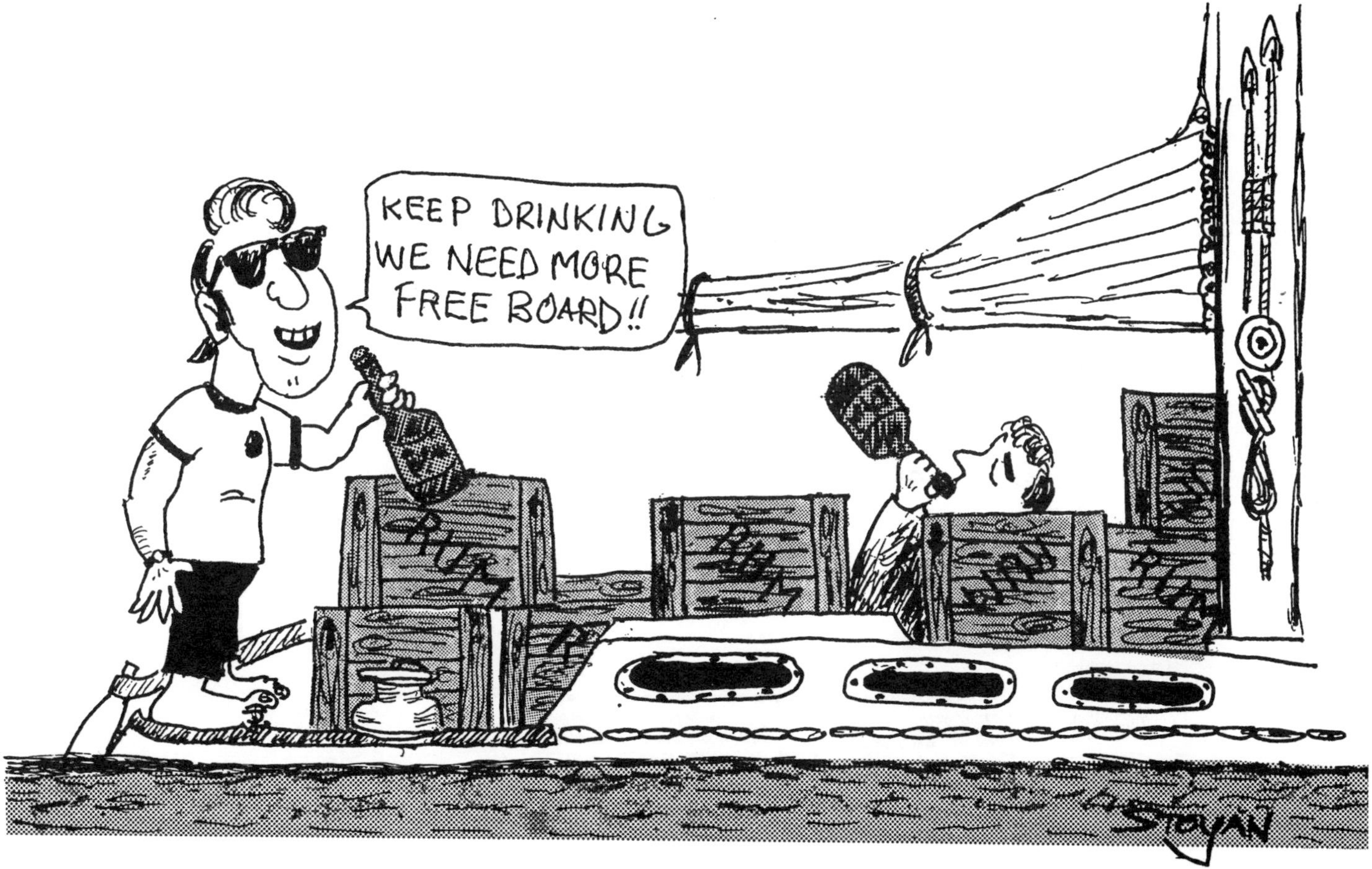
KEEP DRINKING WE NEED MORE FREE BOARD!!
STOYAN

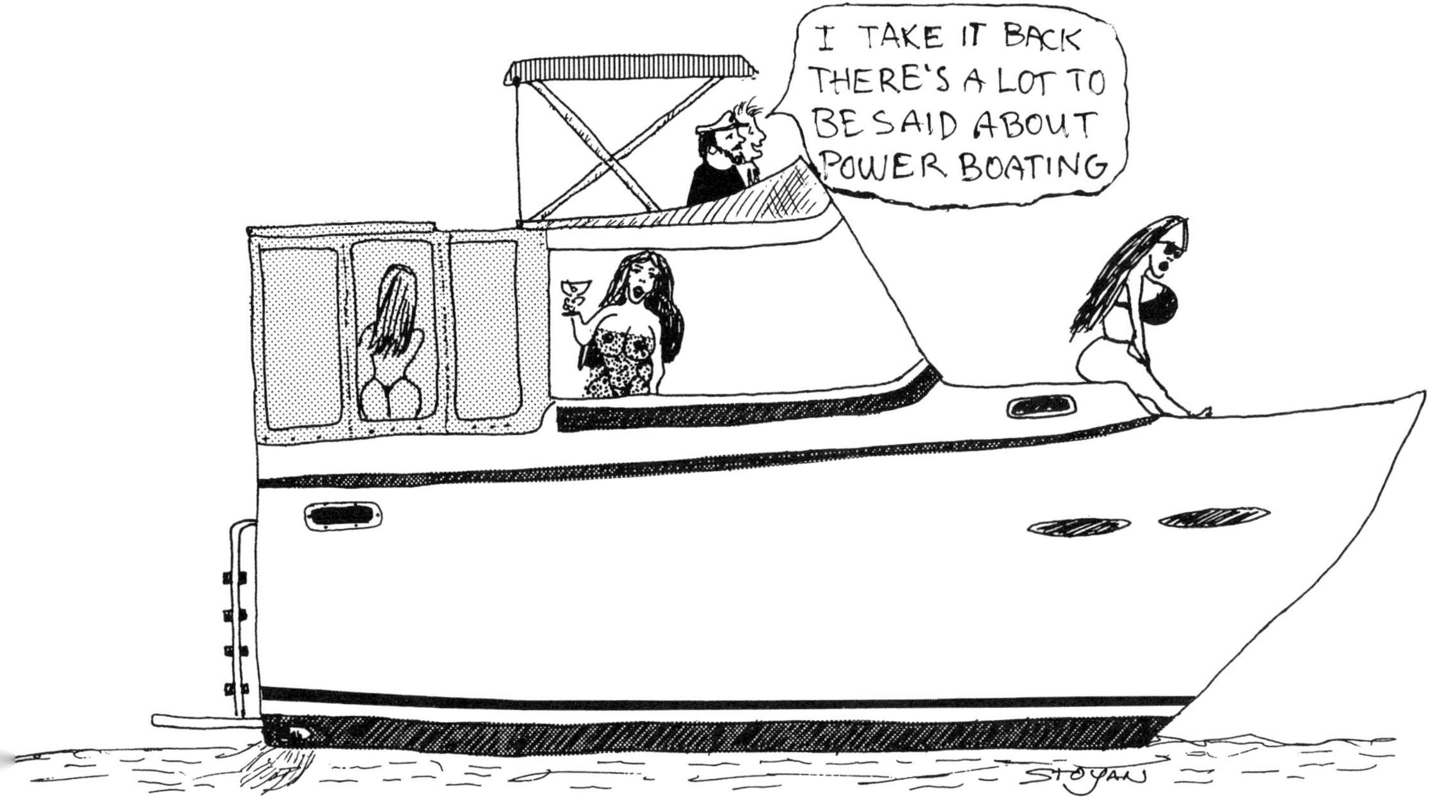
I TAKE IT BACK THERE'S A LOT TO BE SAID ABOUT POWER BOATING
STOYAN

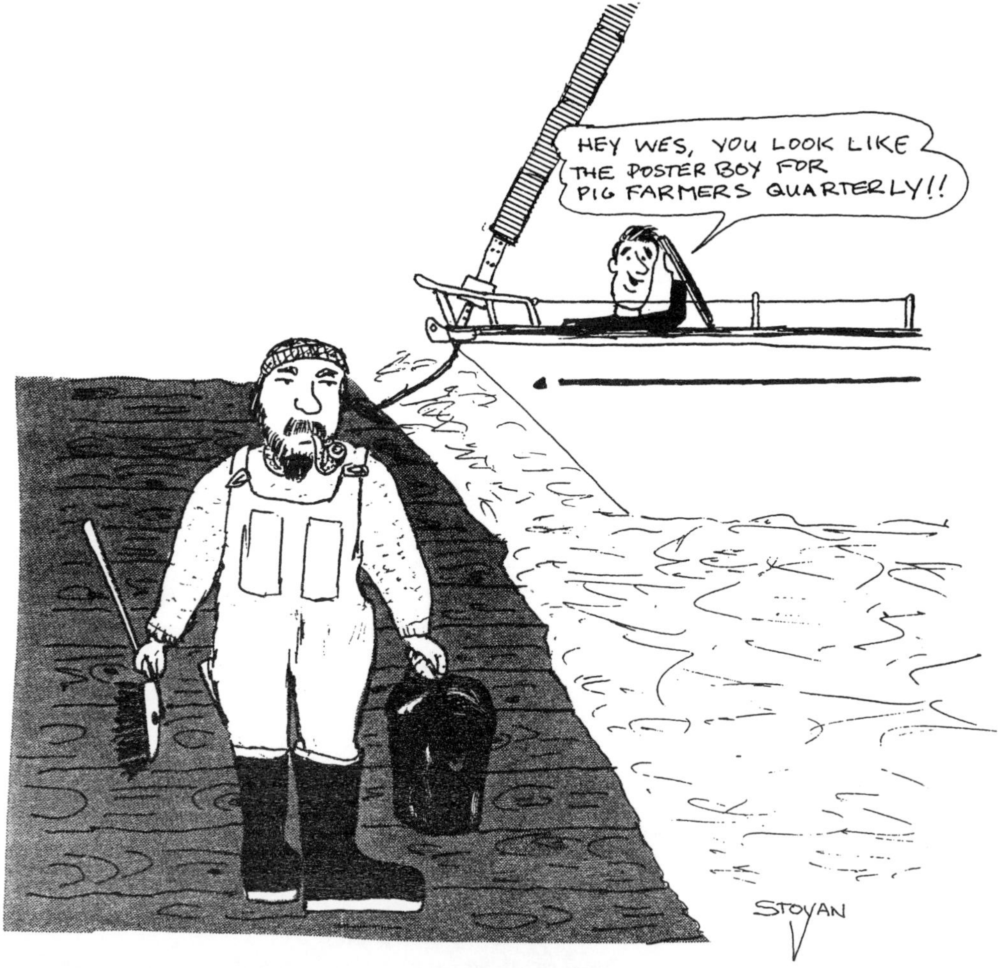
HEY WES, YOU LOOK LIKE THE POSTER BOY FOR PIG FARMERS QUARTERLY!!
STOYAN

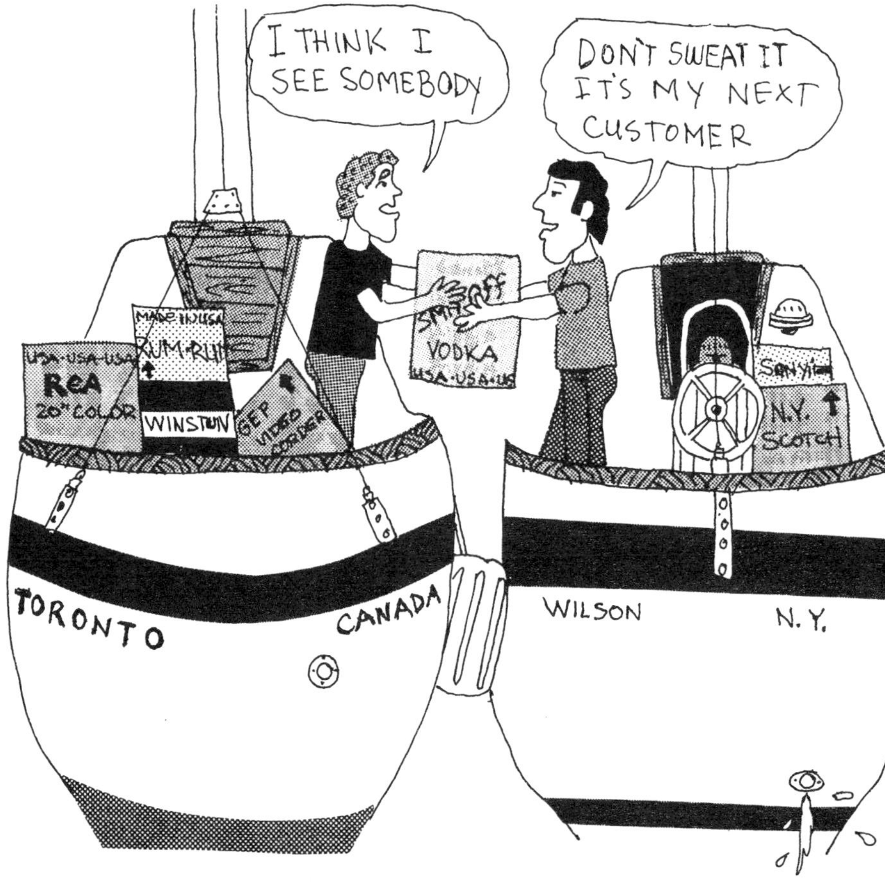
I THINK I SEE SOMEBODY
DON'T SWEAT IT IT'S MY NEXT CUSTOMER
USA-USA-USA
RCA 20" COLOR
WINSTON
VODKA
USA-USA-US
N.Y. SCOTCH
TORONTO
CANADA
WILSON
N.Y.

"FREE TRADE"

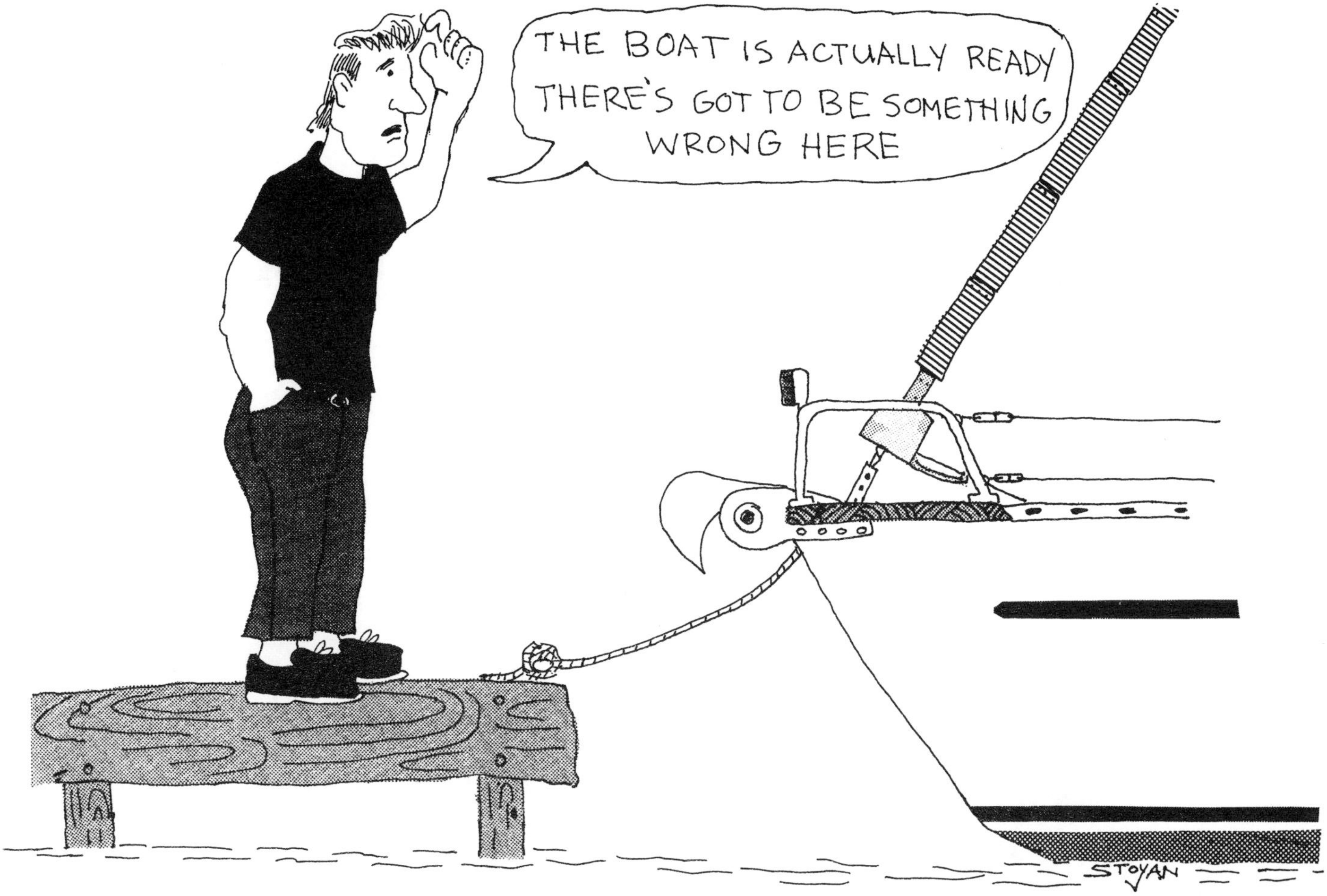
THE BOAT IS ACTUALLY READY THERE'S GOT TO BE SOMETHING WRONG HERE
STOYAN

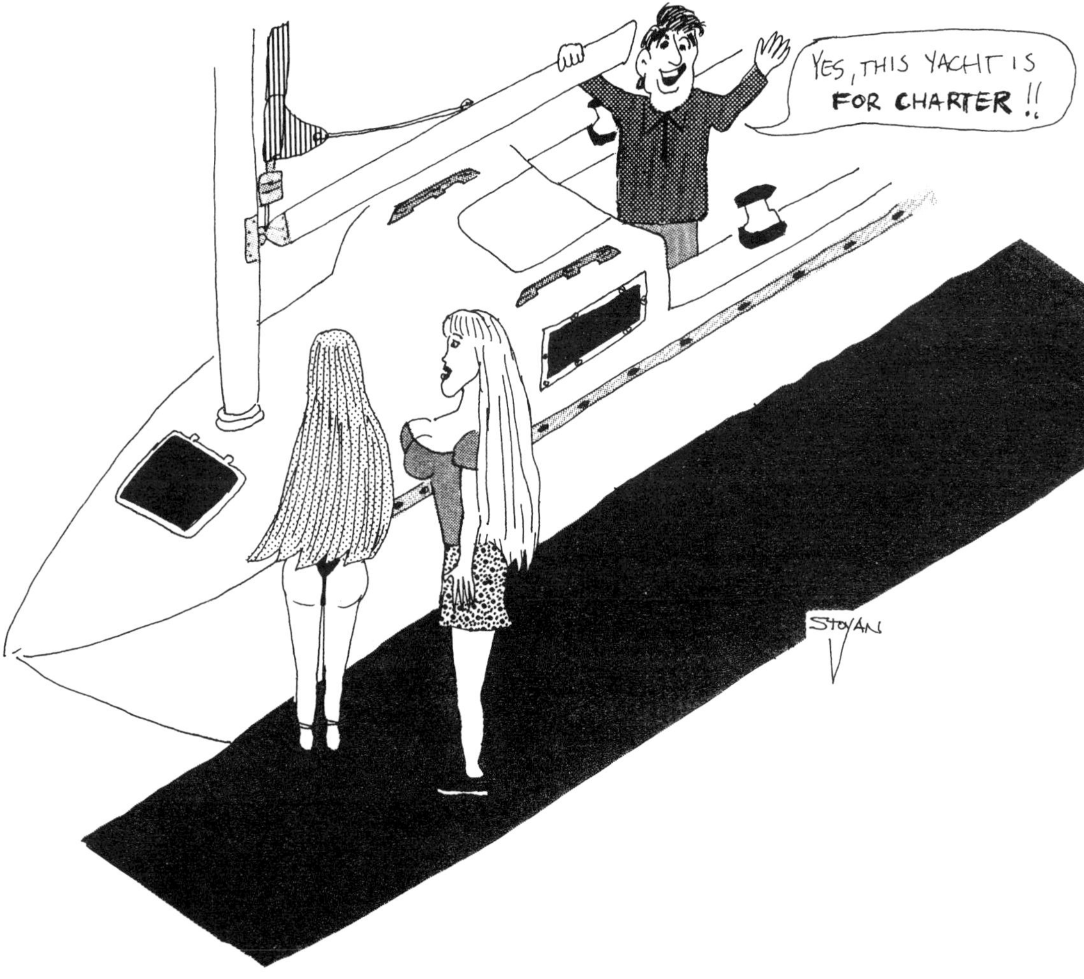
YES, THIS YACHT IS FOR CHARTER !!
STOYAN

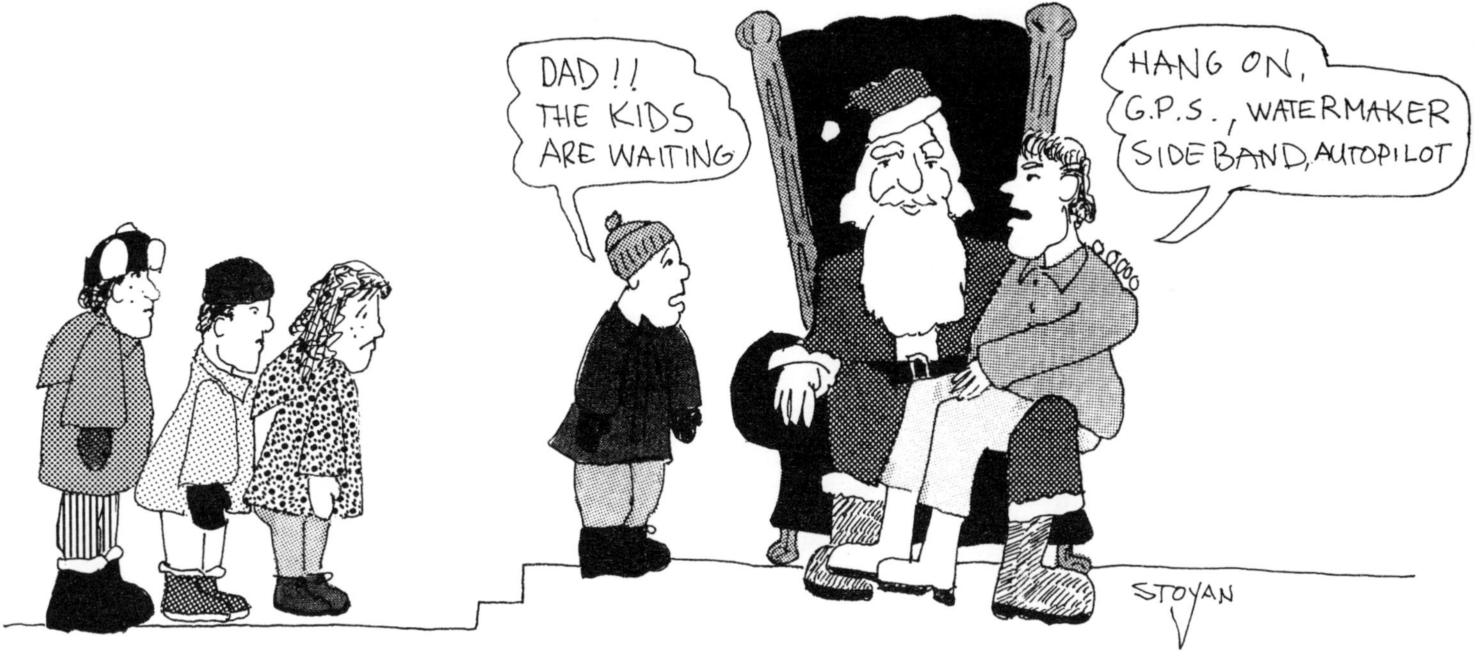
DAD !! THE KIDS ARE WAITING
HANG ON, G.P.S., WATERMAKER SIDEBAND, AUTOPILOT
STOYAN

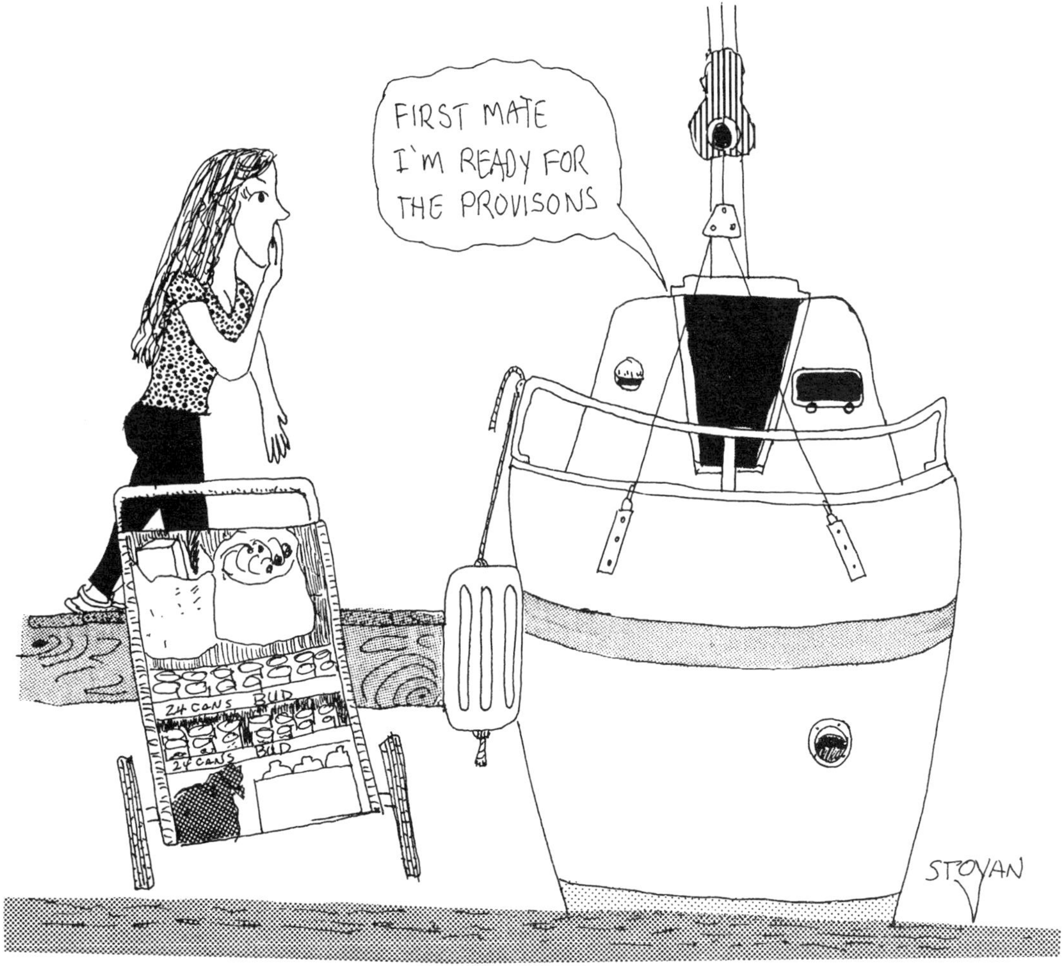
FIRST MATE
I`M READY FOR
THE PROVISONS
24 CANS BUD
24 CANS BUD
STOYAN

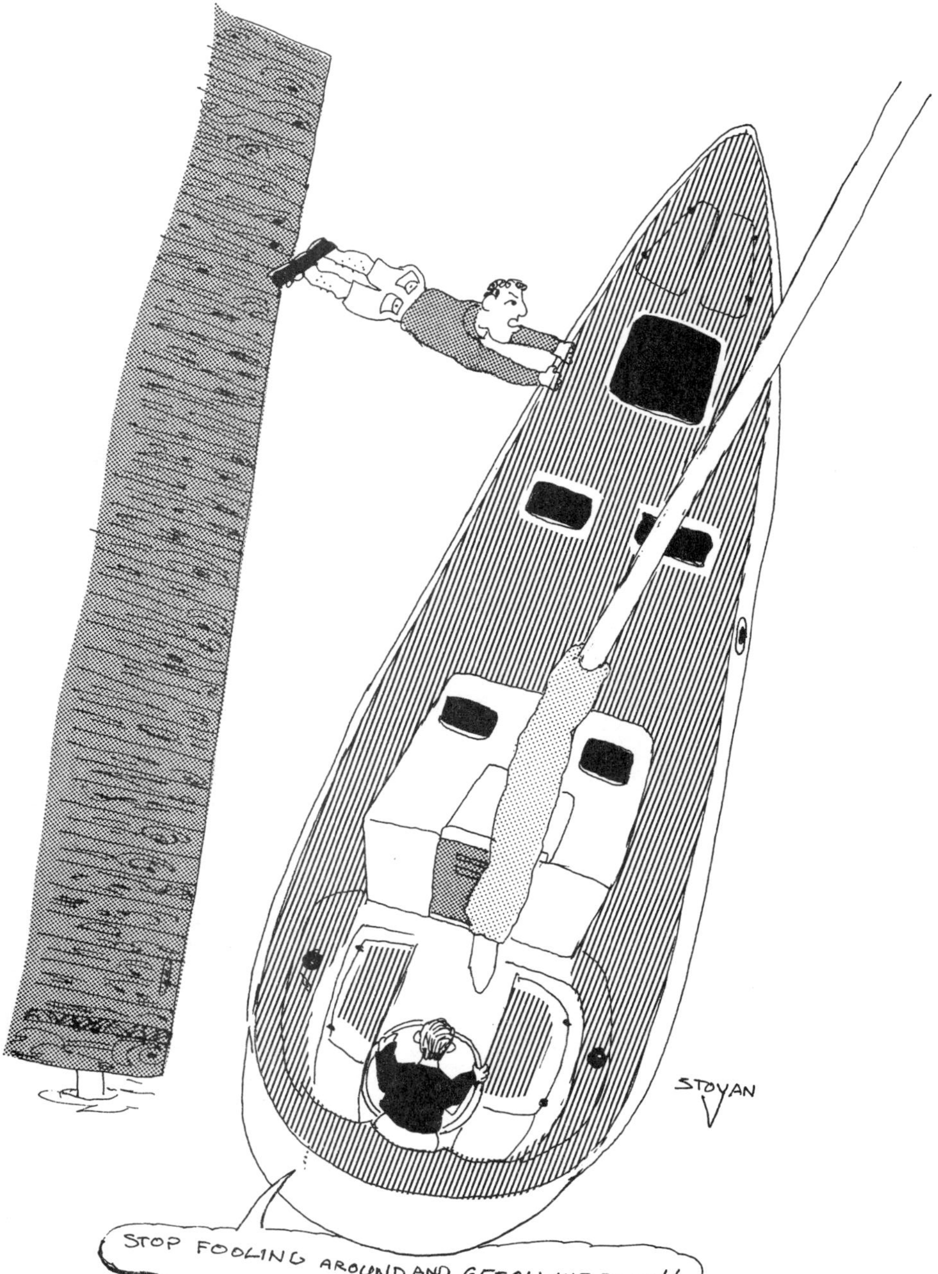
STOP FOOLING AROUND AND GET ON THE BOAT!!
STOYAN

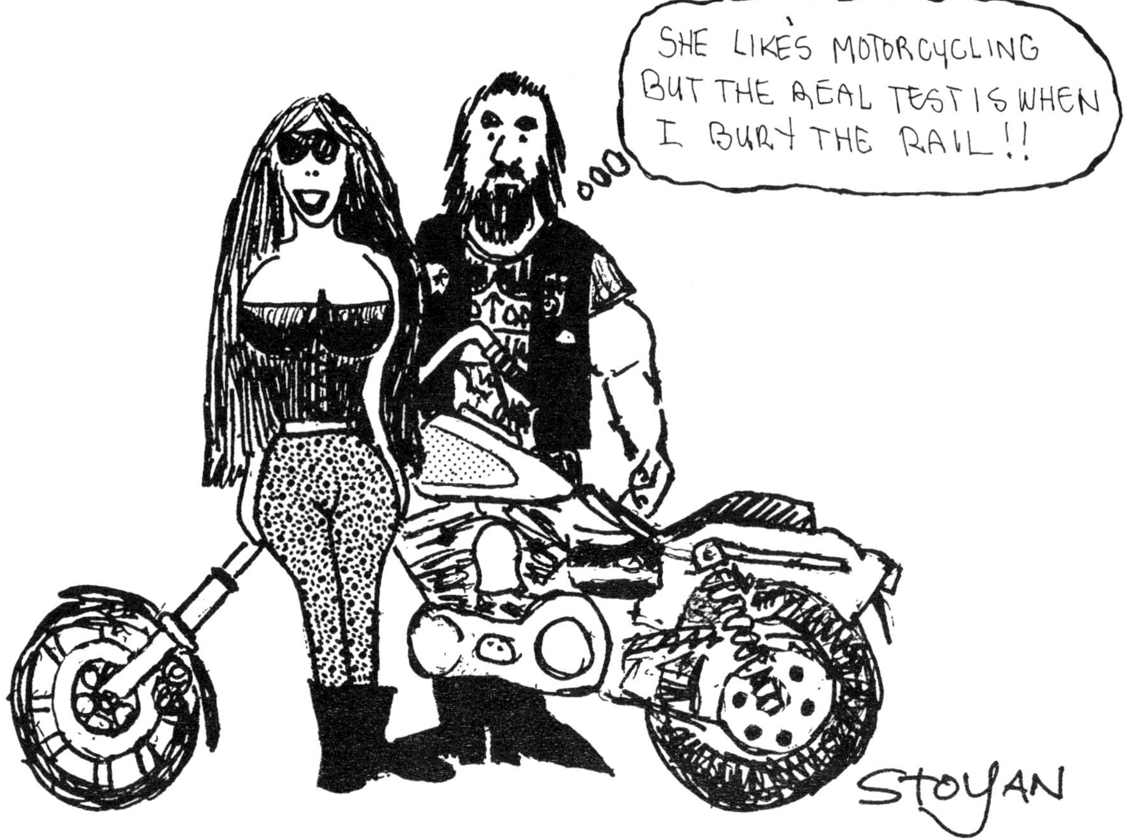
SHE LIKE'S MOTORCYCLING BUT THE REAL TEST IS WHEN I BURY THE RAIL!!
STOYAN

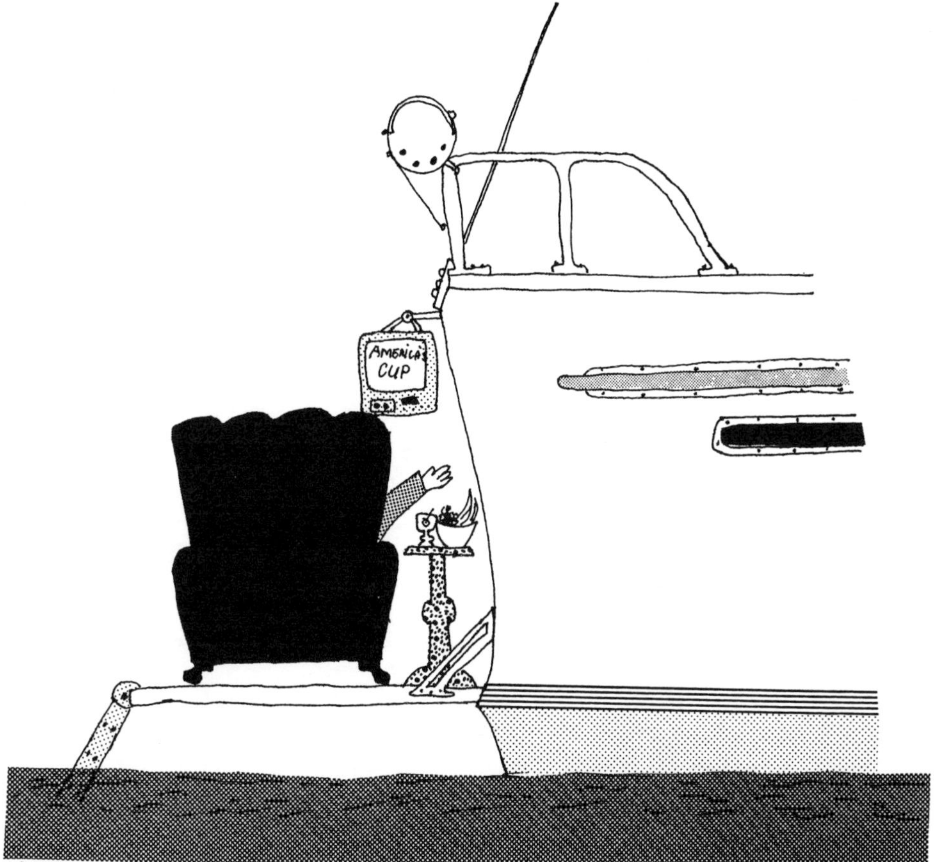
AMERICA'S CUP

HARRIET, THERE IS ENOUGH ROOM... ORDER THAT MATCHING LOVE SEAT!!

STOYAN

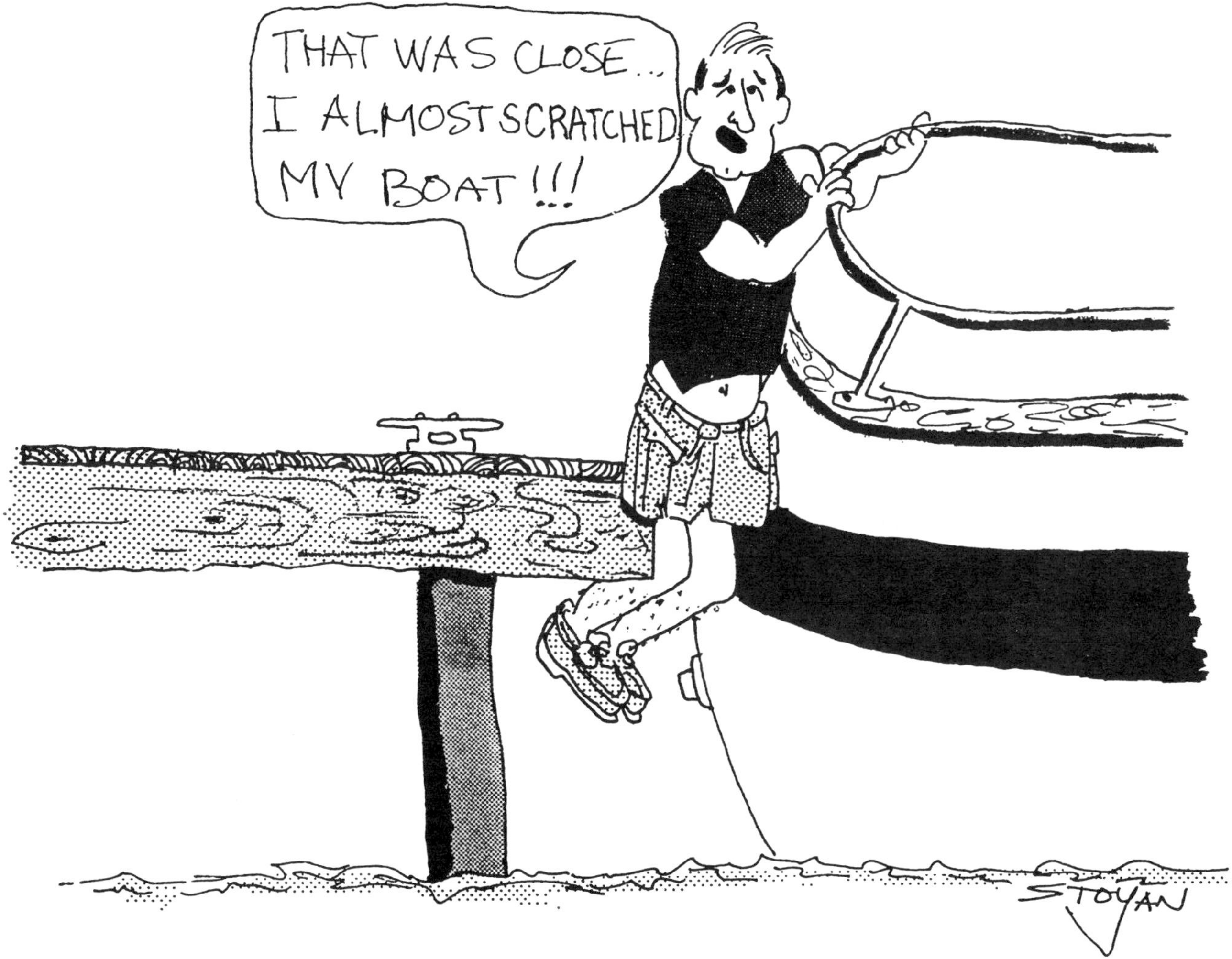
THAT WAS CLOSE...
I ALMOST SCRATCHED
MY BOAT!!!
STOYAN

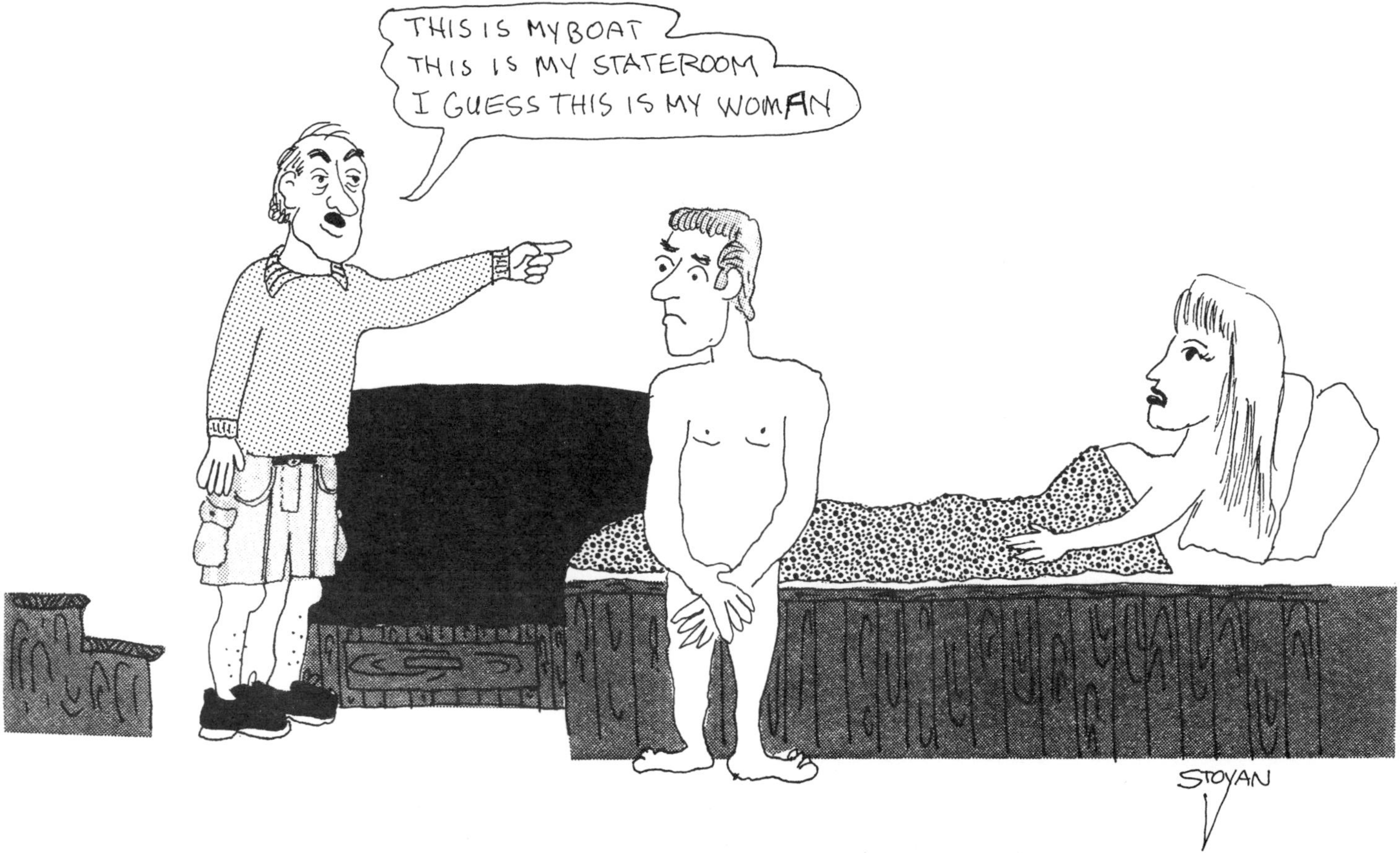
THIS IS MY BOAT
THIS IS MY STATEROOM
I GUESS THIS IS MY WOMAN
STOYAN

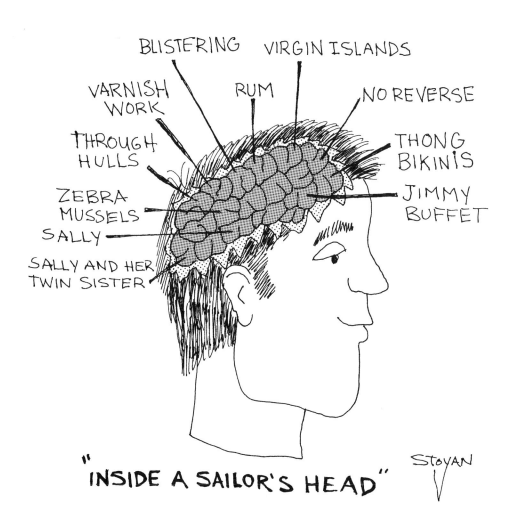

BLISTERING   VIRGIN ISLANDS

VARNISH WORK   RUM   NO REVERSE

THROUGH HULLS   THONG BIKINIS

ZEBRA MUSSELS   JIMMY BUFFET

SALLY

SALLY AND HER TWIN SISTER

"INSIDE A SAILOR'S HEAD"

STOYAN

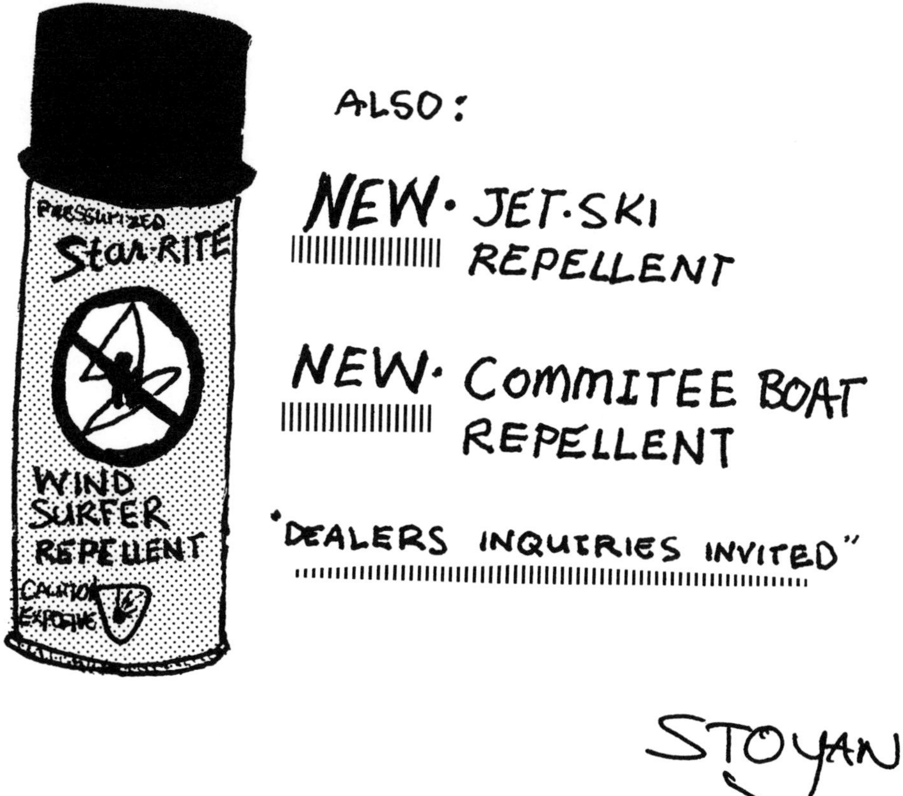
PRESSURIZED
Star-RITE
WIND SURFER REPELLENT
CAUTION EXPLOSIVE
ALSO:
NEW • JET•SKI REPELLENT
NEW • COMMITEE BOAT REPELLENT
"DEALERS INQUIRIES INVITED"
STOYAN

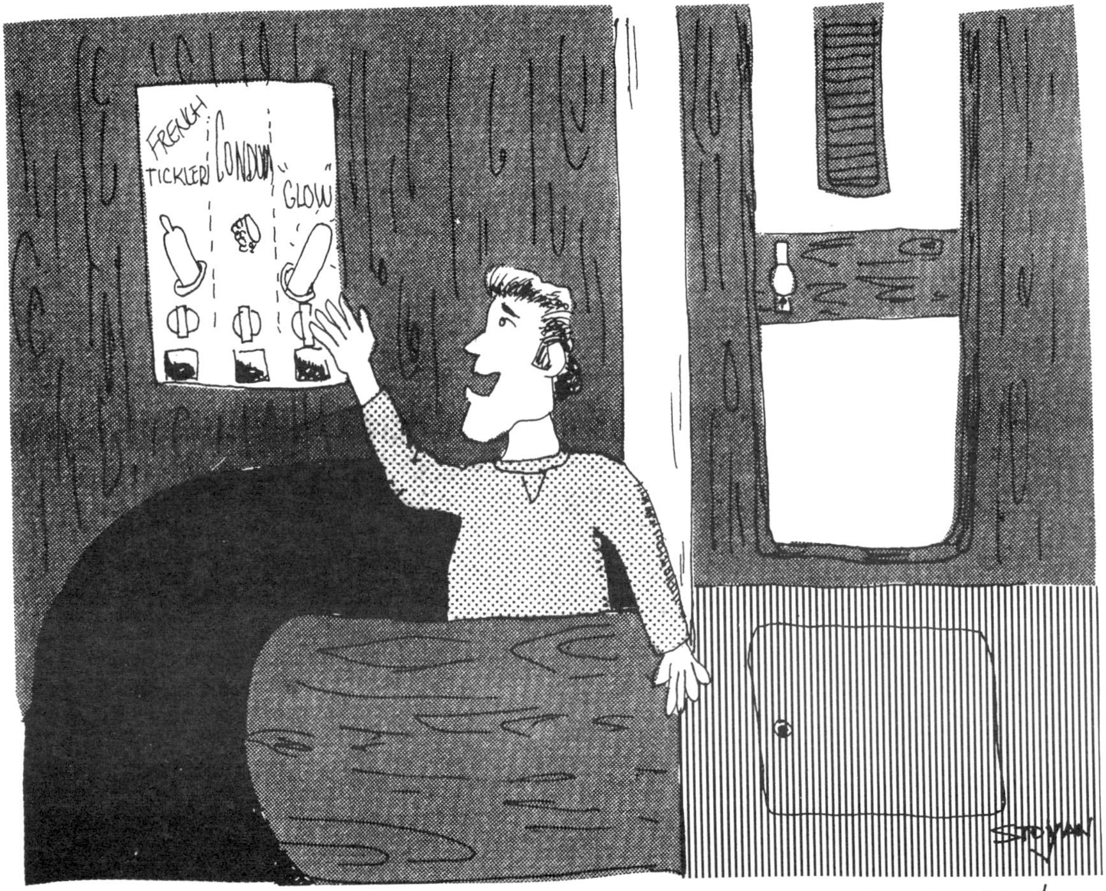
FRENCH TICKLER
CONDOM
"GLOW"

THE CONDOM MACHINE IS JUST PART OF SAFE BOATING!

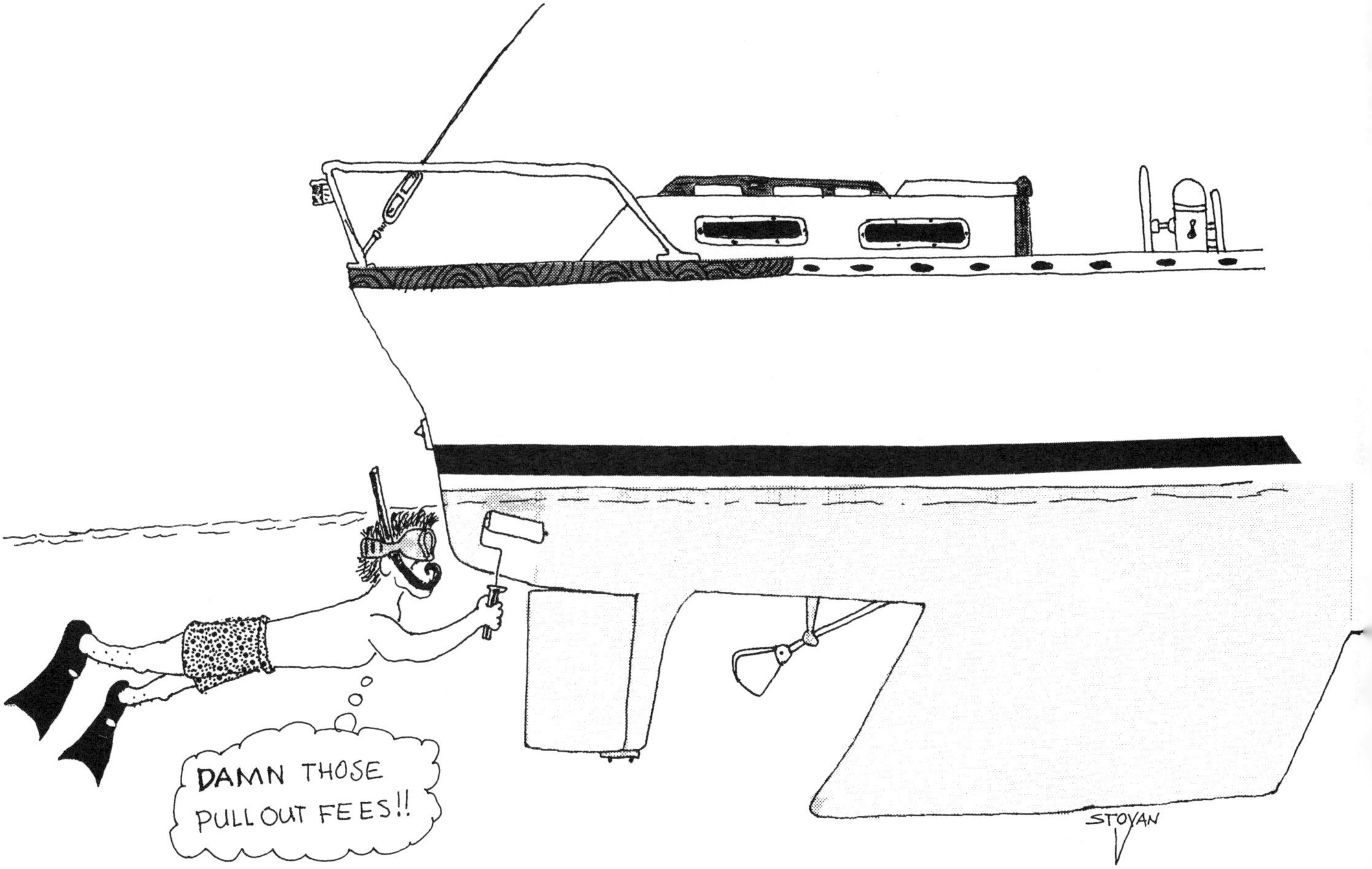
DAMN THOSE PULLOUT FEES!!
STOYAN

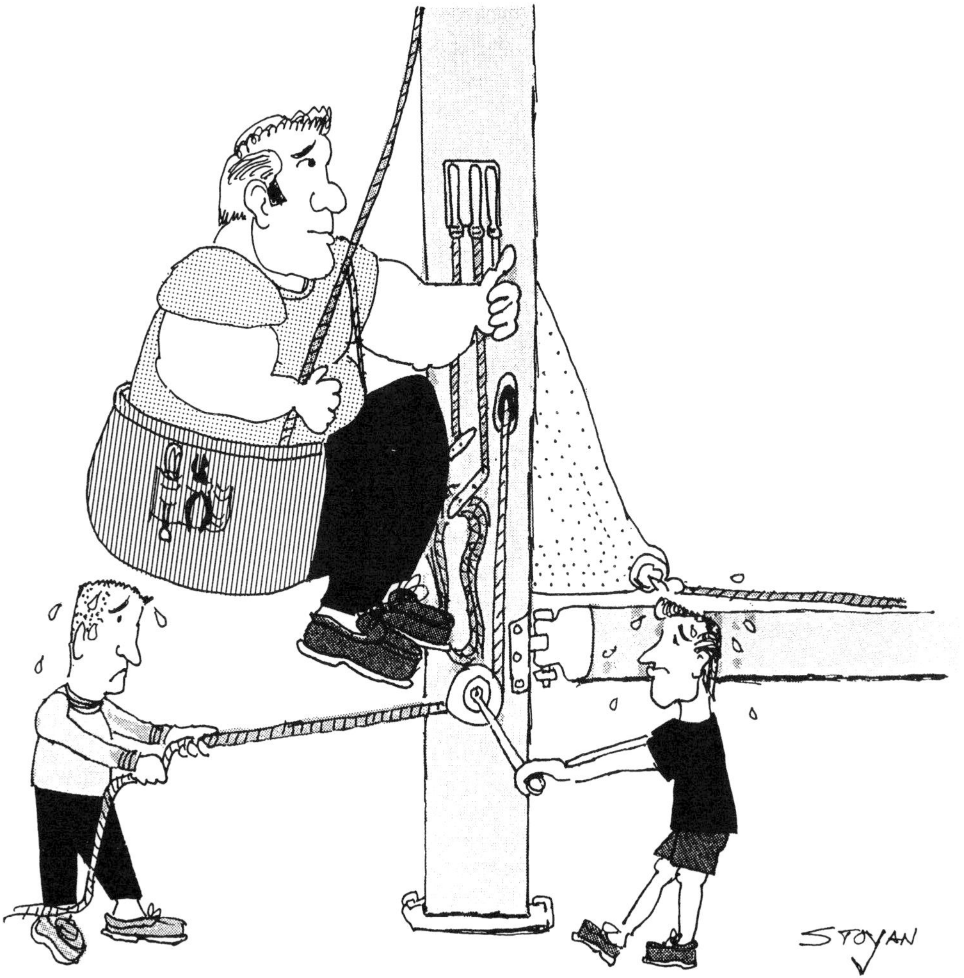
STOYAN

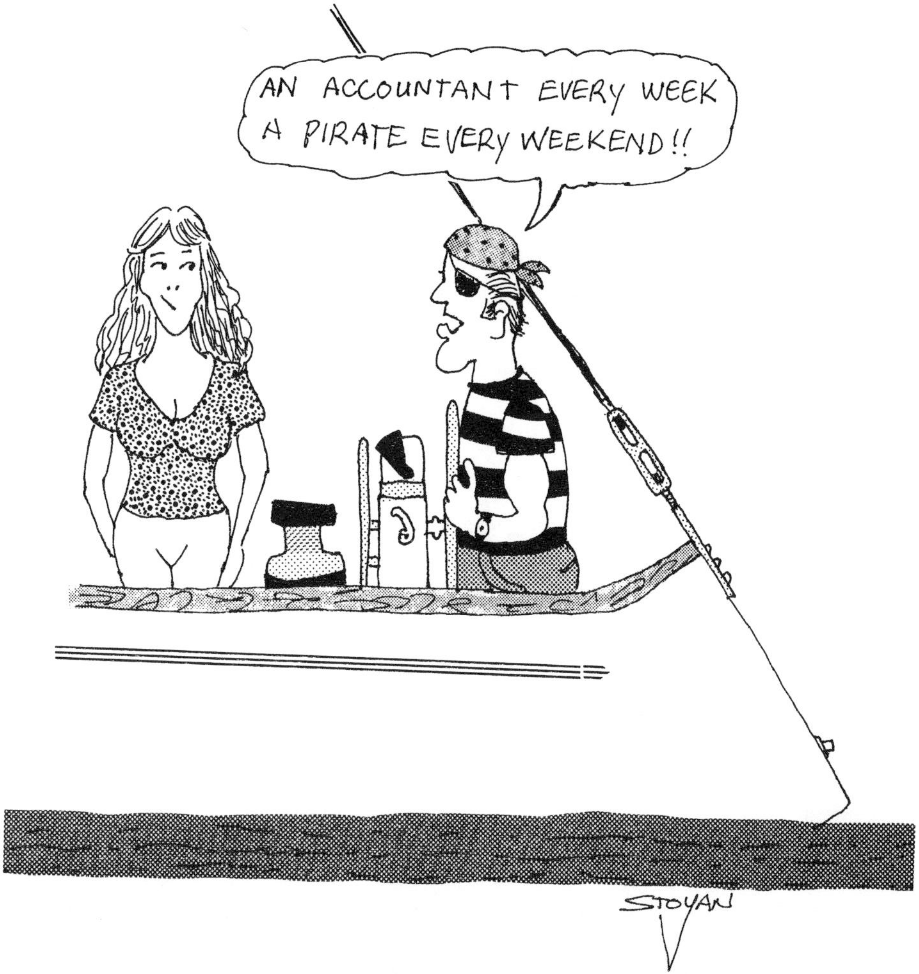
AN ACCOUNTANT EVERY WEEK
A PIRATE EVERY WEEKEND!!
STOYAN

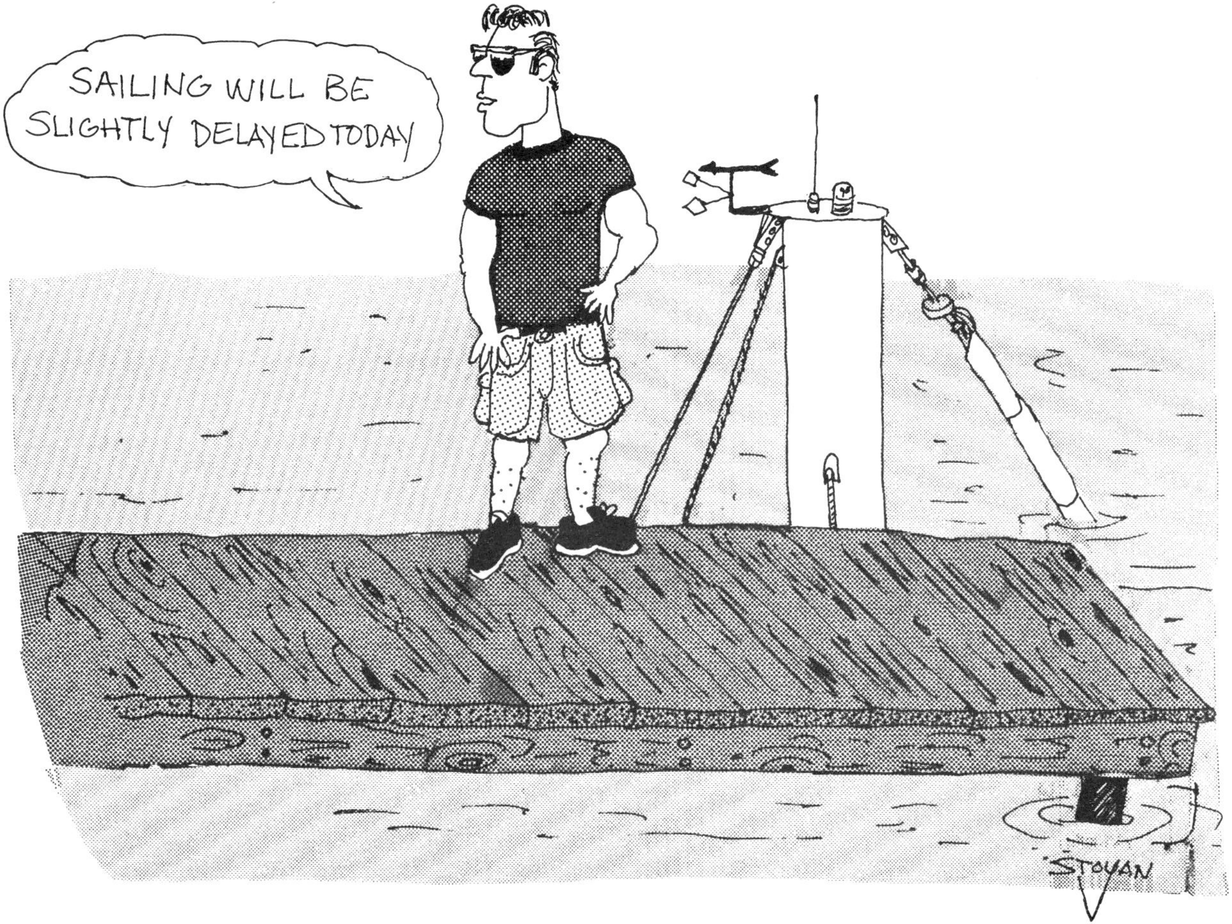
SAILING WILL BE SLIGHTLY DELAYED TODAY
STOYAN

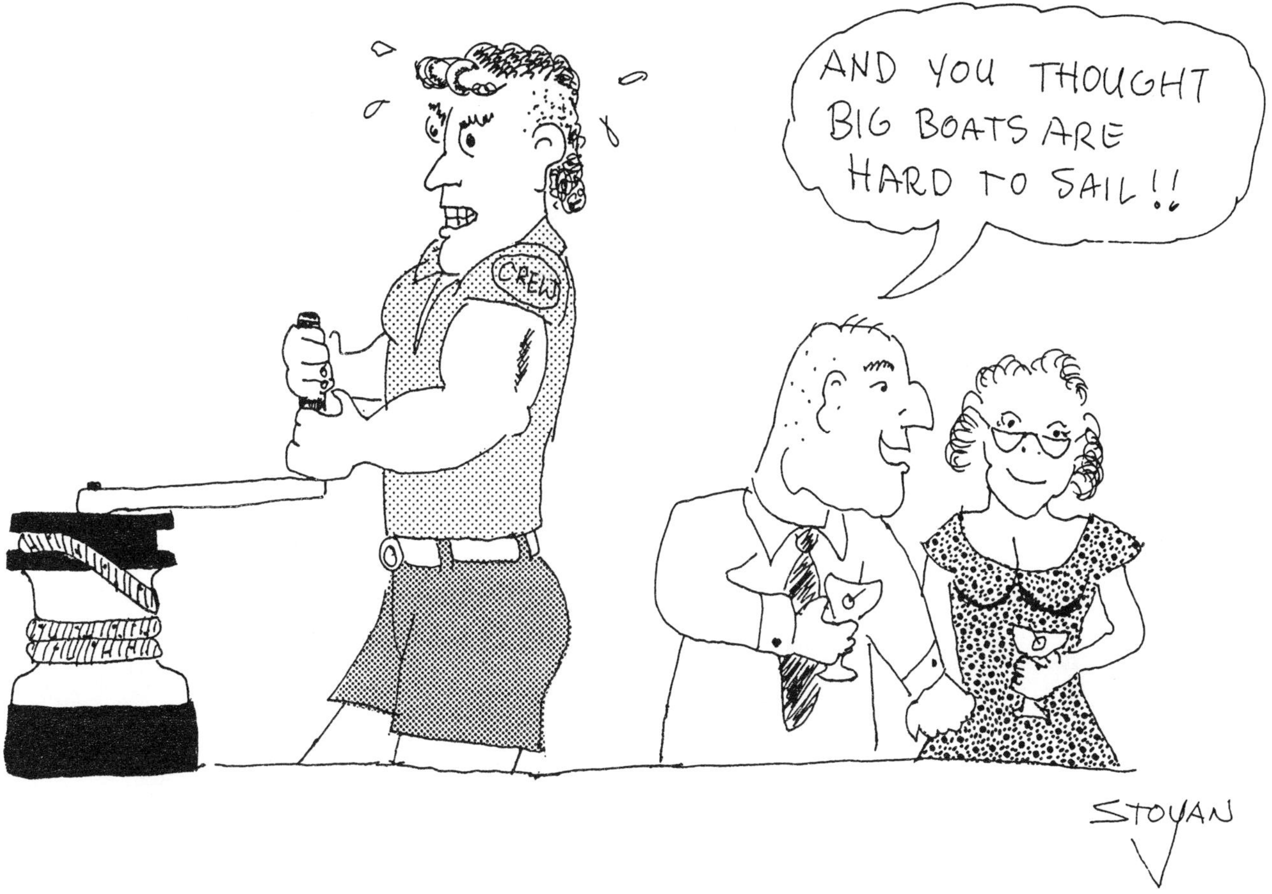
AND YOU THOUGHT BIG BOATS ARE HARD TO SAIL!!
CREW
STOYAN

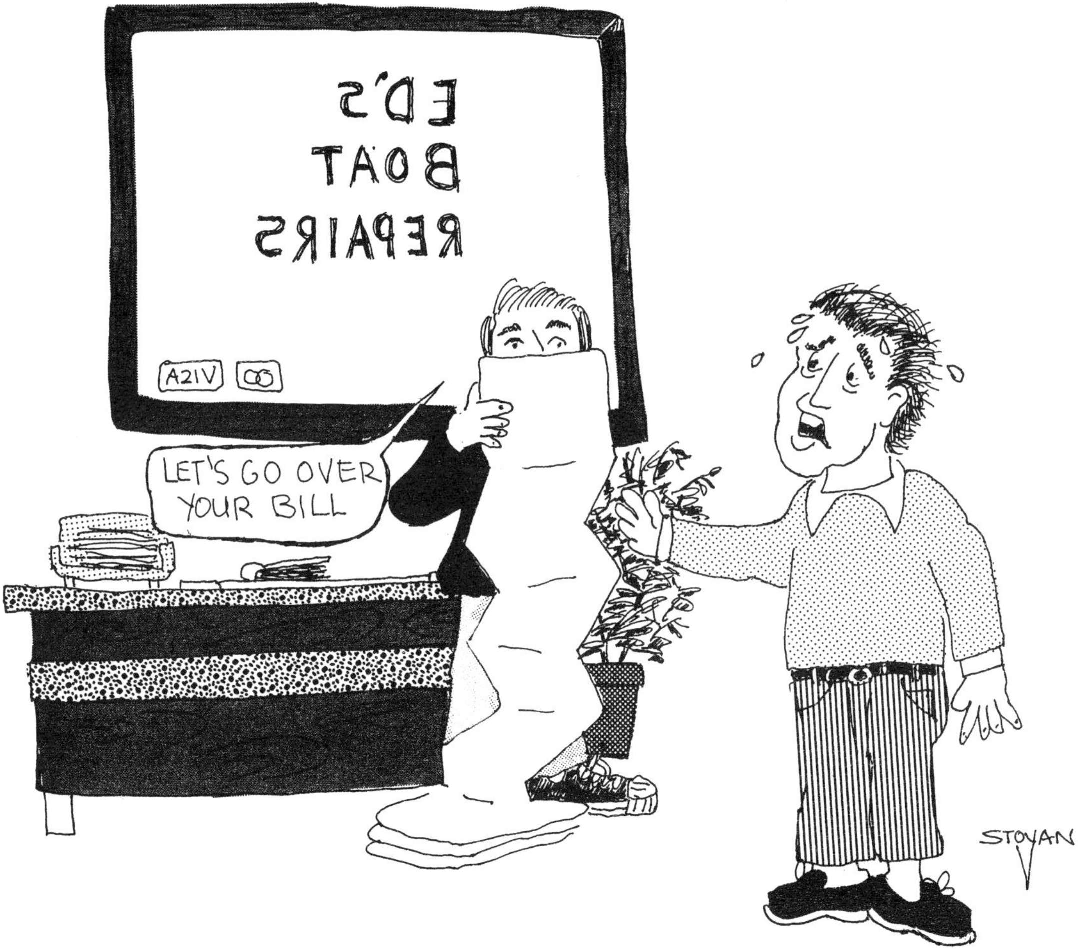
ED'S
BOAT
REPAIRS
LET'S GO OVER YOUR BILL
STOYAN

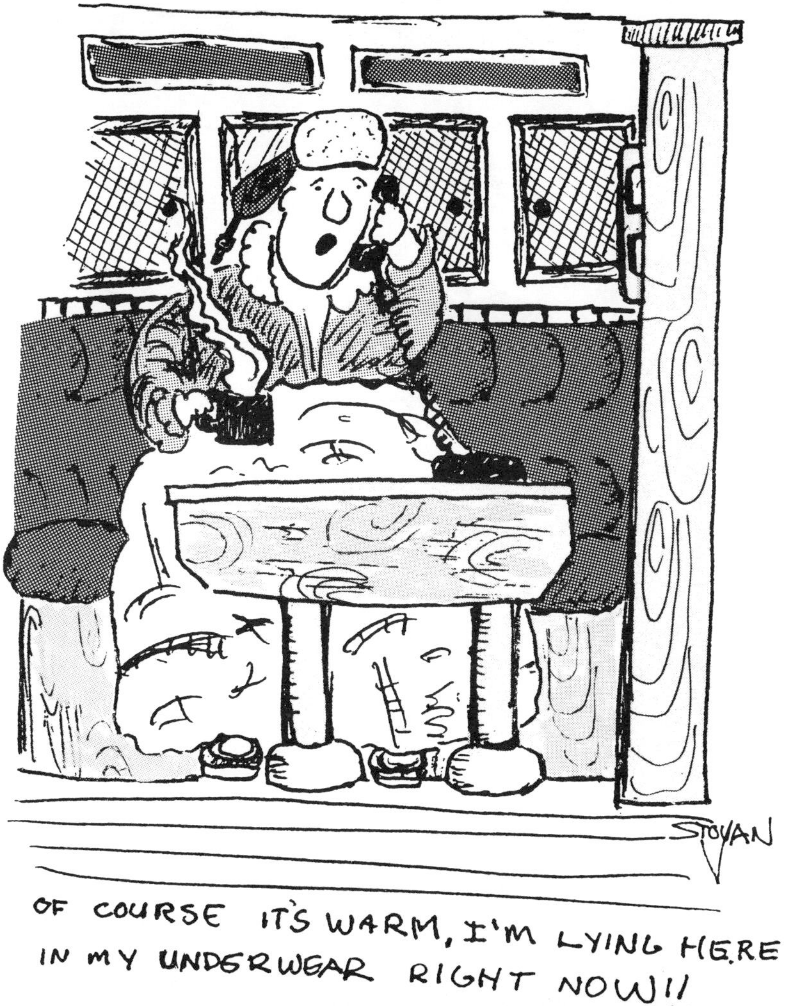
STOYAN

OF COURSE IT'S WARM, I'M LYING HERE
IN MY UNDERWEAR RIGHT NOW!!

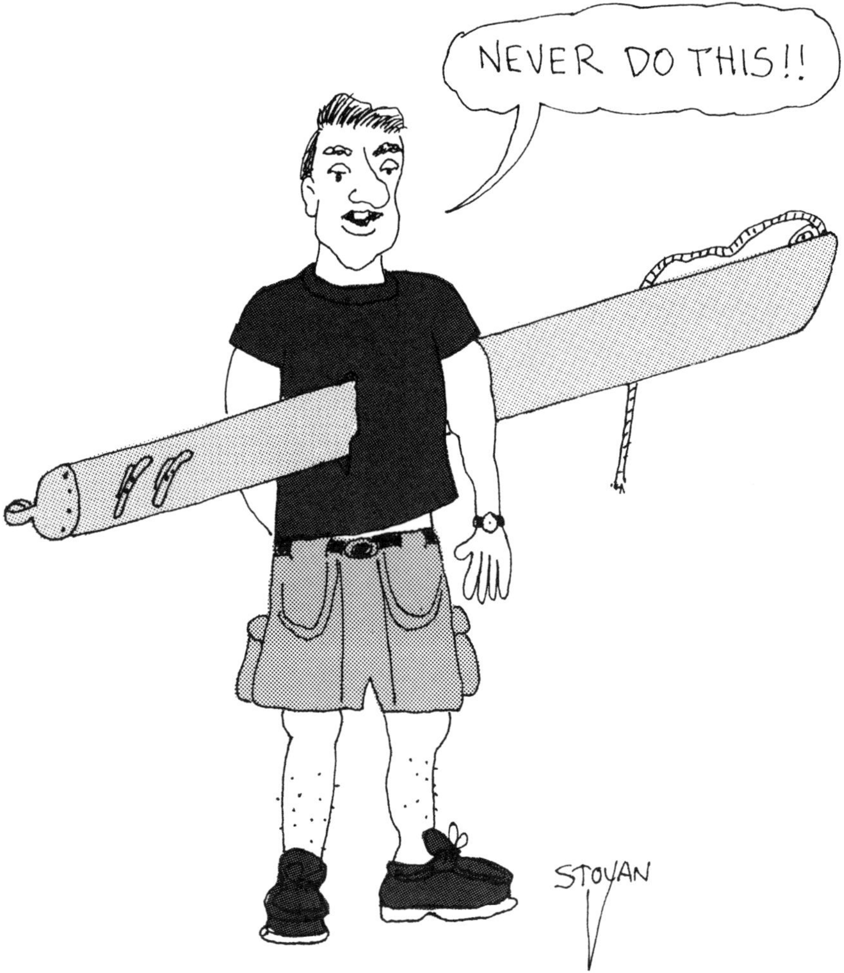
NEVER DO THIS!!
STOYAN

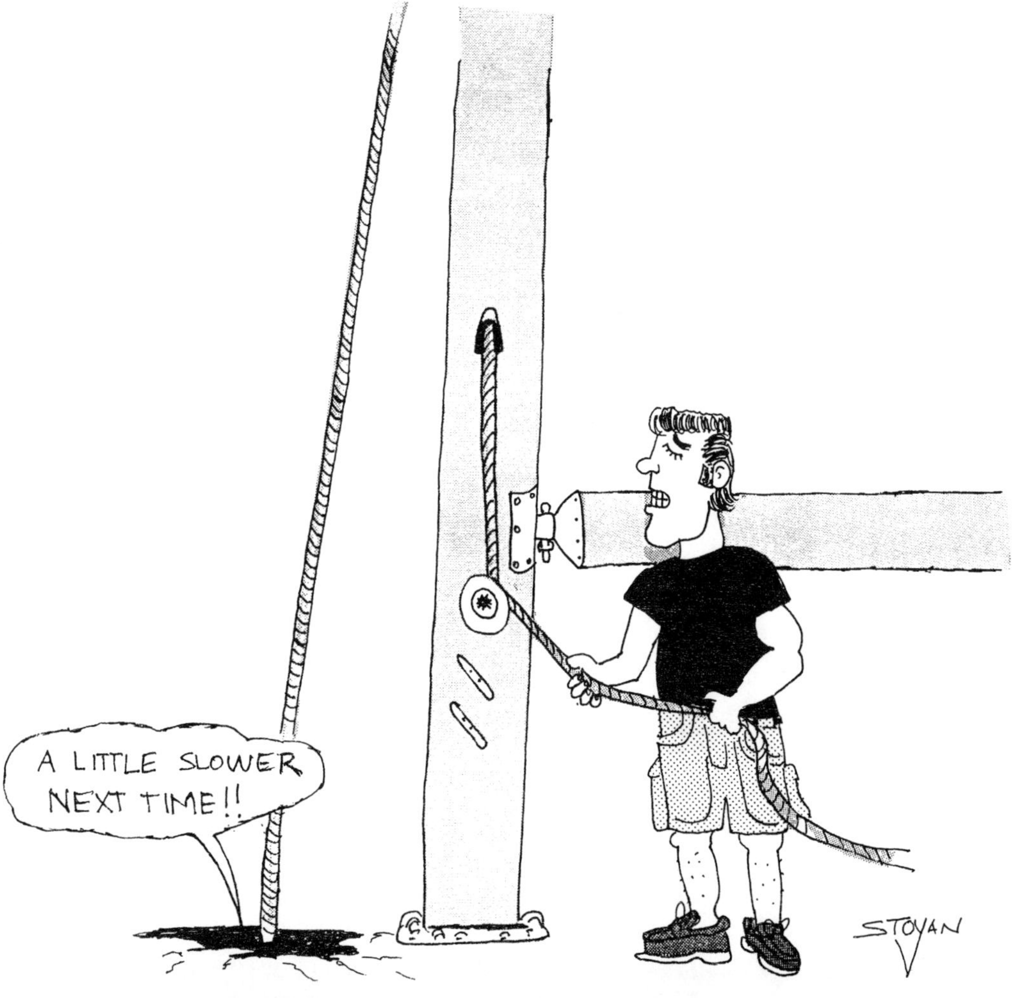
A LITTLE SLOWER NEXT TIME!!
STOYAN

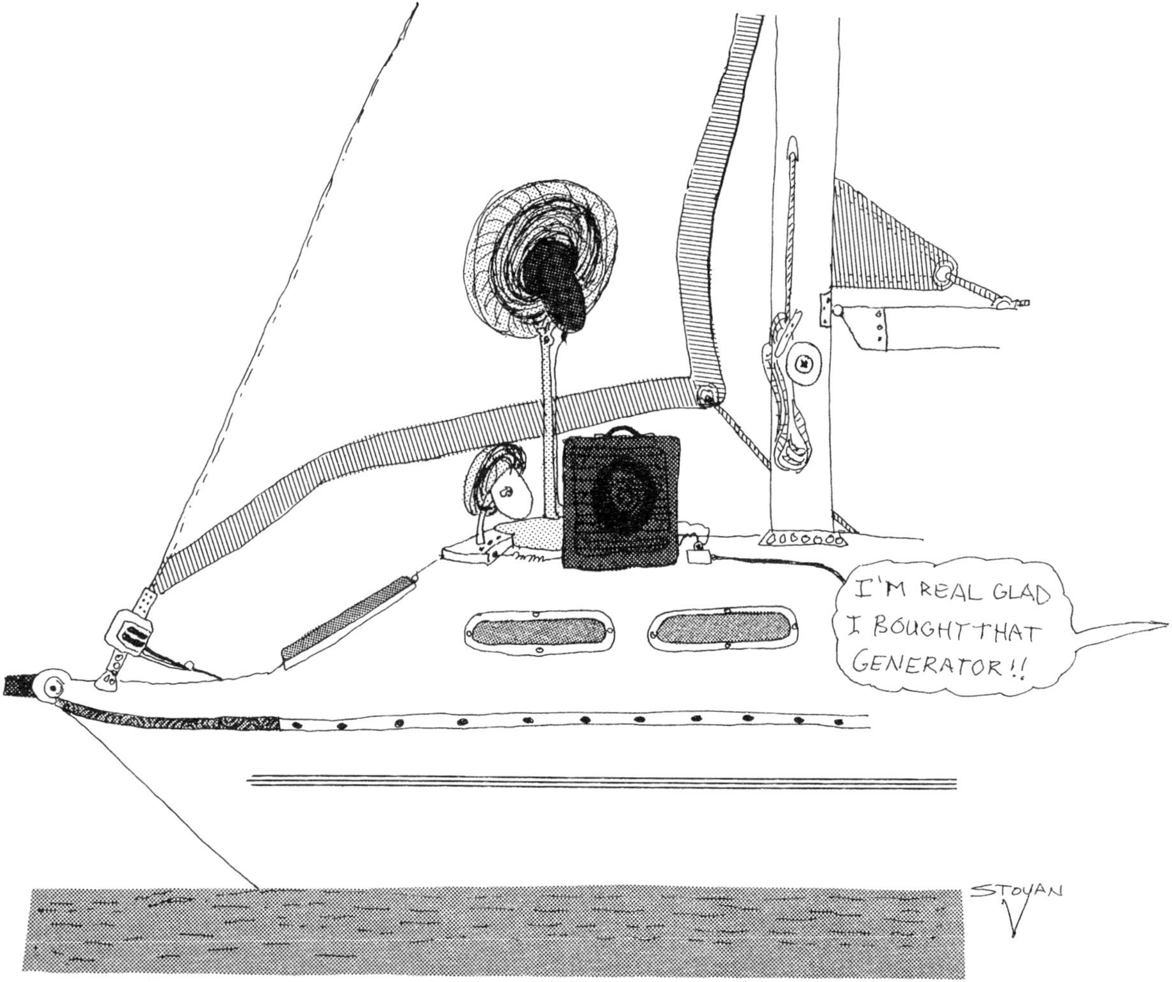
I'M REAL GLAD
I BOUGHT THAT
GENERATOR!!
STOYAN

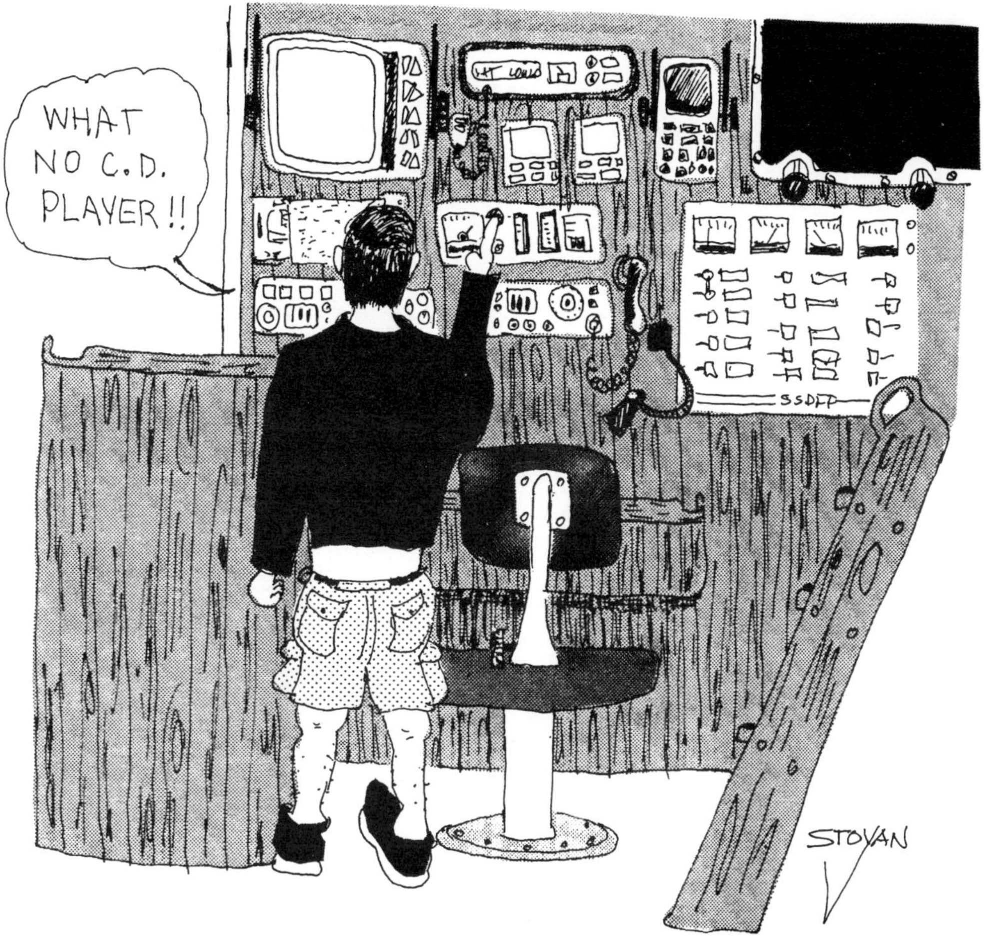
WHAT NO C.D. PLAYER!!
SSDFP
STOYAN

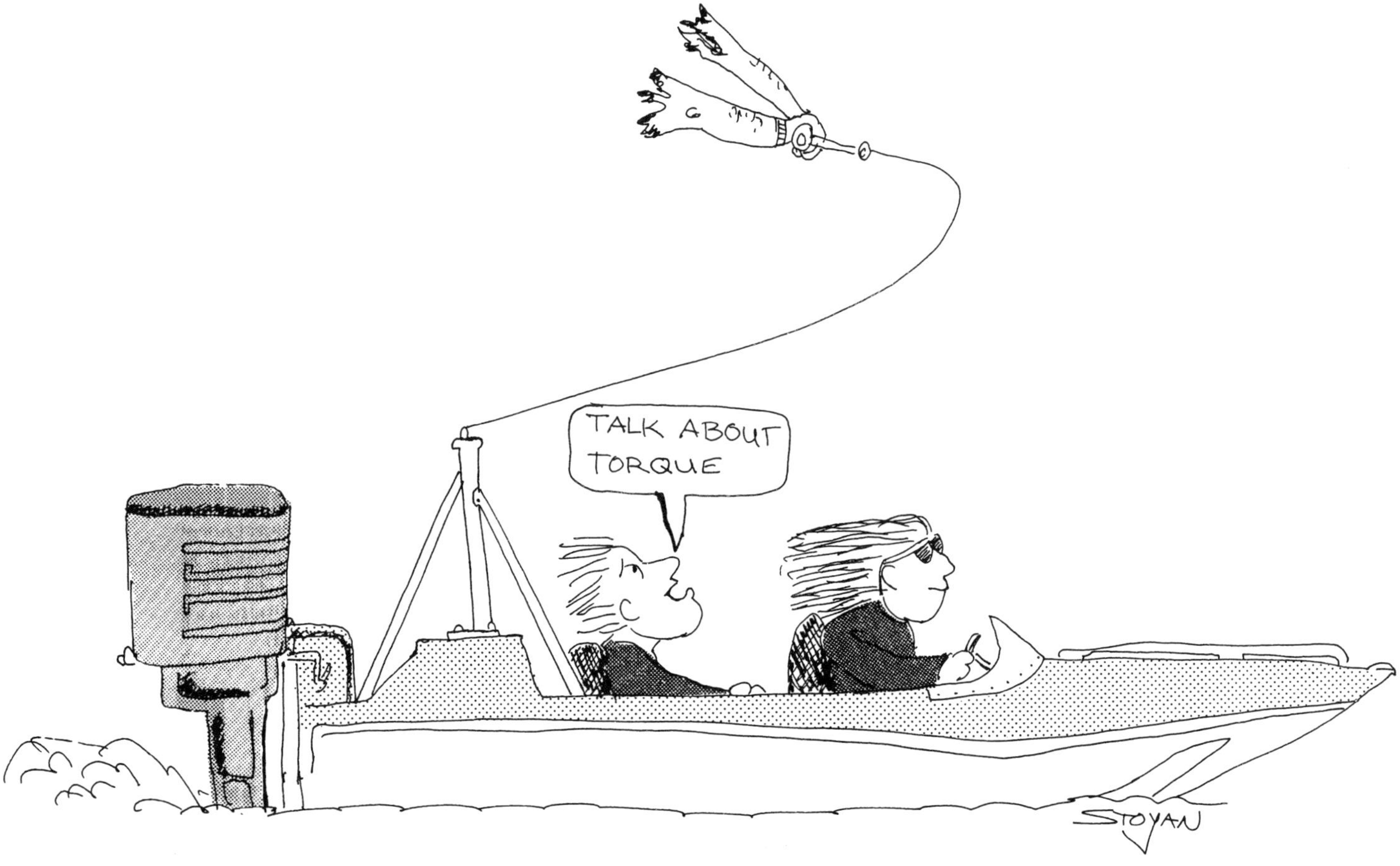
TALK ABOUT TORQUE
STOYAN

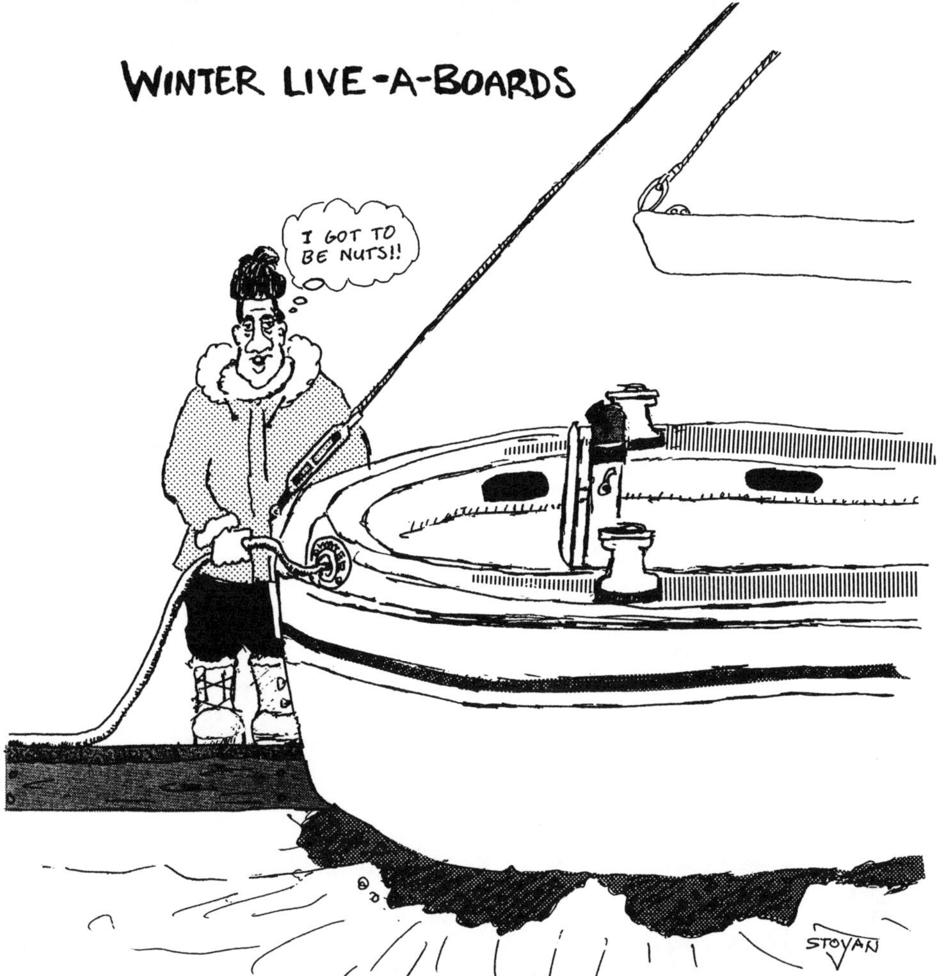
WINTER LIVE-A-BOARDS
I GOT TO BE NUTS!!
STOYAN

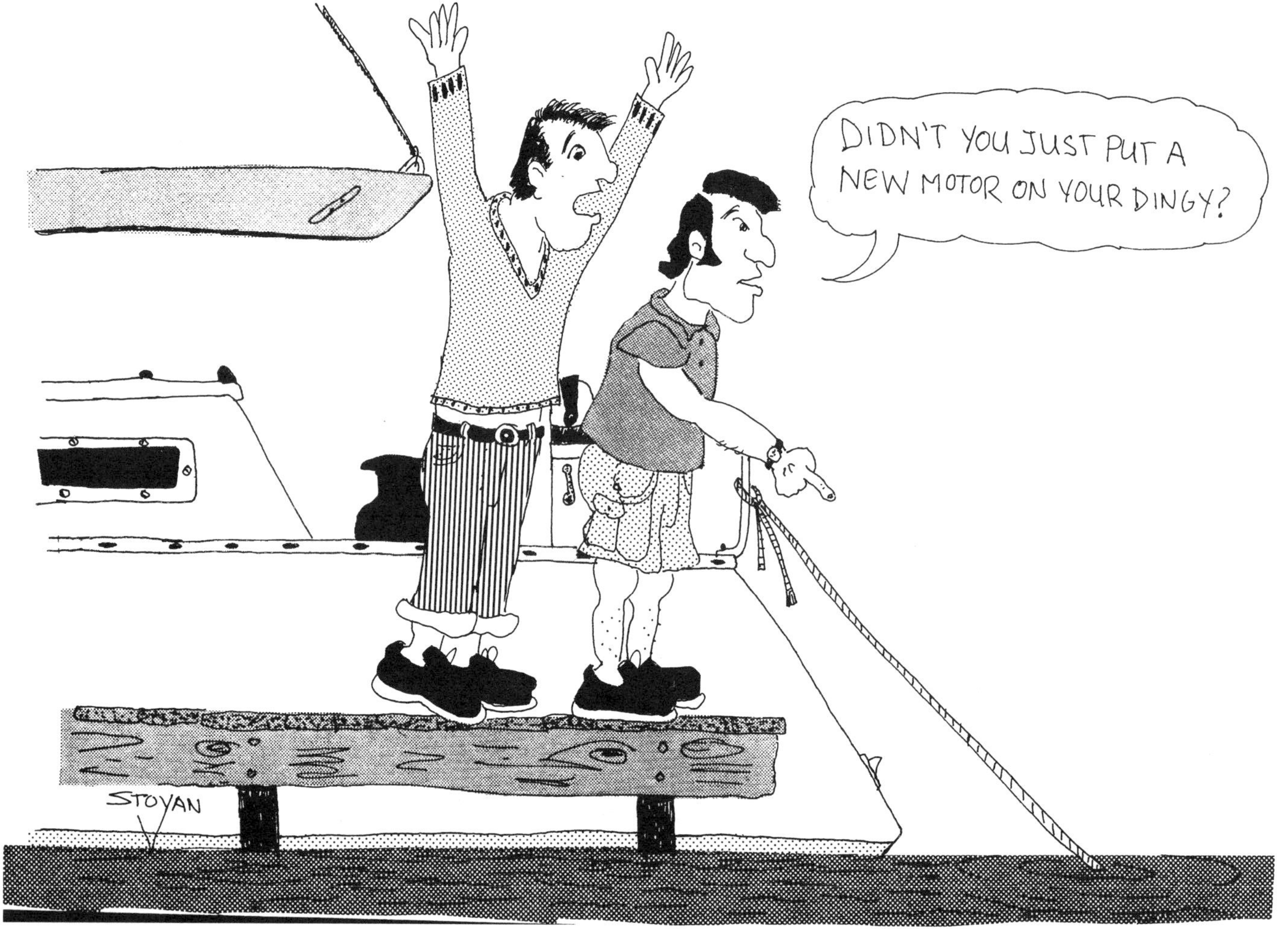
DIDN'T YOU JUST PUT A NEW MOTOR ON YOUR DINGY?
STOYAN

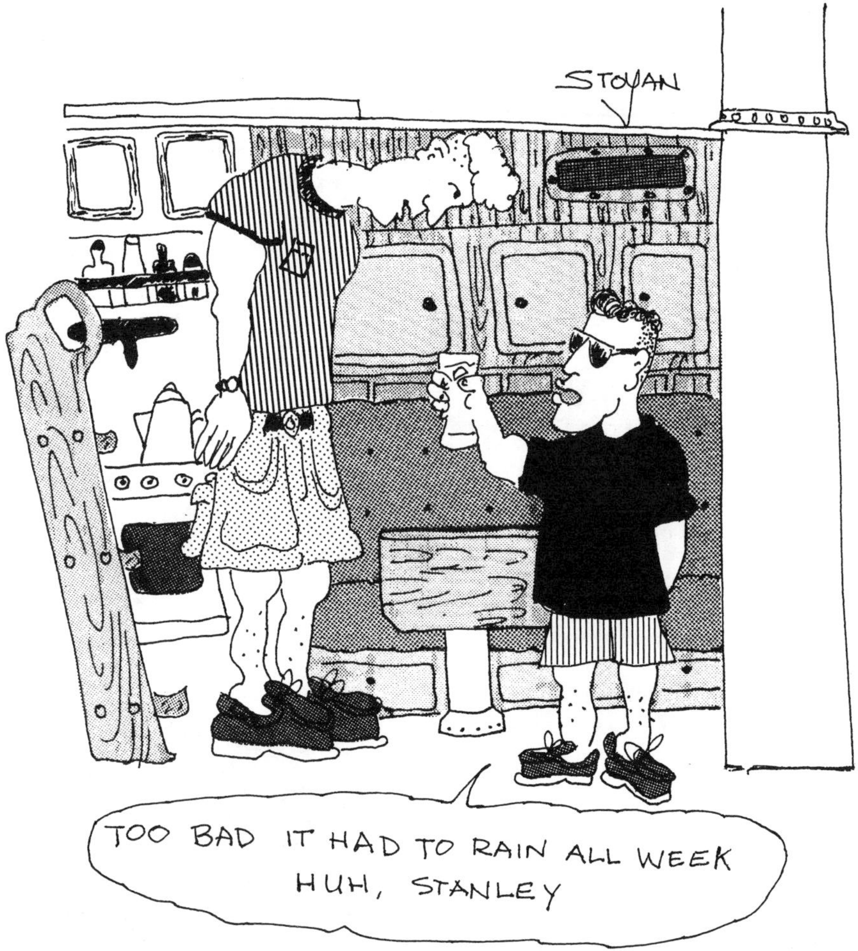
STOYAN
TOO BAD IT HAD TO RAIN ALL WEEK
HUH, STANLEY

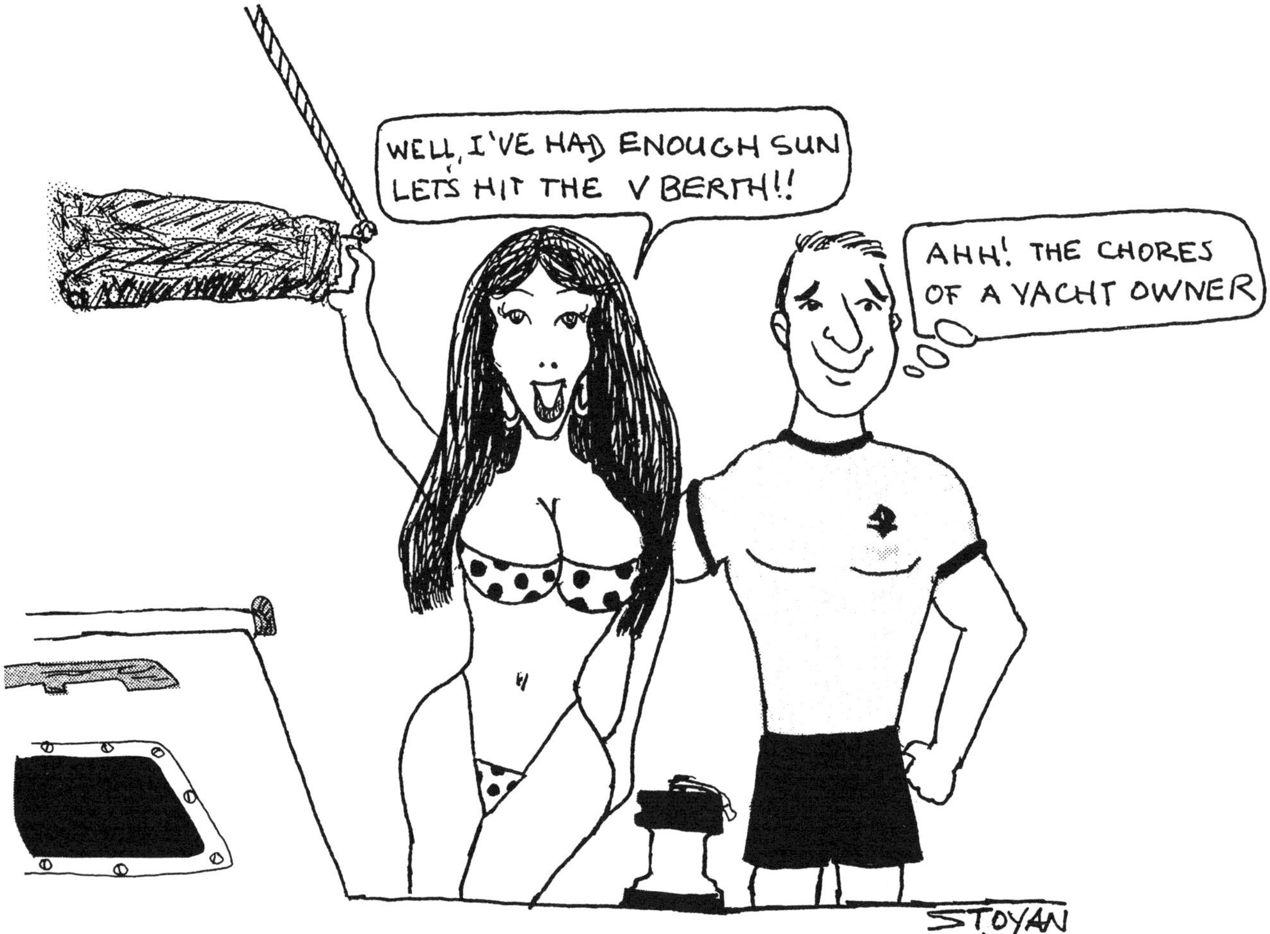
WELL, I'VE HAD ENOUGH SUN LETS HIT THE V BERTH!!
AHH! THE CHORES OF A YACHT OWNER
STOYAN

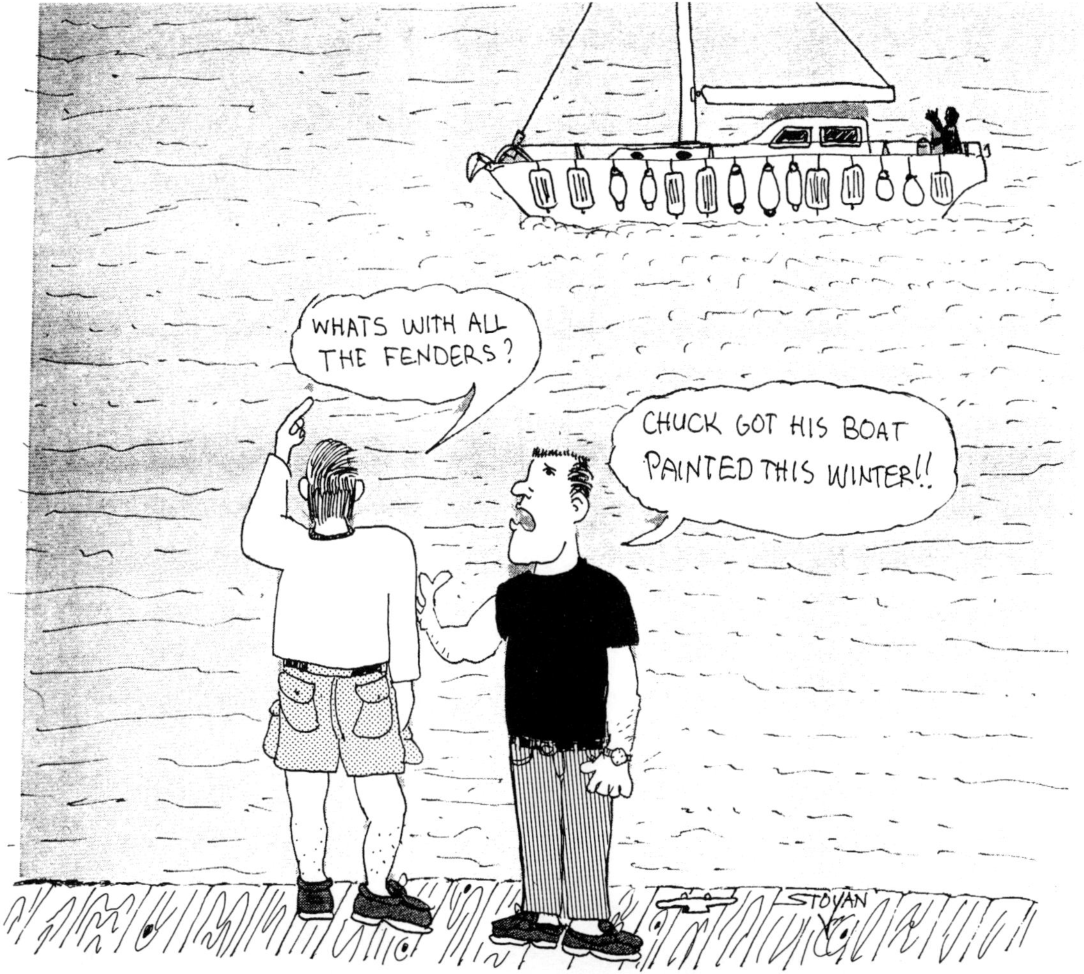
WHATS WITH ALL THE FENDERS?
CHUCK GOT HIS BOAT PAINTED THIS WINTER!!
STOYAN

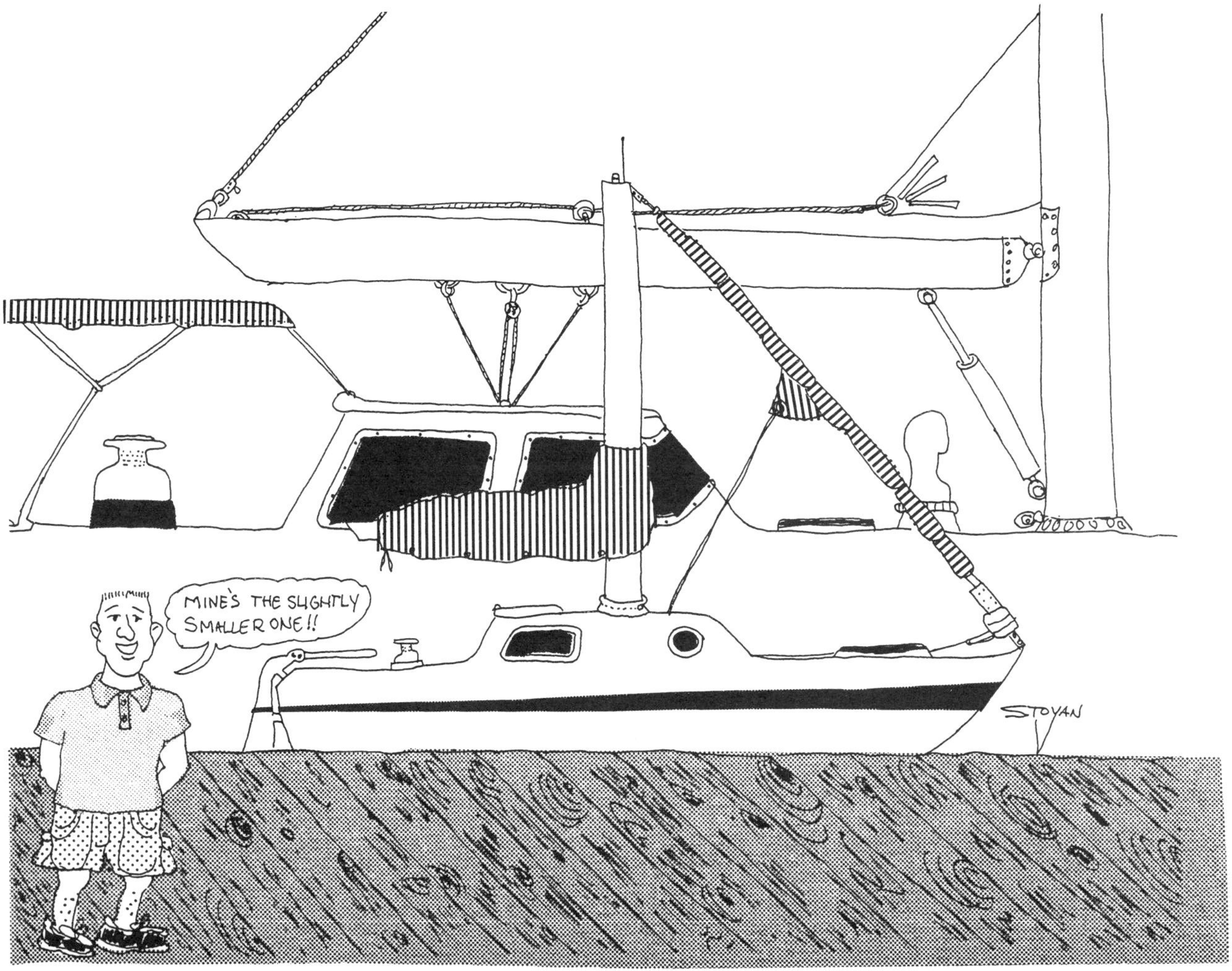
MINE'S THE SLIGHTLY SMALLER ONE!!
STOYAN

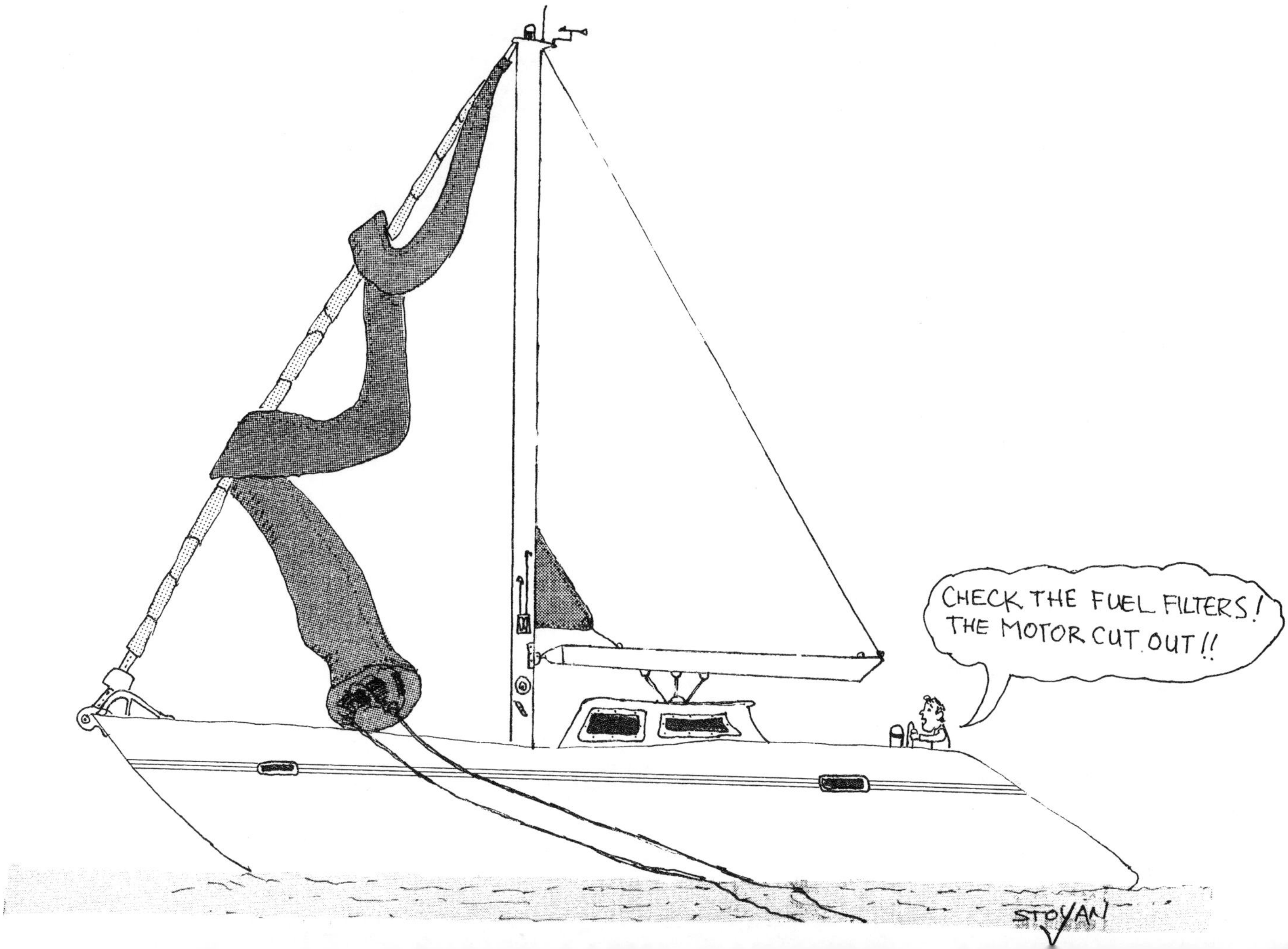
CHECK THE FUEL FILTERS! THE MOTOR CUT OUT!!
STOYAN

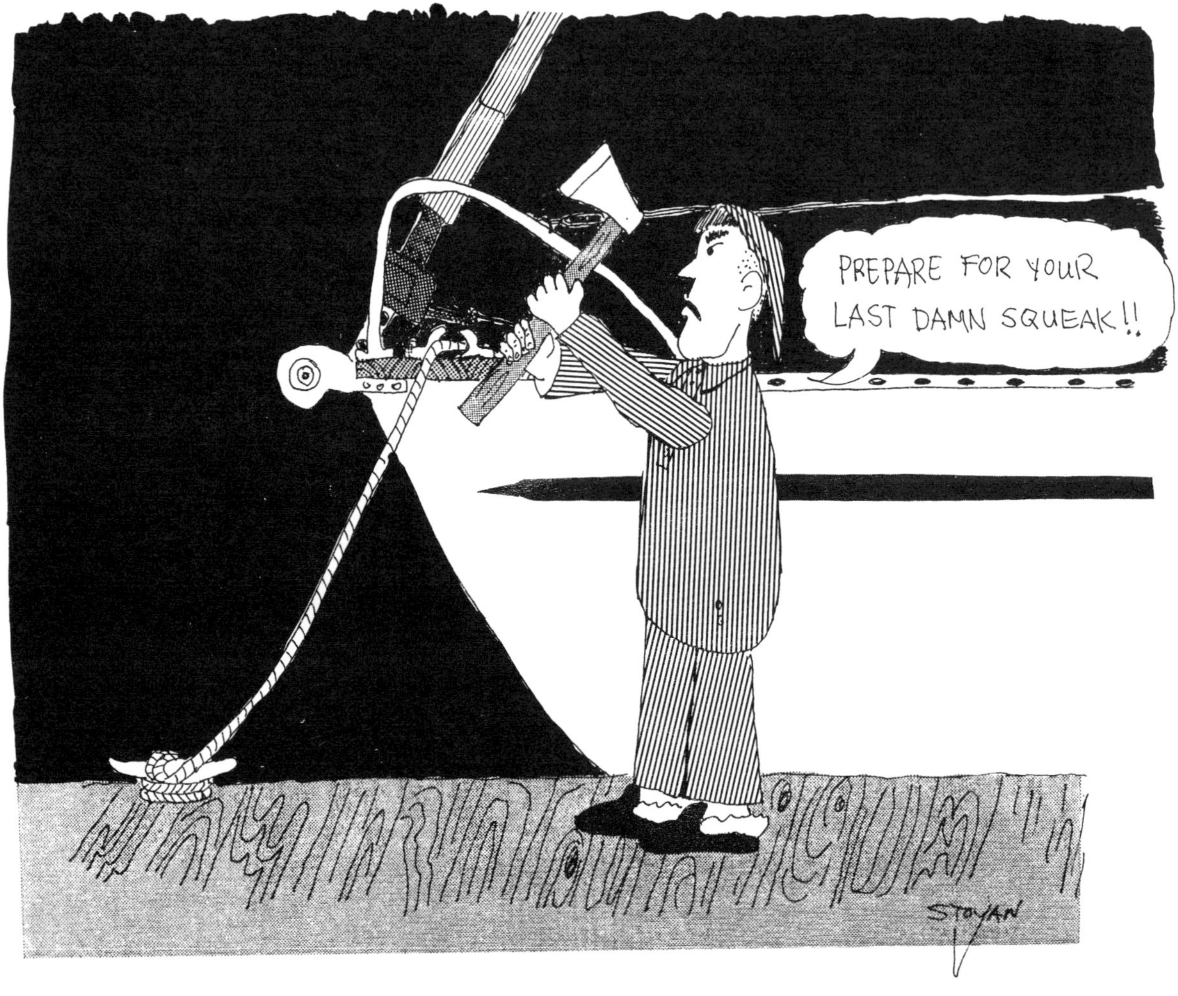
PREPARE FOR YOUR LAST DAMN SQUEAK!!
STOYAN

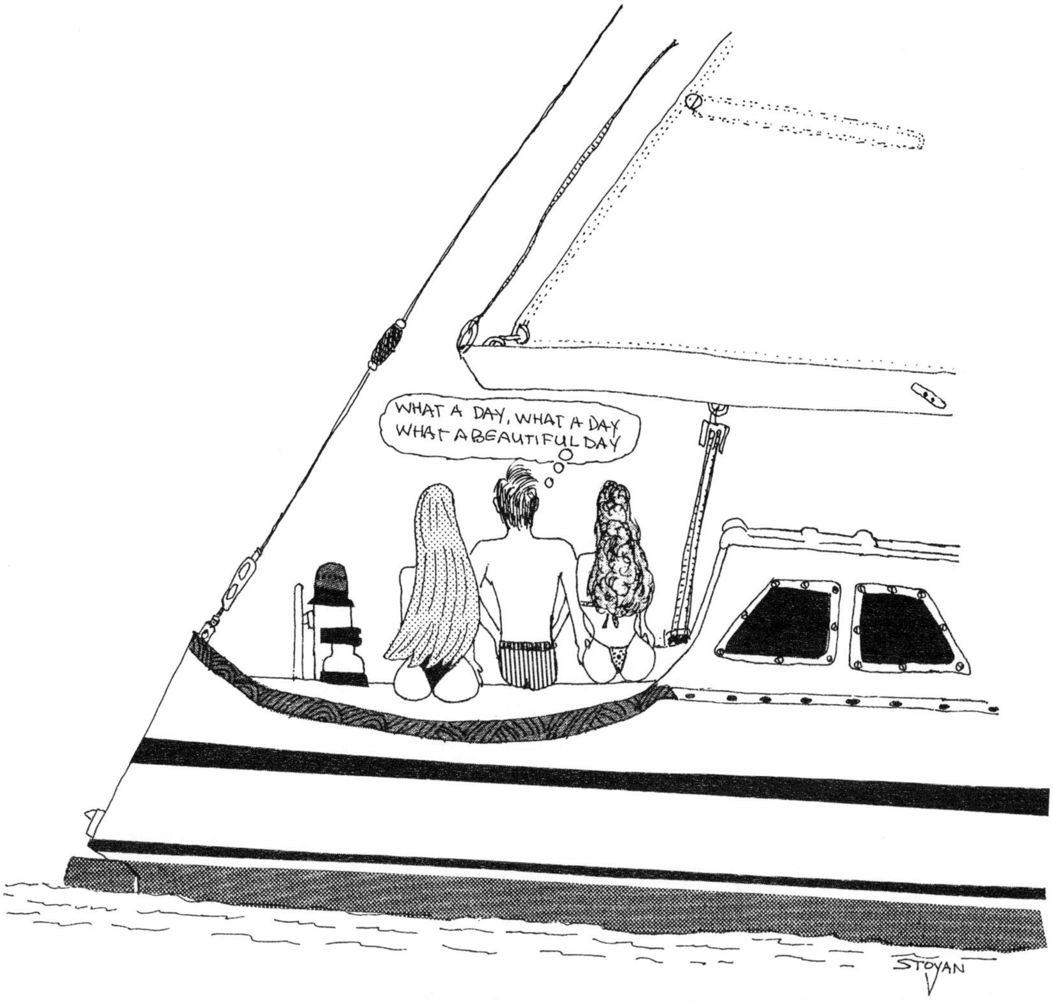
WHAT A DAY, WHAT A DAY
WHAT A BEAUTIFUL DAY
STOYAN

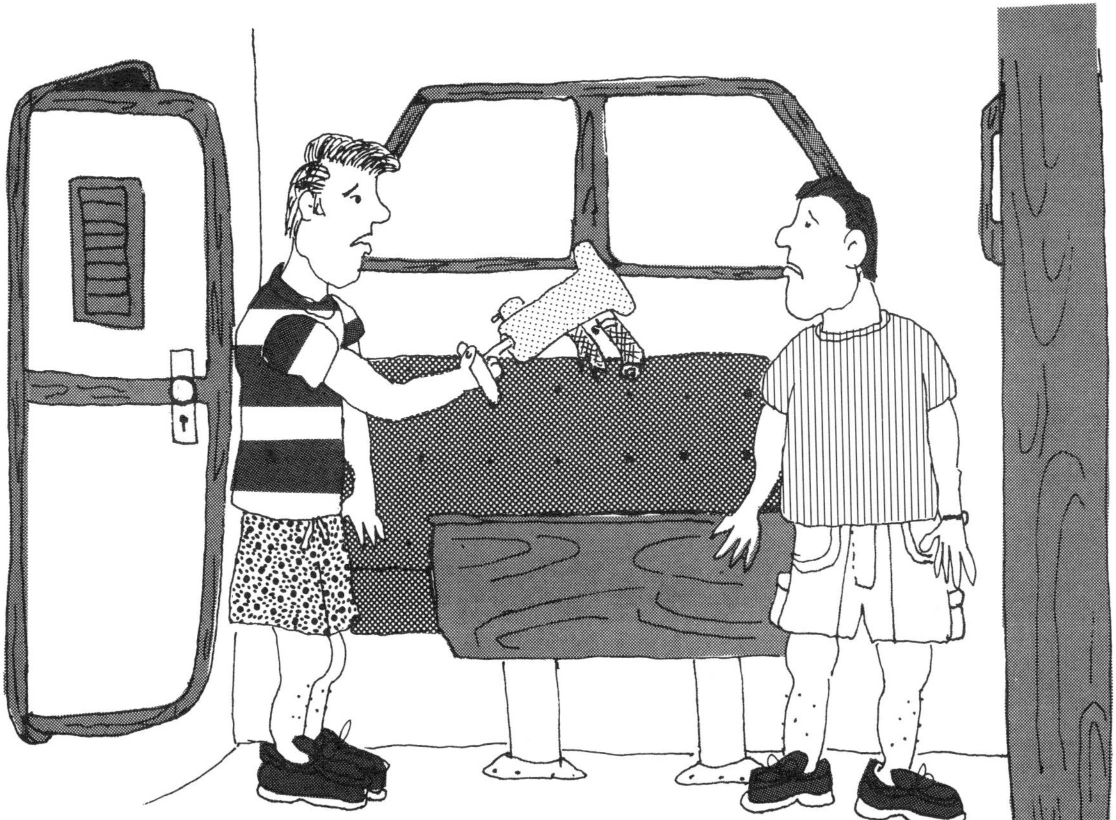

THIS PART CAME OFF YOUR HEAD!!

STOYAN

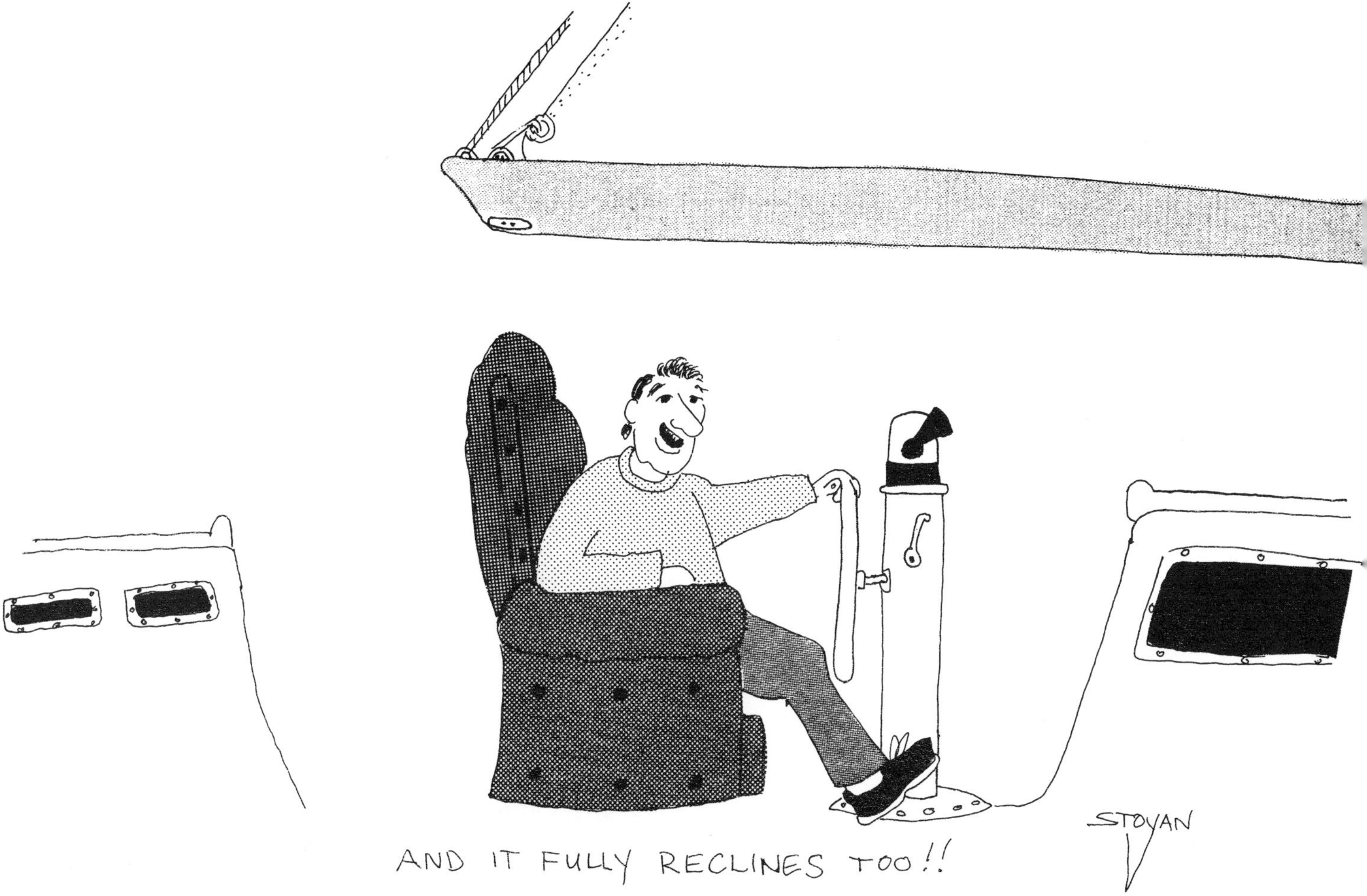

AND IT FULLY RECLINES TOO!!

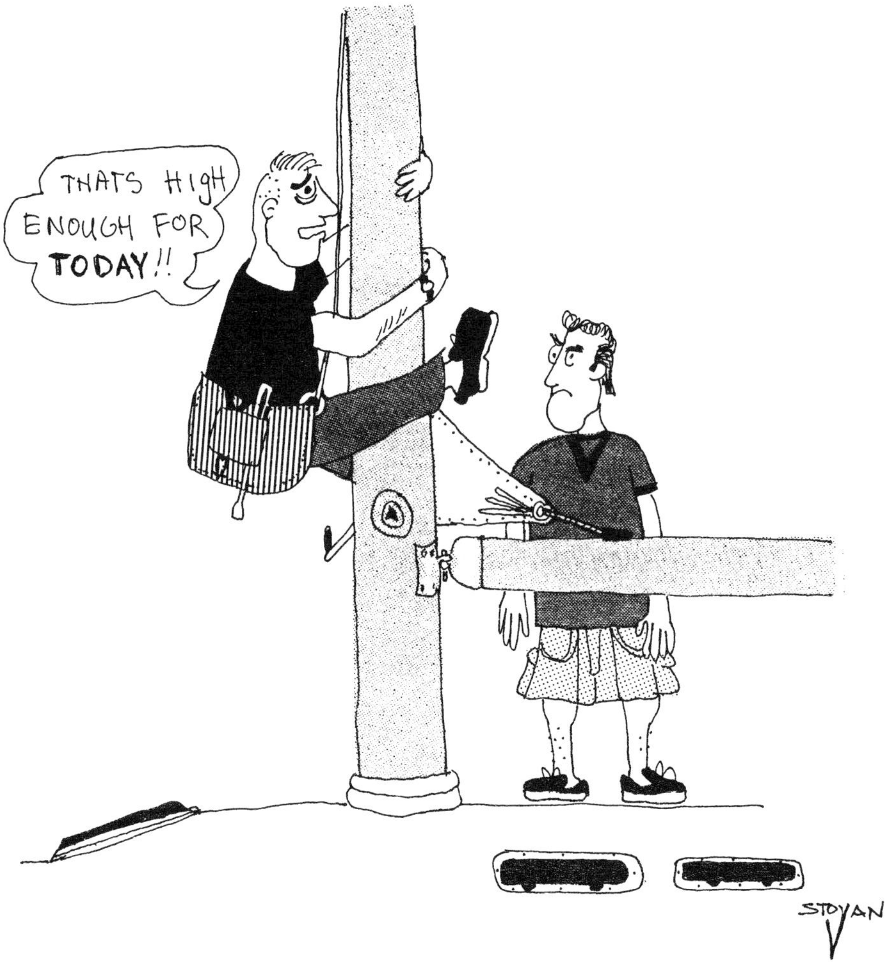
THATS HIGH ENOUGH FOR TODAY!!
STOYAN

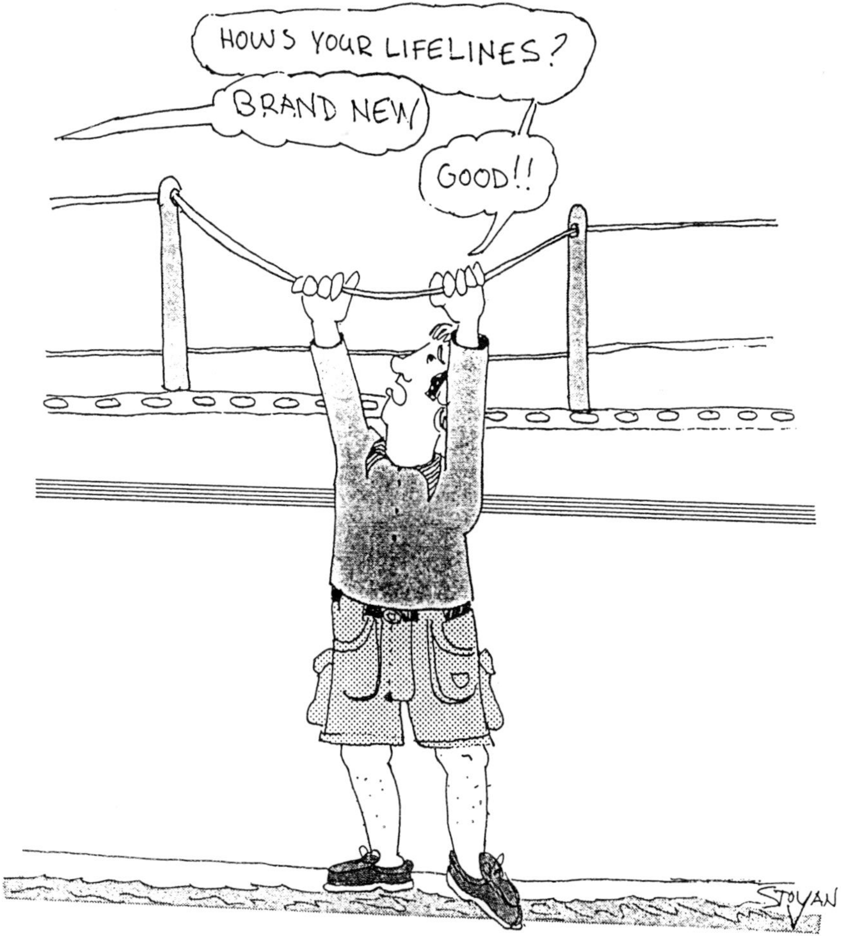
HOWS YOUR LIFELINES?
BRAND NEW
GOOD!!
STOYAN

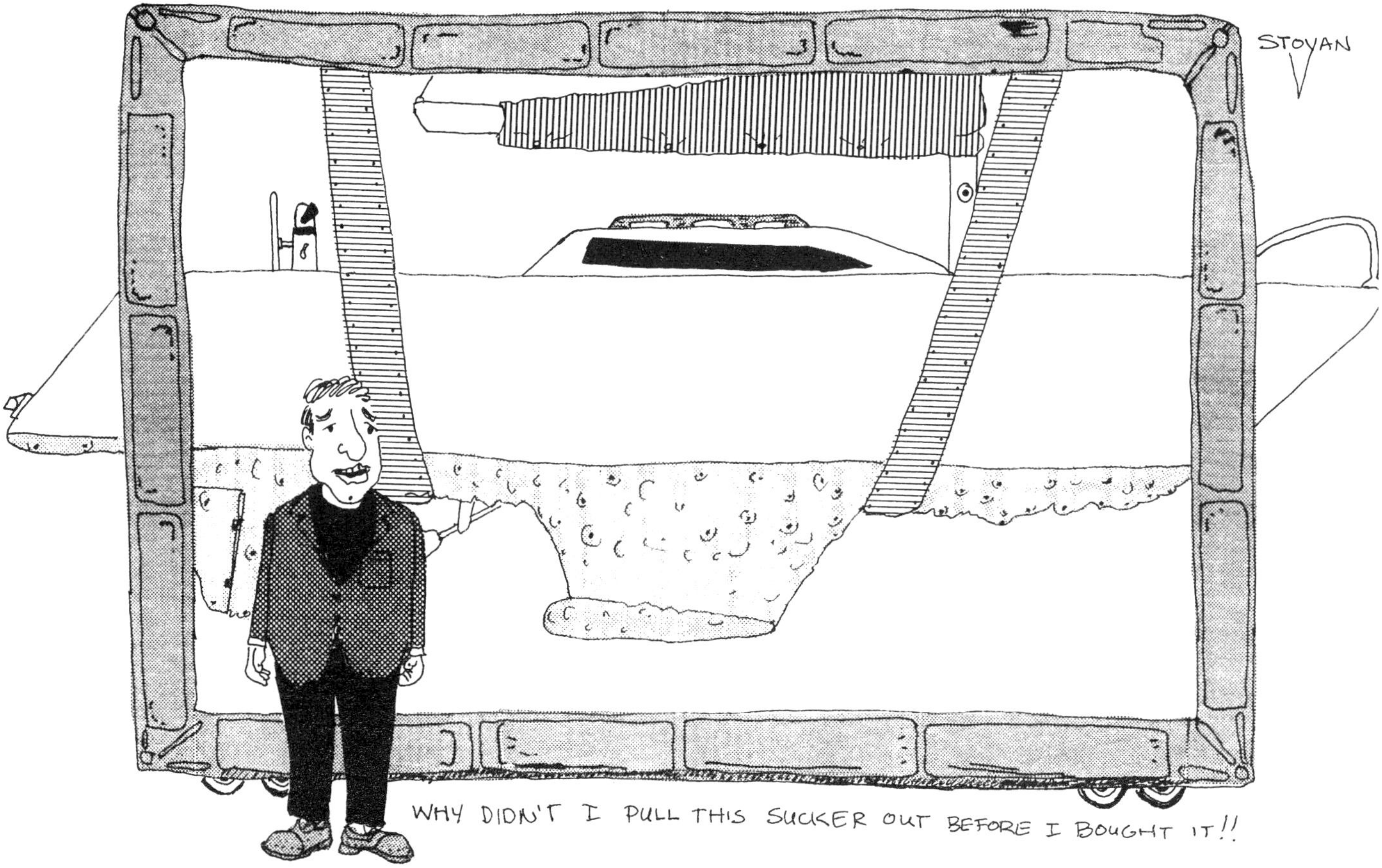
STOYAN
WHY DIDN'T I PULL THIS SUCKER OUT BEFORE I BOUGHT IT!!

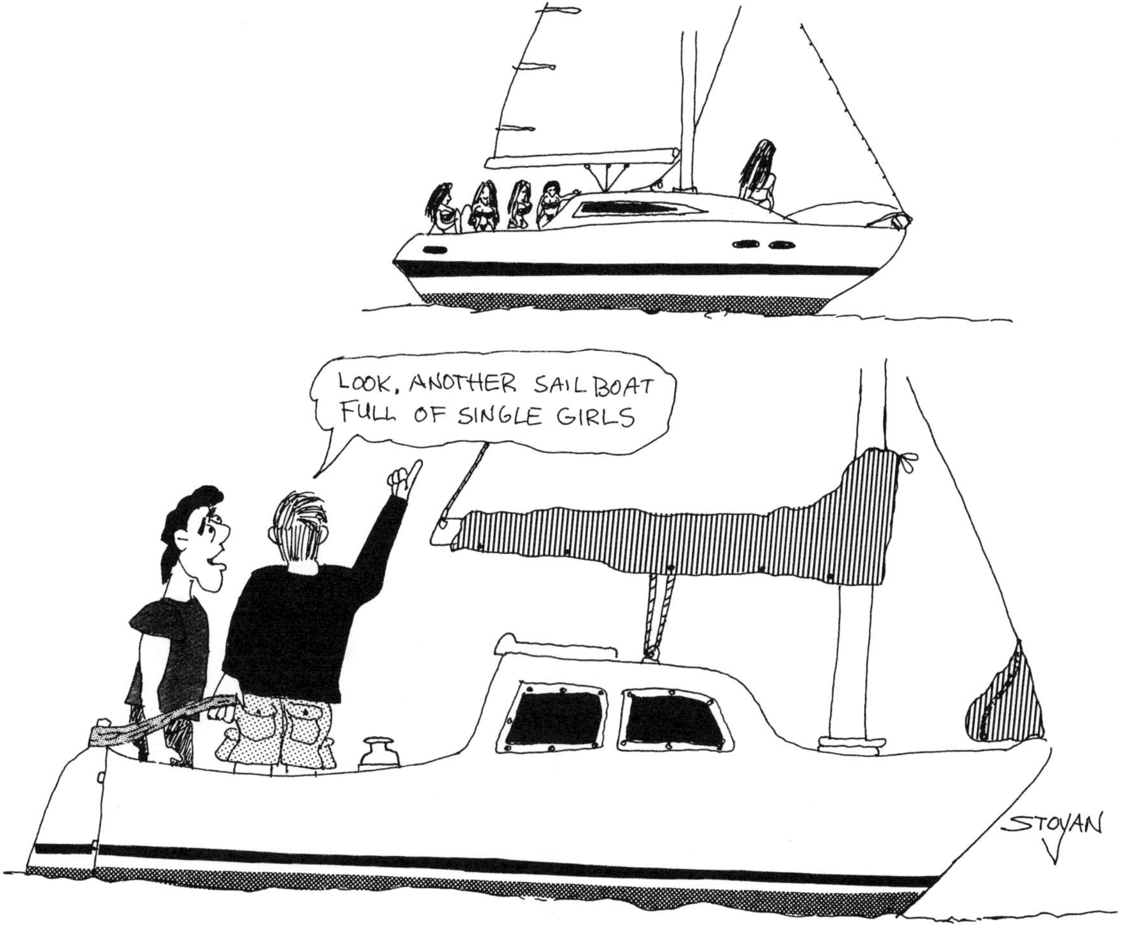
LOOK, ANOTHER SAILBOAT FULL OF SINGLE GIRLS
STOYAN

"THE IMPOSSIBLE"

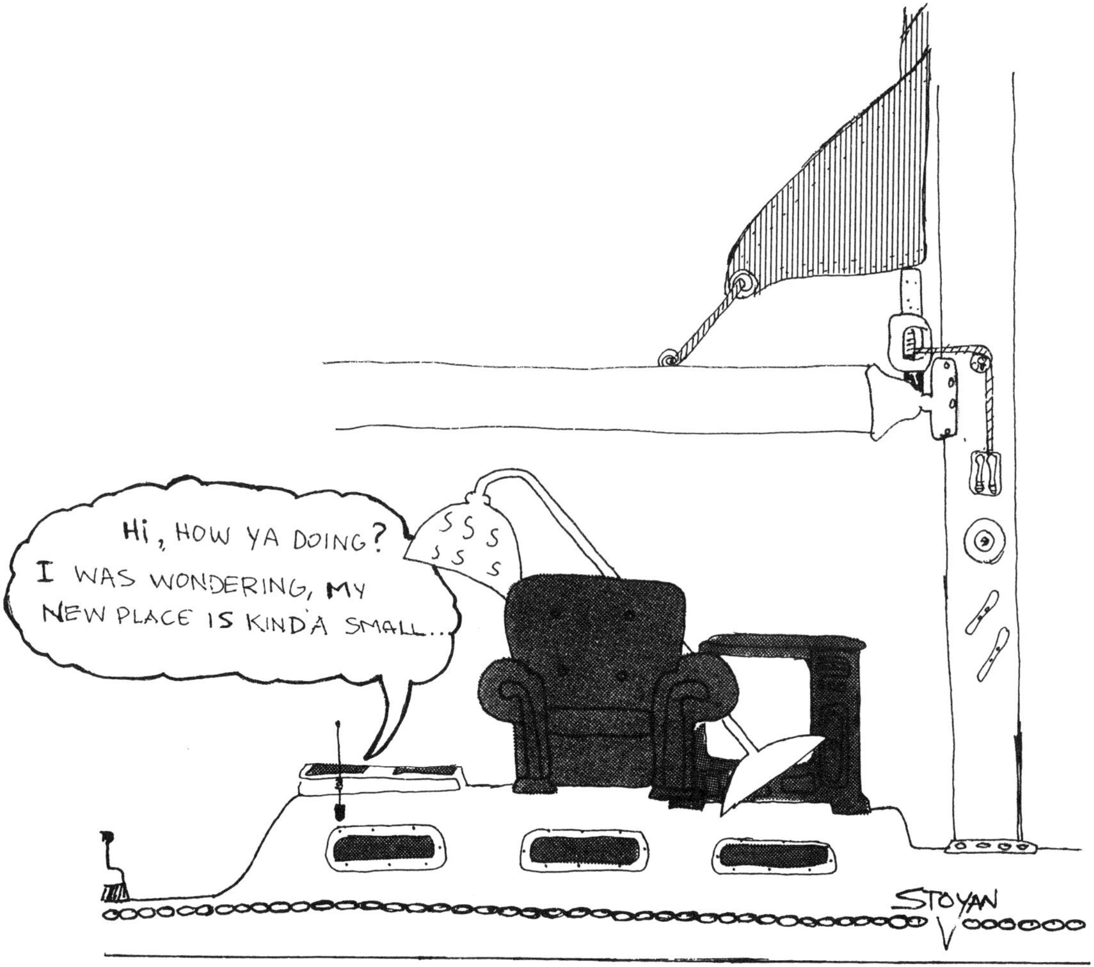
Hi, HOW YA DOING? I WAS WONDERING, MY NEW PLACE IS KIND'A SMALL...
STOYAN

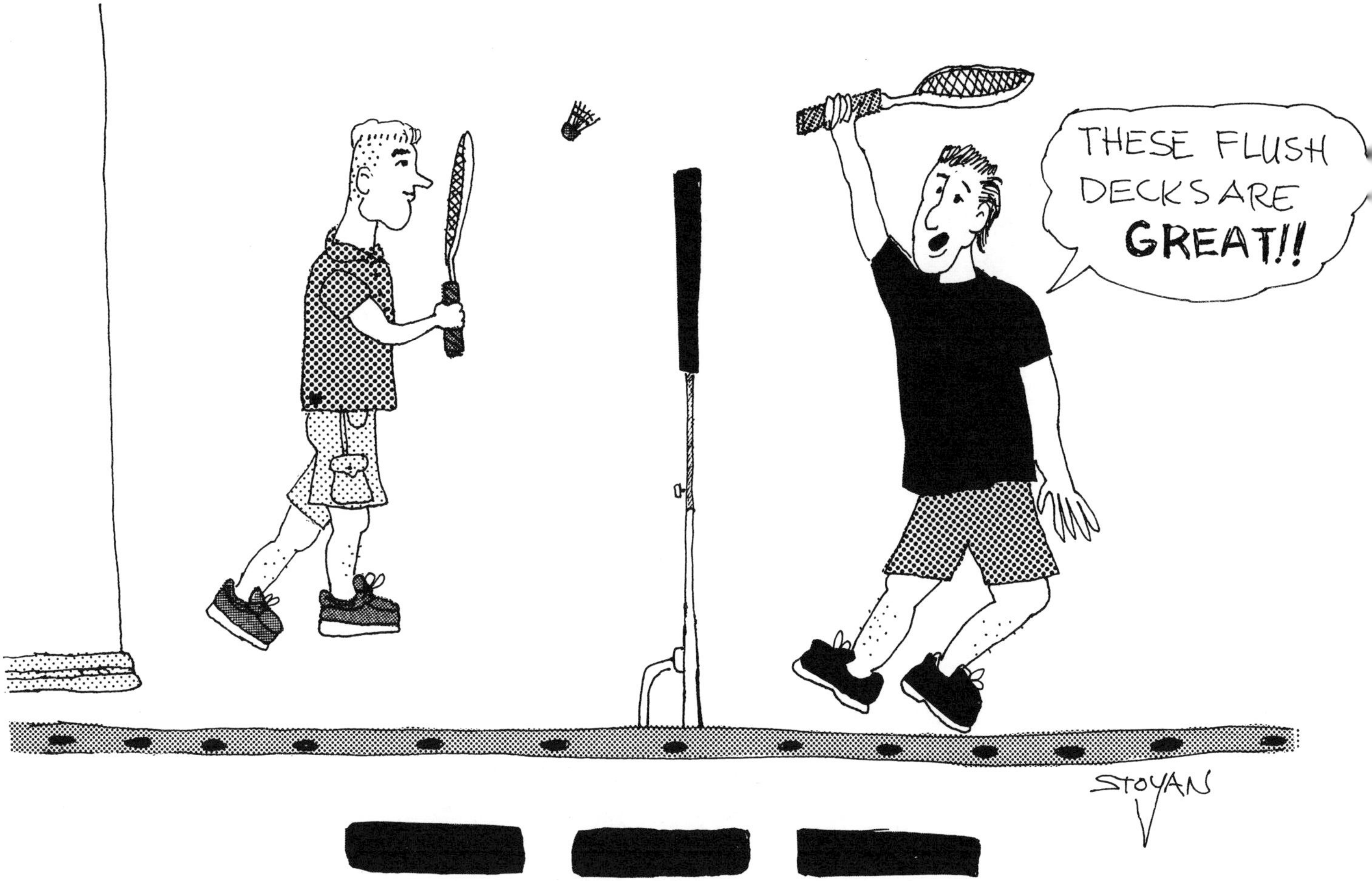
THESE FLUSH DECKS ARE GREAT!!
STOYAN

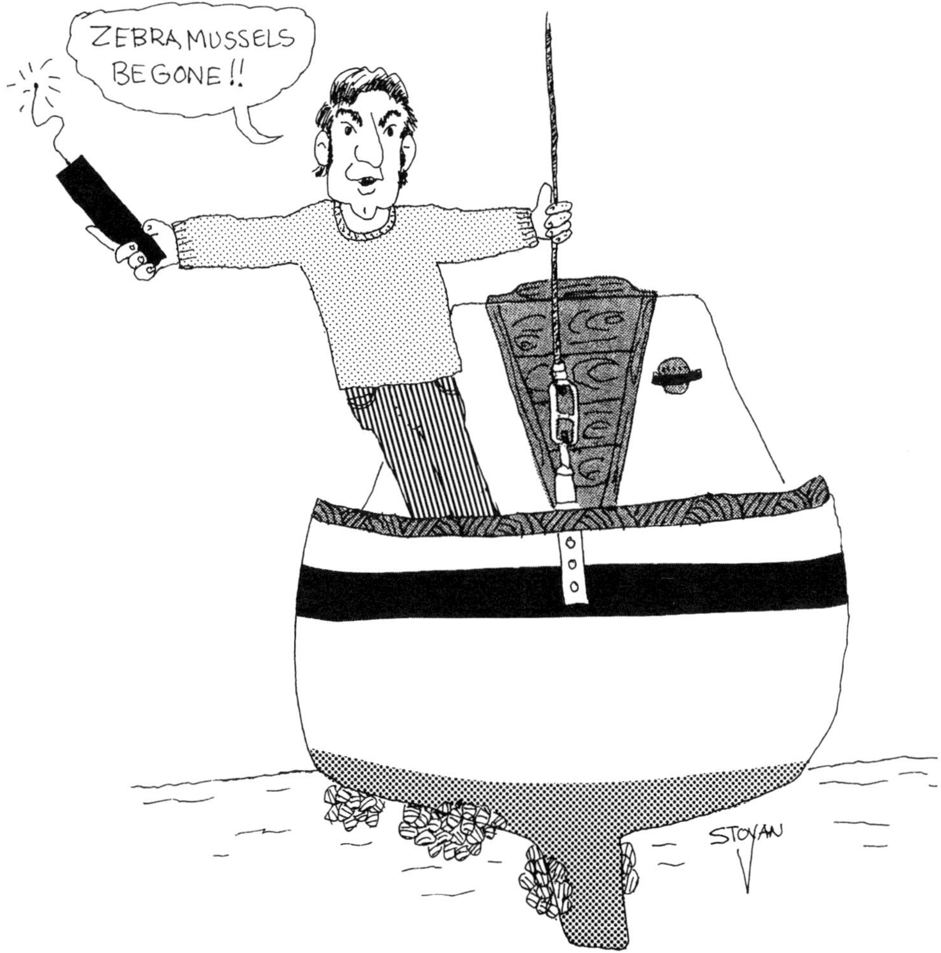
ZEBRA MUSSELS BEGONE!!
STOYAN

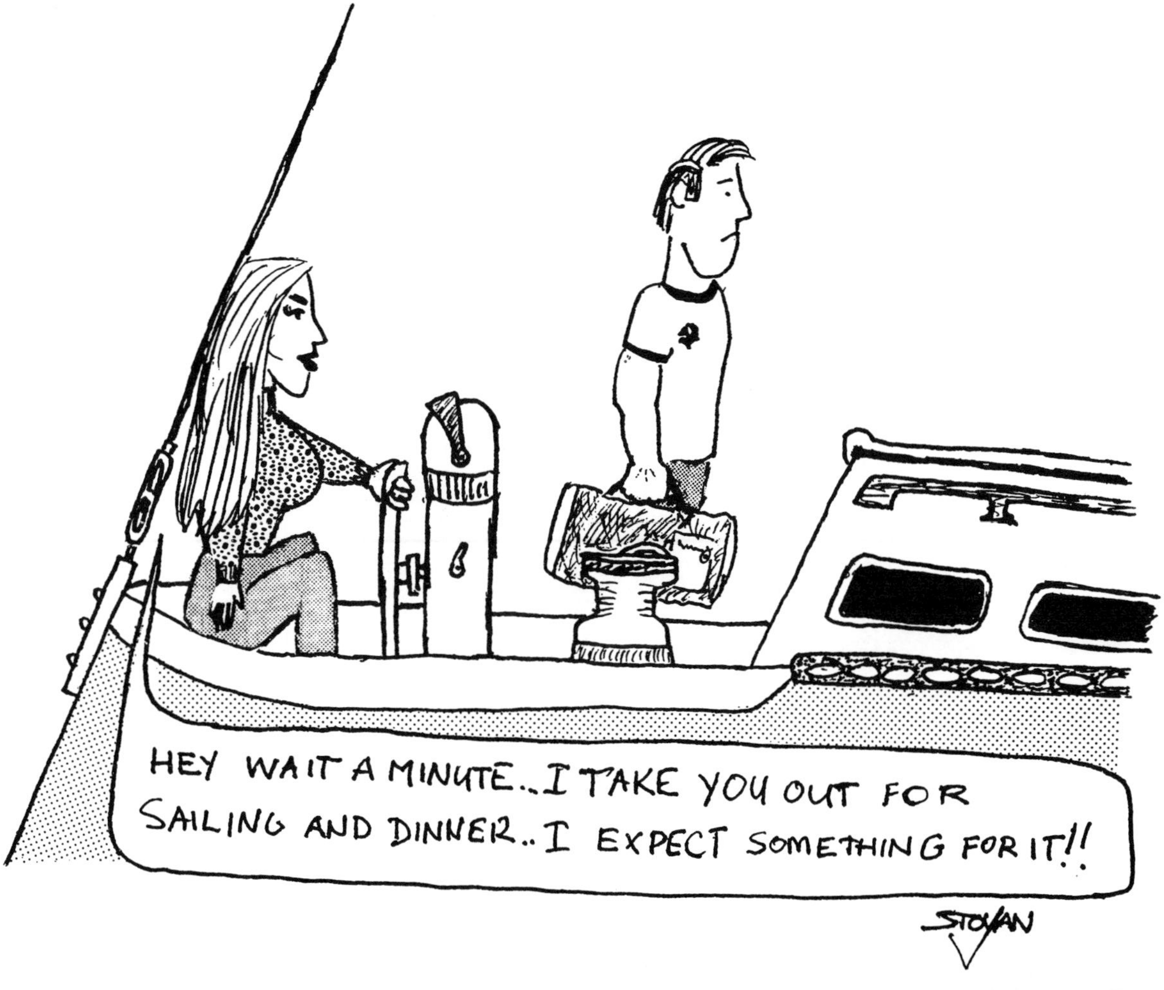
HEY WAIT A MINUTE.. I TAKE YOU OUT FOR SAILING AND DINNER.. I EXPECT SOMETHING FOR IT!!
STOYAN

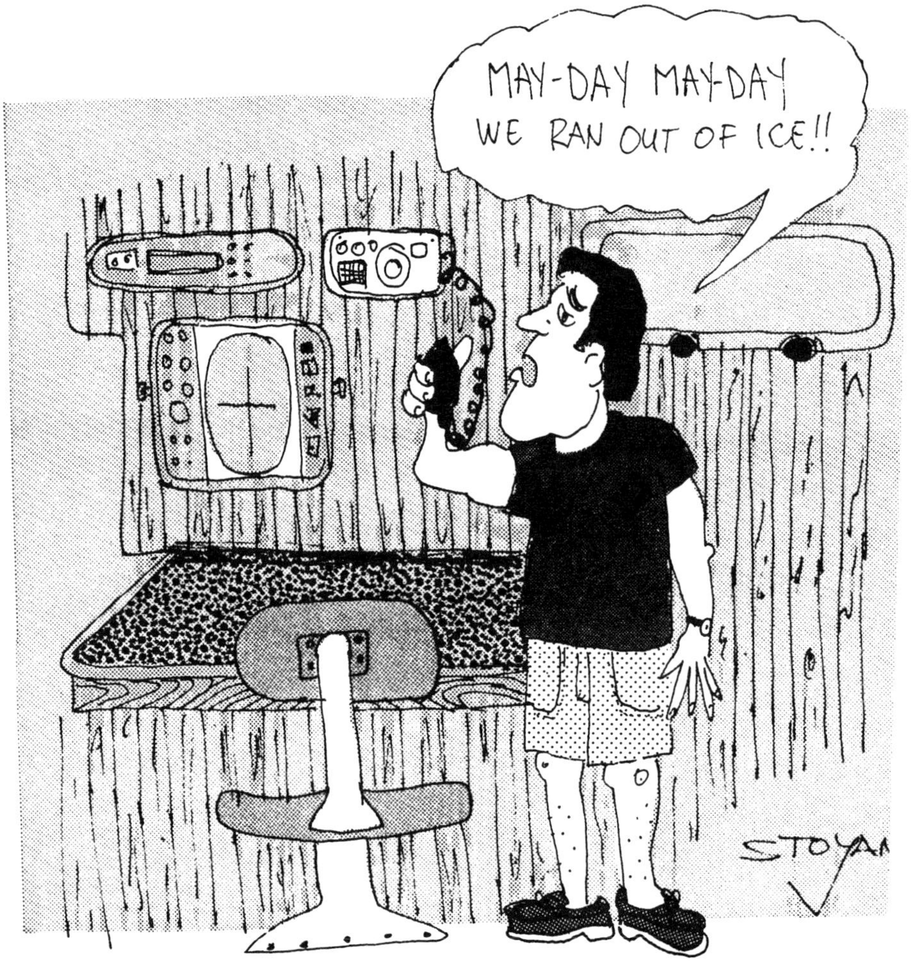
MAY-DAY MAY-DAY
WE RAN OUT OF ICE!!

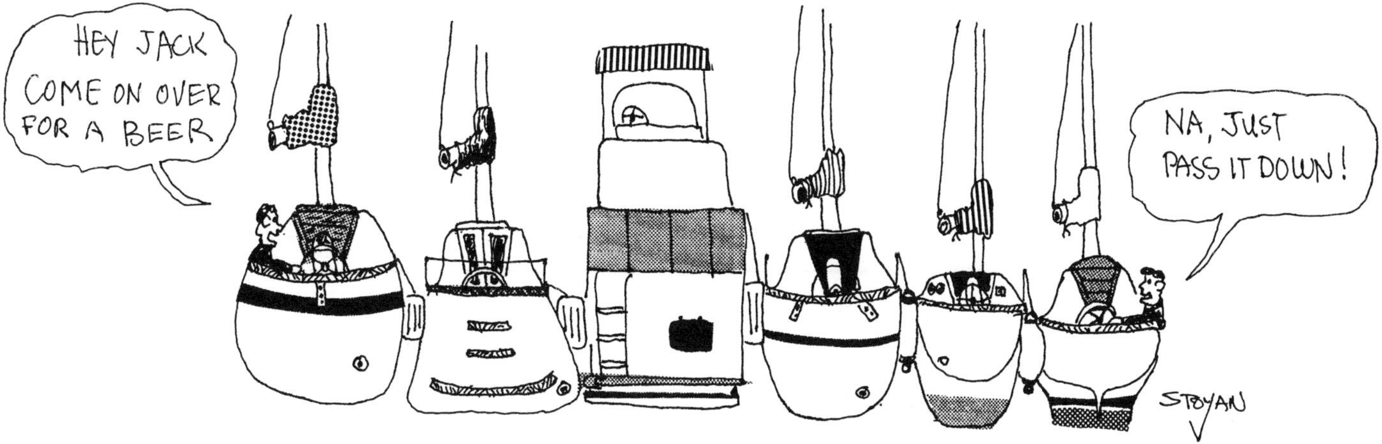
HEY JACK COME ON OVER FOR A BEER
NA, JUST PASS IT DOWN!
STOYAN

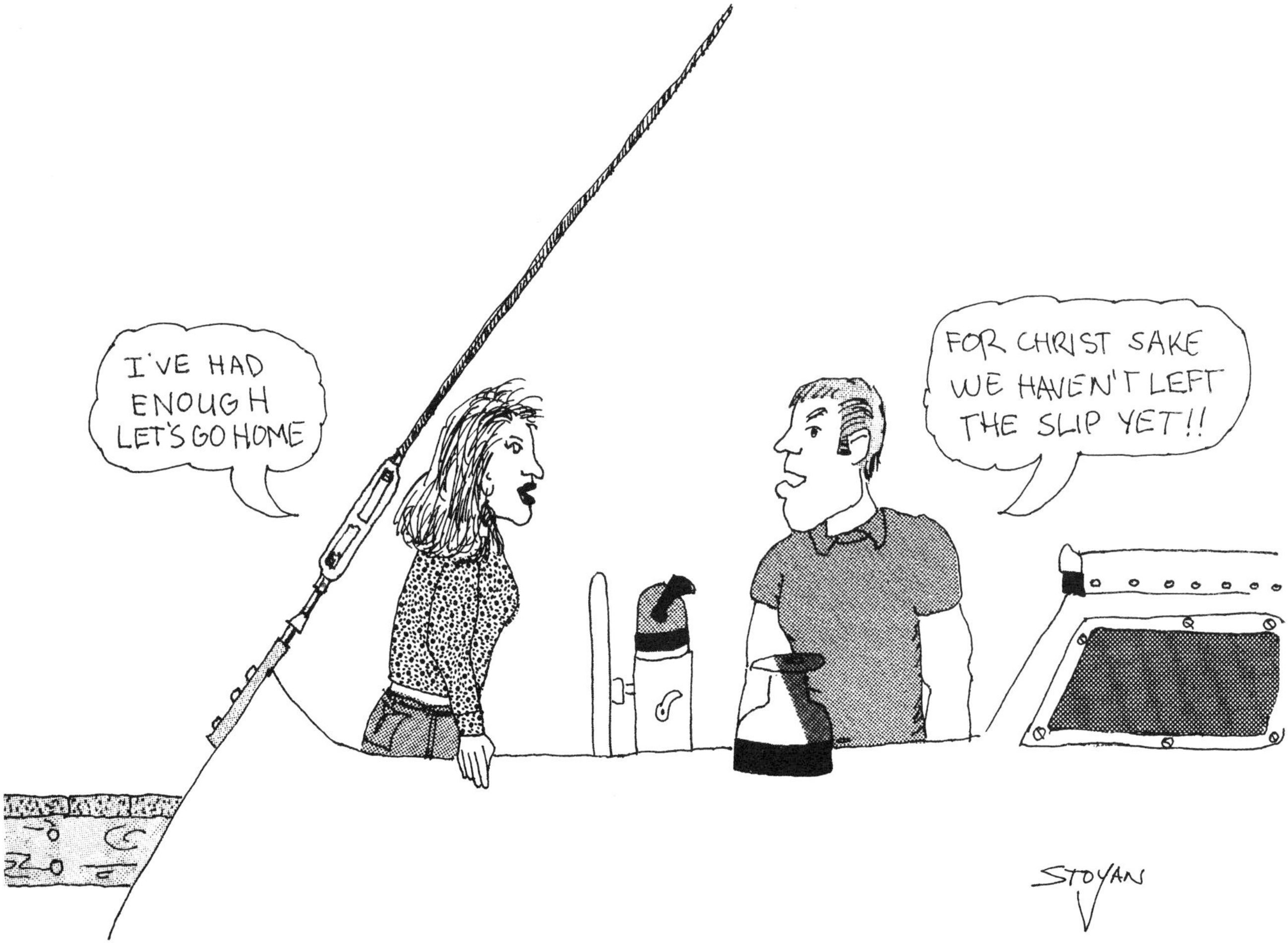
I'VE HAD ENOUGH LET'S GO HOME
FOR CHRIST SAKE WE HAVEN'T LEFT THE SLIP YET!!
STOYAN

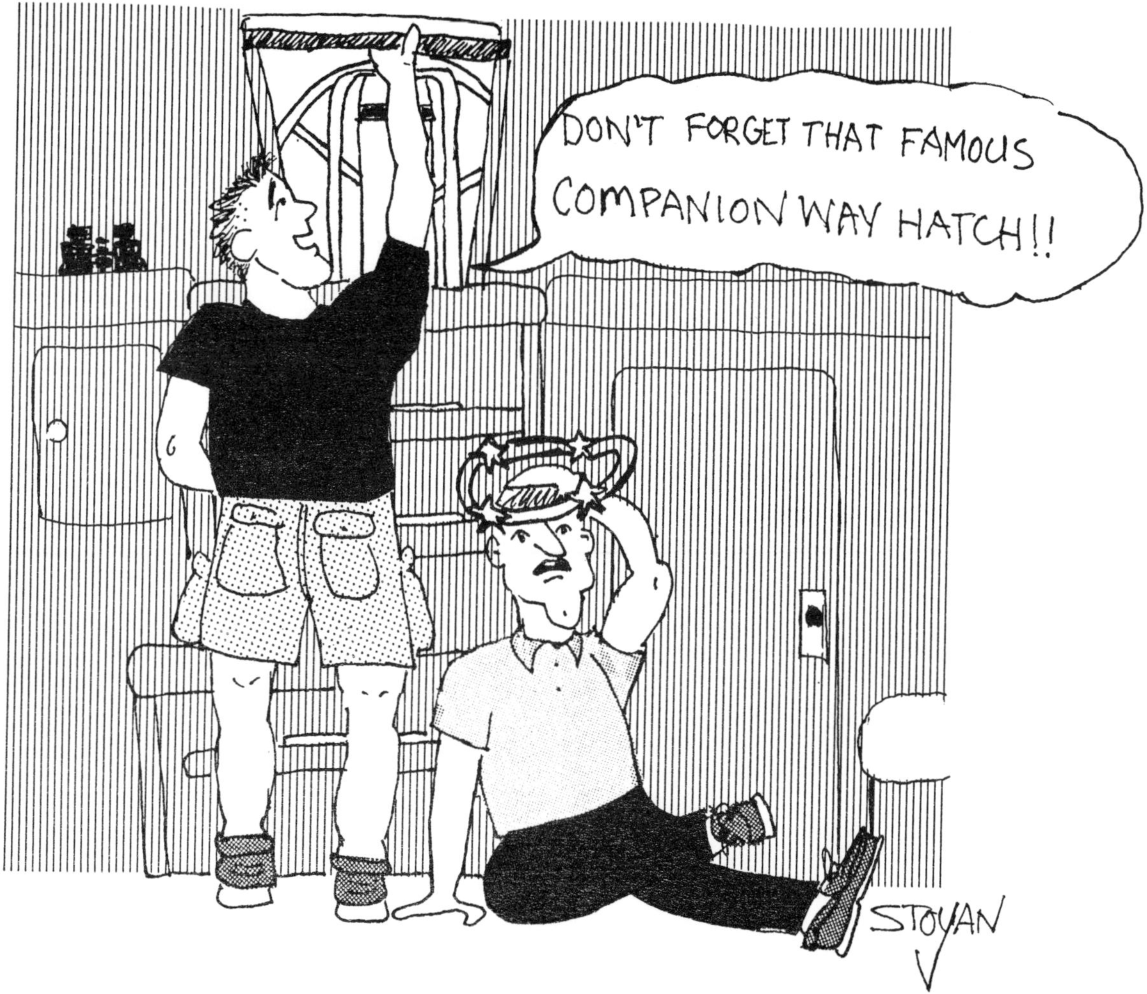
DON'T FORGET THAT FAMOUS COMPANION WAY HATCH!!
STOYAN

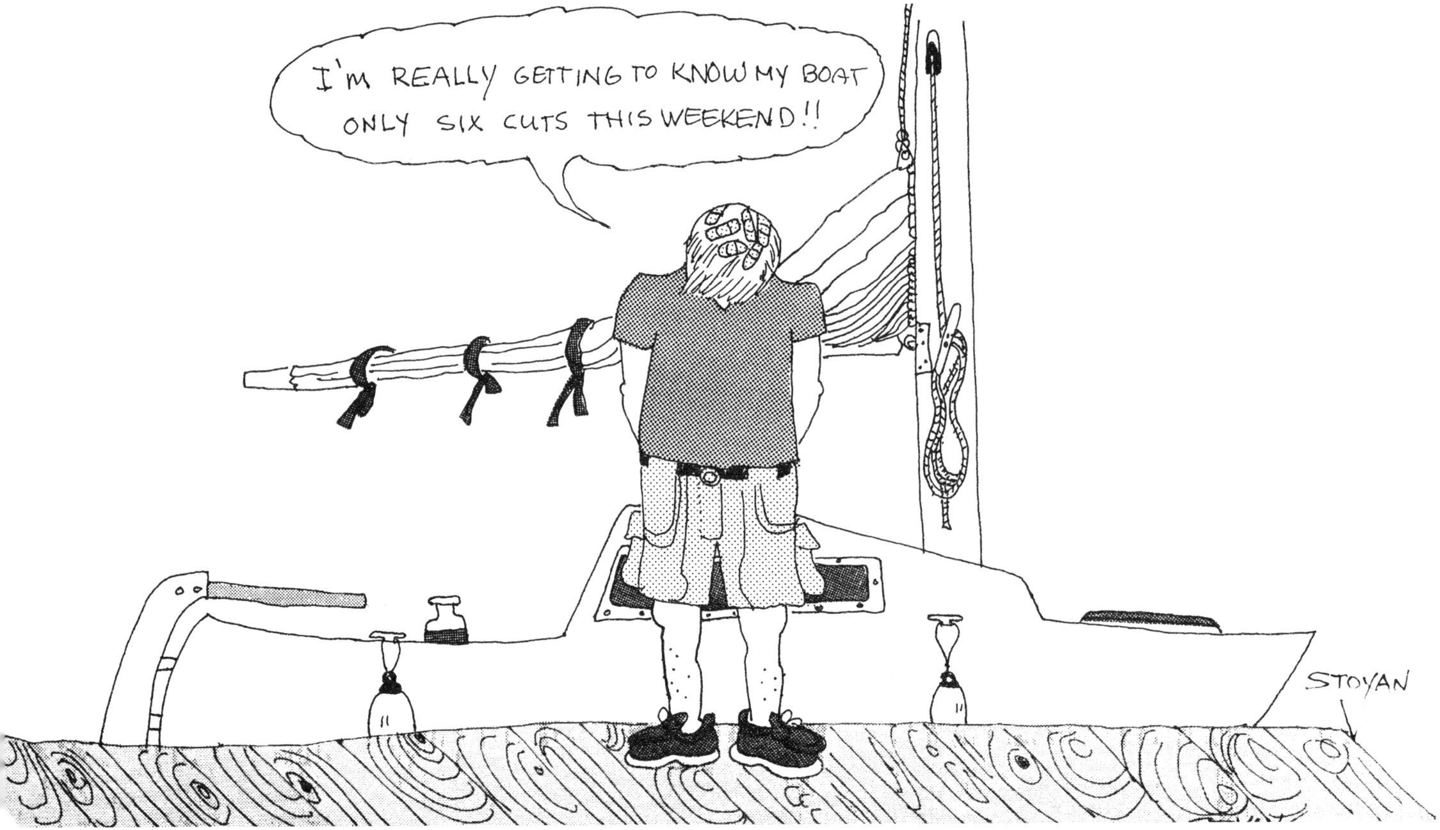
I'M REALLY GETTING TO KNOW MY BOAT
ONLY SIX CUTS THIS WEEKEND!!
STOYAN

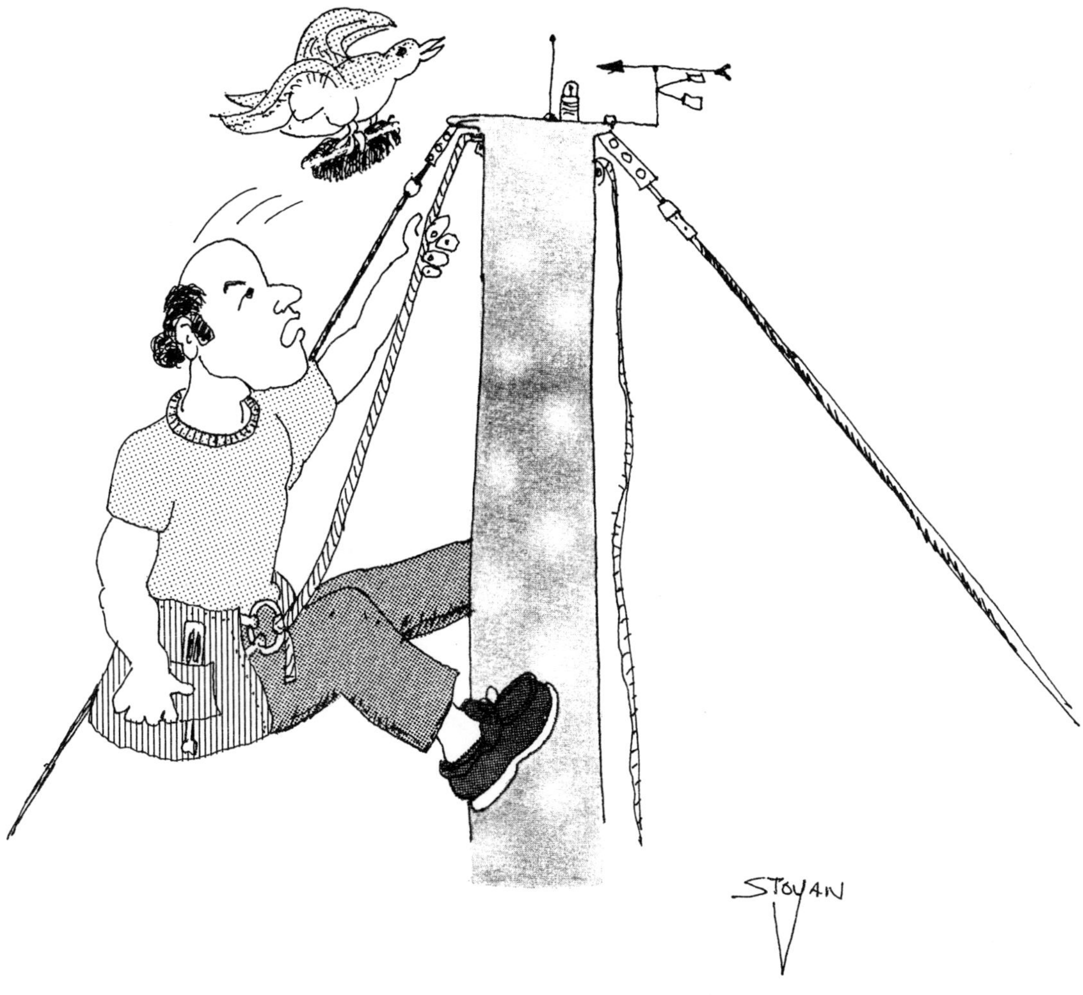
STOYAN

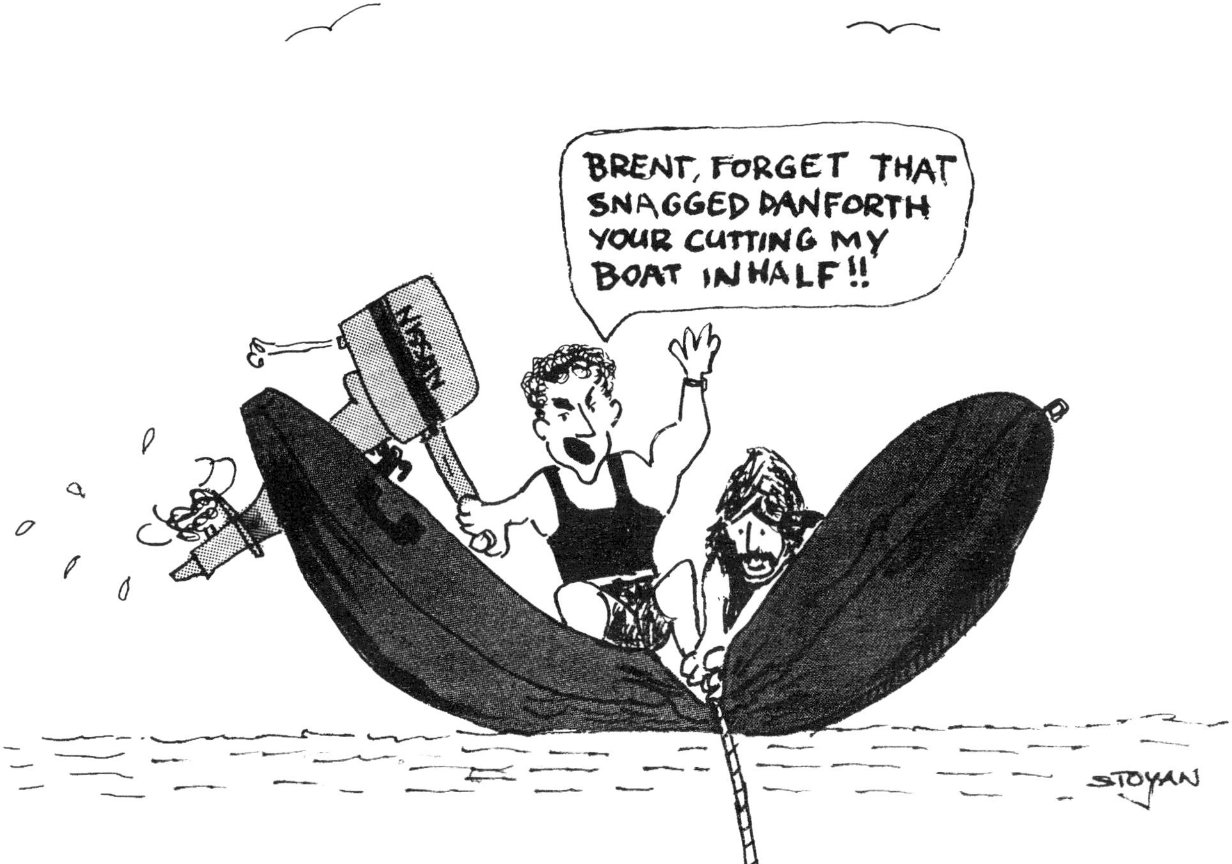
BRENT, FORGET THAT SNAGGED DANFORTH YOUR CUTTING MY BOAT IN HALF!!
STOYAN

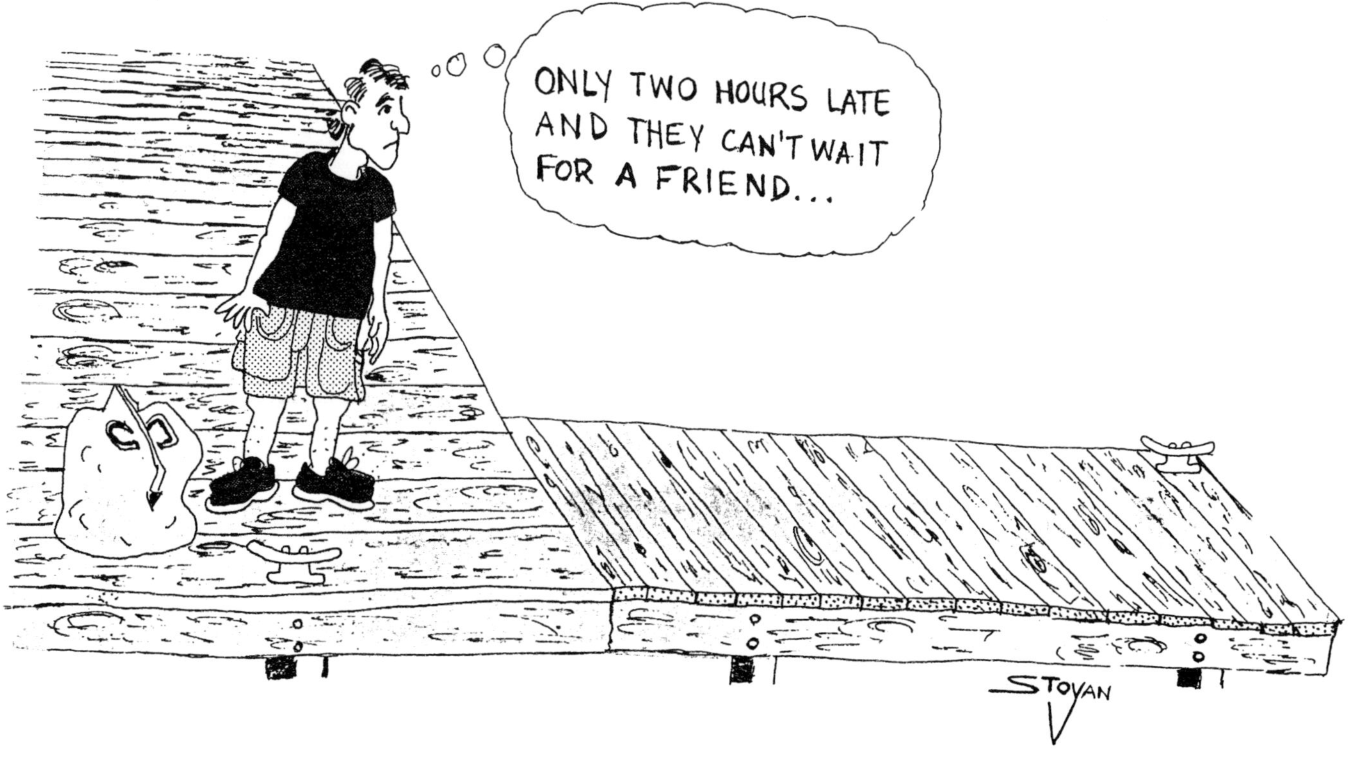
ONLY TWO HOURS LATE AND THEY CAN'T WAIT FOR A FRIEND...
STOYAN

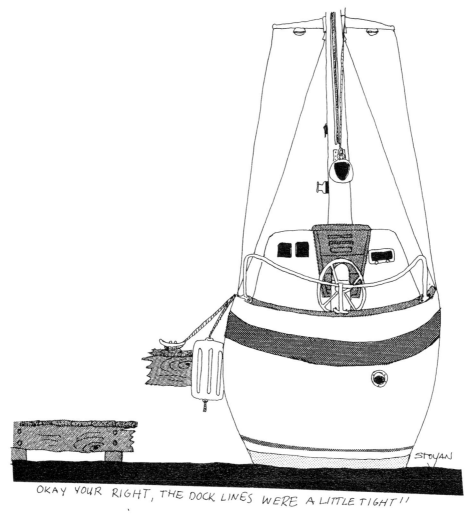

OKAY YOUR RIGHT, THE DOCK LINES WERE A LITTLE TIGHT!!

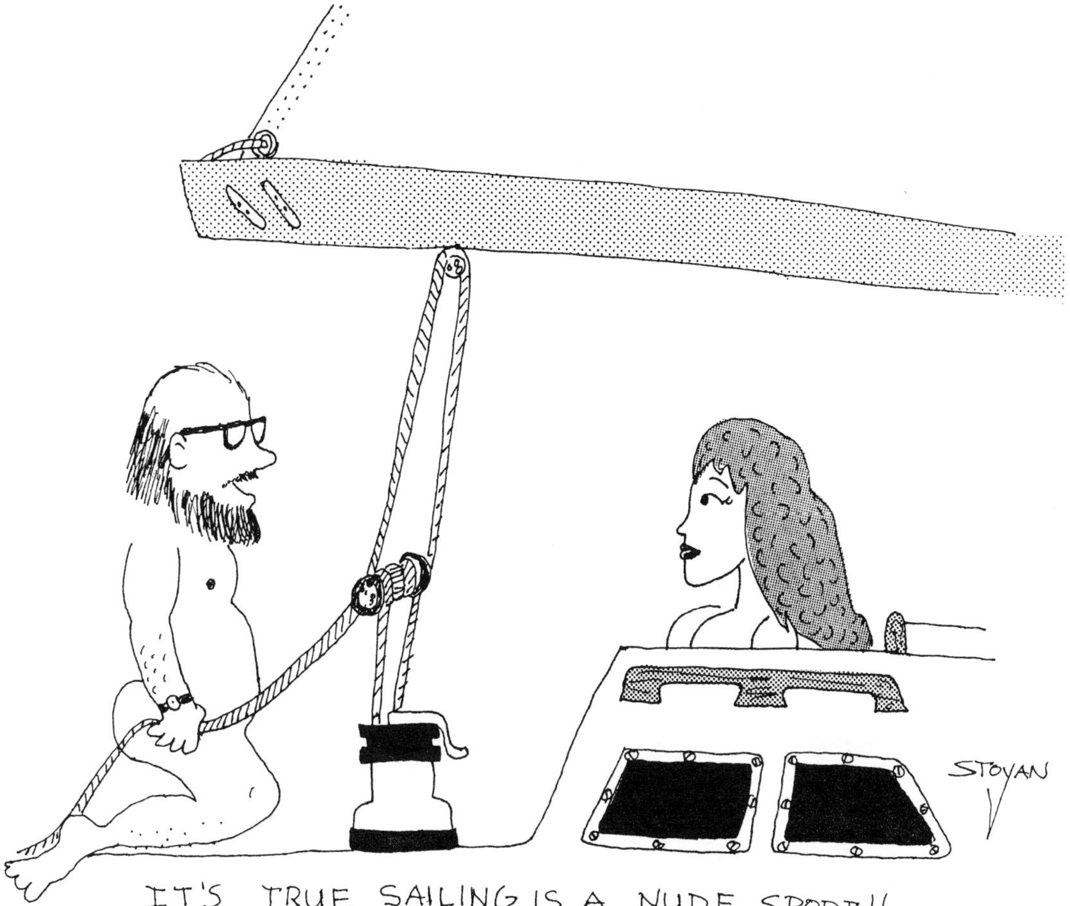
STOYAN

IT'S TRUE SAILING IS A NUDE SPORT!!

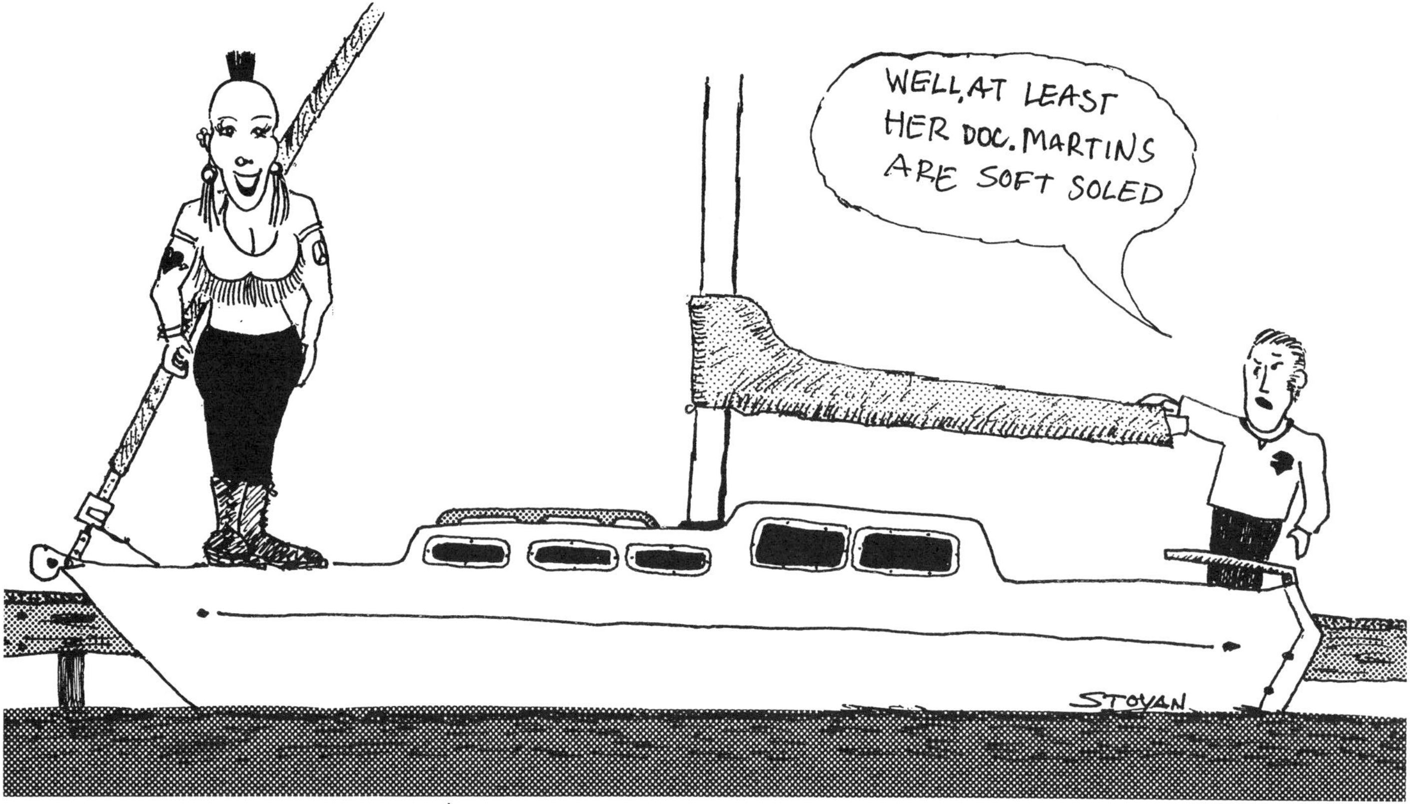
WELL, AT LEAST HER DOC. MARTINS ARE SOFT SOLED
STOYAN

"THE BLIND DATE"

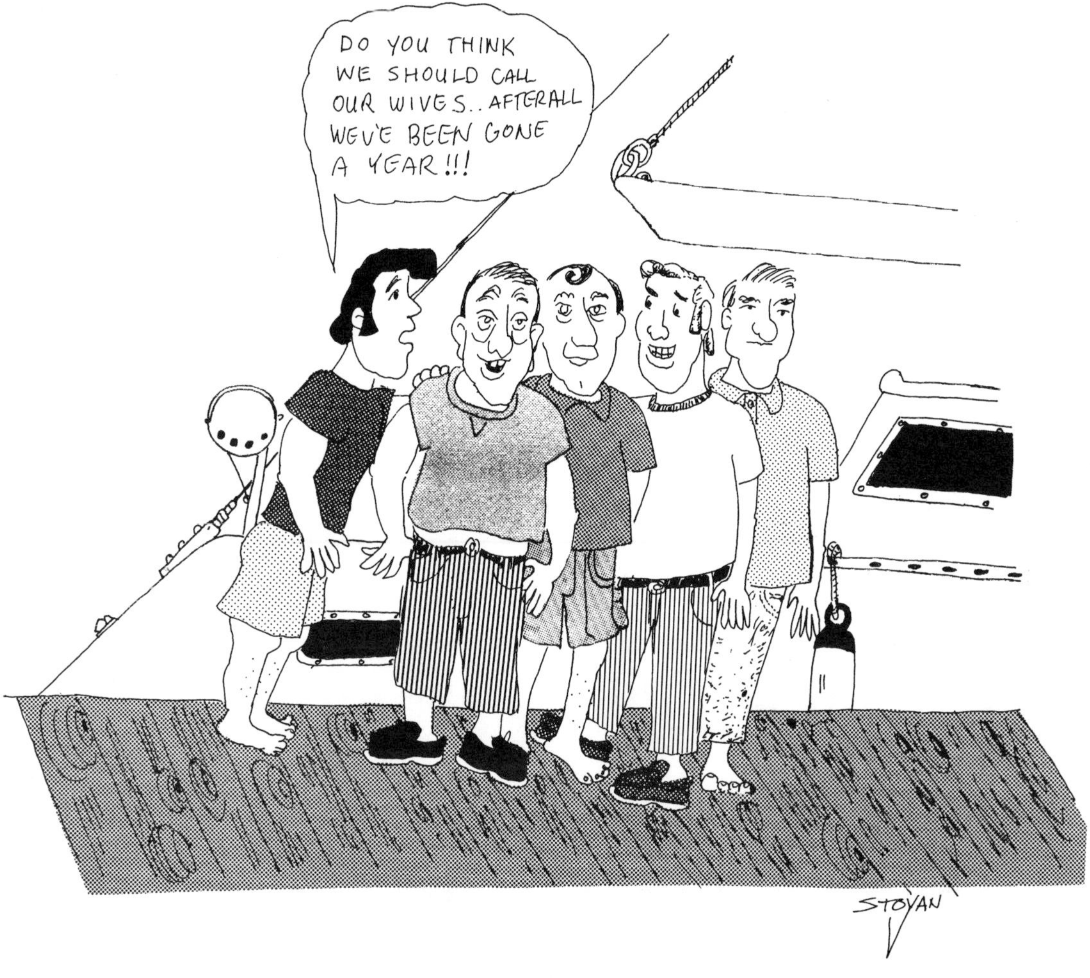
DO YOU THINK WE SHOULD CALL OUR WIVES.. AFTERALL WEV'E BEEN GONE A YEAR!!!
STOYAN

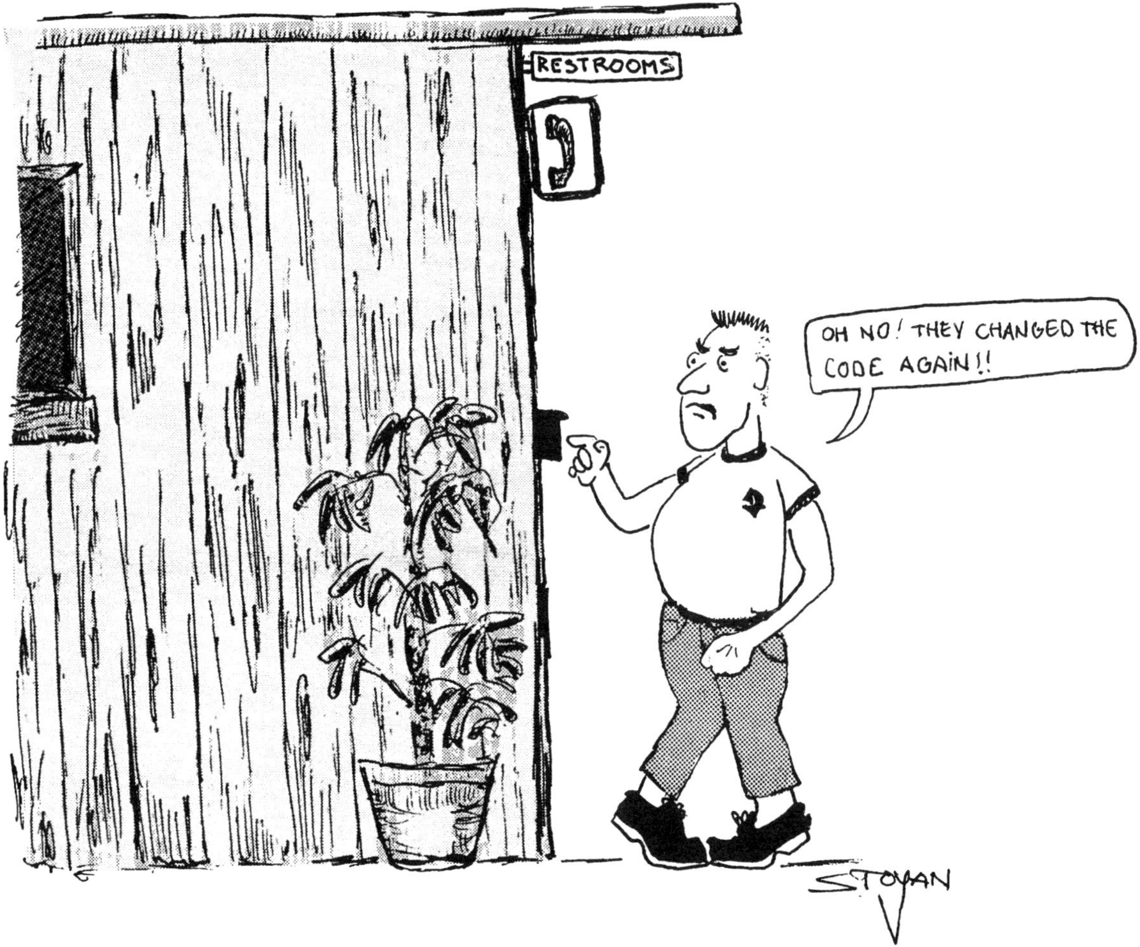
RESTROOMS
OH NO! THEY CHANGED THE CODE AGAIN!!
STOYAN

3 EASY WAYS TO ORDER

PHONE	FAX	MAIL
TOLL FREE 1-800-638-9557 Have your credit card ready. 24 hours	(416) 431-5343 24 hours	DINKADOLLY Publishing P.O. Box 275 Station "D" Scarborough, ON Canada M1R 5B7

Please send me ( ) copies of The Bent Bulkhead, at $9.95 each.

I understand , I may return the book(s) for full refund - for any reason, no questions asked.

Company Name _____

Name _____

Address _____

City _____ **State** _____ **Zip** _____

Sales tax: Canadian orders add 7% G.S.T. 8% P.S.T.

Shipping: Book rate: $1.00 per book. Air mail orders add $2.00 per book
(Allow 3-4 weeks for surface delivery)

Payment: ☐ Check ☐ Money Order ☐ Visa ☐ Master Card ☐ AMEX

Thank-you for your order

Card number _____

Name on card _____ **Exp. date** _____